KU-241-926

THE WESTERN FRONT

RICHARD HOLMES

BOOKS

3 5 7 9 10 8 6 4

First published in 1999 to accompany the BBC television series
The Western Front. This paperback edition first published 2008.

Published by BBC Books, an imprint of Ebury Publishing.
A Random House Group Company

Copyright © Richard Holmes 1999

Richard Holmes has asserted his right to be identified as the author of this Work
in accordance with the Copyright, Designs and Patents Act 1988

All rights reserved. No part of this publication may be reproduced, stored in a retrieval system,
or transmitted in any form or by any means, electronic, mechanical, photocopying,
recording or otherwise, without the prior permission of the copyright owner.

The Random House Group Limited Reg. No. 954009

Addresses for companies within the Random House Group
can be found at www.randomhouse.co.uk

A CIP catalogue record for this book is available from the British Library.

ISBN 978 1 84607 582 7

The Random House Group Limited supports the Forest Stewardship Council (FSC),
the leading international forest certification organization. All our titles that are printed
on Greenpeace approved FSC certified paper carry the FSC logo. Our paper
procurement policy can be found at www.rbooks.co.uk/environment

Mixed Sources
Product group from well-managed
forests and other controlled sources
www.fsc.org Cert no. TT-COC-2139
© 1996 Forest Stewardship Council

Commissioning editors: Sheila Ableman and Christopher Tinker
Designer: Jonathan Baker at Seagull Design
Production: David Brimble
Maps: Angela Wilson at All Terrain Mapping

Printed in the UK by CPI Cox & Wyman, Reading, RG1 8EX

PICTURE CREDITS

BBC Books would like to thank the following for providing photographs
and for permission to reproduce copyright material.
Plate section 1 e.t. archive: page 8 (top right); Hulton Getty: pages 1 (both), 4 (top), 5 (top),
7 (bottom), 8 (top left); Imperial War Museum: pages 2 (both), 3 (both), 4 (bottom),
5 (middle and bottom), 6 (both), 7 (top and middle).
Plate section 2 Hulton Getty: pages 2 (top) and 3 (bottom); Imperial War Museum: pages 1 (both),
2 (bottom), 3 (top), 4–5 (all), 6 (both), 7 (both) and 8.

AUTHOR'S NOTE

Both Allied and German Armies were numbered, so to avoid unneccessary confusion I have referred
to Allied Armies using 1st, 2nd, 3rd etc, and First, Second and Third etc for German Armies.

CONTENTS

INTRODUCTION

I am haunted by the Western Front: there is no other word for it. Yet the family connection is thin. My father was a boy during the First World War, which transformed jolly uncles into entries in lengthening casualty lists. He visited its battlefields in the late 1920s, and I still have some of his photographs, taken before the dignified memorials to the missing were complete, and when some graves were still marked by crosses, not chiselled head-stones. I grew up in a part of Staffordshire which remembered the sacrifices of the local Territorial division, 46th North Midland, its bad day at Gommecourt on 1 July 1916 balanced by its triumphant breaking of the Hindenburg Line in September 1918.

If my family was touched by the war, it was bruised far less than many. A headstone near Cambrai commemorates a decorated infantry corporal in his thirties. His family proudly added the inscription telling us that he was one of five brothers that fell, every one a hero. Sergeant George Lee, Royal Field Artillery, killed on 5 September 1916, lies beside his son, Corporal Robert Frederick Lee, a member of the same battery, killed on the same day at the age of nineteen. And in Flatiron Copse Cemetery, in the shadow of Mametz Wood on the Somme, lie three pairs of brothers.

BACK TO THE FRONT

I first visited the Western Front in my early twenties. I remember standing under the Menin Gate at Ypres, with its almost 55,000 names of soldiers missing in the Ypres salient – where Allied trenches bulged into German lines east of the town – before 16 August 1917; as I stood there, buglers of the local fire brigade

ENGLAND

Dover
Folkestone

Zeebrugge
Ostend
Dunkirk
Calais
Roulers
Boulogne
St Omer
Poperinghe
Ypres
Menin
BELGIU
Armentières
Montreuil
Béthune
Lille
Tournai
Brussels
Mons
Loos
La Bassée
Lens
Arras
Charler
Abbeville
Doullens
Bapaume
Maubeuge
Cambrai
Landrècies
R. Somme
Albert
Le Cateau
Dieppe
Amiens
Villers-
Bretonneux
Péronne
St Quentin
Guise
Le Havre
Montdidier
Noyon
R. Oise
Charleville-Mézie
Laon
Rouen
Compiègne
R. Oise
Coucy-le-
Château
Craonne
Soissons
R. Aisne
Chantilly
Villers-Cotterêts
Rhein
R. Seine
Château-Thierry
Epernay
Meaux
R. Marne
Versailles
Paris
Châlons-sur-Marne
Vitry-le-François
R. Seine
FRANCE

N
W — E
S

0   50 Miles
0   50 Kilometres

Frontiers as in 1914

**THE WESTERN FRONT
1914–18**

OLLAND

R. Meuse

Maastricht

iège

ur

nt

GERMANY

LUXEMBOURG

R. Moselle

an

Trier

enay

Luxembourg

Lorraine

Verdun

Metz

Morhange

niel

Nancy

Sarrebourg

Bar-le-
Duc

R. Rhine

R. Meuse

R. Moselle

Alsace

Epinal

Belfort

Montbéliard

sounded the Last Post. They had done so every night since 11 November 1929, with an interlude during the German occupation of 1940–4. Among the audience were many veterans of the war, mostly white-haired and spry, with First World War medals shining on their chests. Here was a Military Medal, there the purple and white of the Military Cross.

The war had ended just fifty-one years before: I was closer in time to it then than I am now to the Normandy landings of 1944. Veterans were neither hard to find, nor reticent when you found them. One stocky Welshman, with a South Wales Borderers badge on his blazer, pulled me up sharply when I started talking about something airily academic like the dissemination of information within the unit. He was a platoon sergeant. The officer read the map: he ensured that the boys followed in good order. 'Dissemination of bloody information,' the veteran mimicked in an English accent. Then his memories were back to the front, and his lilt was back to the valleys. 'Lousy as rooks, we was,' he said. 'Lousy as bloody rooks.'

Since then I have been back to the front perhaps three times a year for the intervening thirty, and in the process I must have spent as long on it as many of the combatants. When I began, there were hardly any graves of soldiers younger than I was. Now I am hard-pressed to find one older, and the growing weight of my own mortality seems to bend me closer to the men whose deaths I chronicle. I know Ypres in the autumn, slipping back almost guiltily for a hot bath and a good dinner – French quality and German portions – as early evening chills Polygon Wood, Nonne Bosschen and Hill 60. Then there is the Somme in high summer, skylarks and poppies now as then, the iron harvest of unexploded shells at roadside collecting points still somehow as fecund as ever. Across into the French sector, there is the mournful ridge of the Chemin des Dames, speckled with memorials to an army that wasted so much French manhood by pitting raw courage against earth and concrete.

Through the forest of the Argonne lies Verdun, to my mind the most shocking of all the front's shocking battlefields. Business takes me to the Musée-Memorial at Fleury-devant-Douaumont (one of the many destroyed villages on the battlefield) every year, but I cannot take the museum's audio-visual show any more, with Brahms's *German Requiem* crashing out like a barrage and the faces of Lorraine peasants, sons and daughters of this butchered landscape, staring out from the sepia slides. Still the front snakes on, down to St-Mihiel, where souvenir hunters creep about the *tranchée du soif* ('thirst trench'), to emerge with shell nosecaps and steel helmets. Beyond it the hills rise and the blue line of the Vosges – almost a Holy Grail to pre-war patriotic Frenchmen schooled to the need to recapture the provinces of Alsace and Lorraine, lost to the Germans after the Franco-Prussian war of 1870–1 – fills the horizon. From the charnel hill of the *Hartmannswillerkopf*, known as *Le Vieil Armand* to the *poilus* ('hairy ones') who fought there, you can see the Alps.

Sometimes the front line cut through villages, like a border drawn by a malign boundary commission, leaving the inn in Allied hands and the school in German. West of Lille it ran through coalfields, trenches bisecting hard-faced rows of miners' cottages, barbed wire and barricades sealing tunnels below. It went through woods, curled across downland, slashed farms and great estates, sugar-factories, backyards and brickfields. At Mametz, on the Somme, it even desecrated the village cemetery: there was a German machine-gun dug snugly (and indestructibly) under the concrete plinth supporting the crucifix.

The front ran from the Swiss border to the North Sea. Its length varied with the ebb and flow of battle, but was usually about 460 miles (736 kilometres). Its defences were as varied as the landscape it crossed. In some places – like Neuve Chapelle, below Aubers Ridge in Flanders – the water-table was too high for trenches to be dug to full depth, so they were built up to form 'high command' trenches. Veterans of the North-West Frontier of India were reminded of the sangars – chest-high stone redoubts – built there as defences. The easy digging of the Ypres salient meant that trenches there required careful revetting to shore up their sides and prevent them from caving in: Somme chalk was harder to dig but more robust. The dimension of no man's land, the debatable ground between the Allied and German barbed wire, also varied. It might be a few yards, so that whispered messages were in danger of being overheard by attentive enemies and rifle-grenades could be fired between trenches, or a few hundred yards, which left abundant scope for grim little patrol actions between the lines. There were places, such as marshy areas on the fringes of rivers, where there were no trenches at all, but wire curled down into the water to deter infiltration.

There was not even consistency as far as mutual hostility was concerned. The front had quiet sectors and dangerous ones. The latter were often areas where the loss of even a small piece of ground had tactical, and even political, significance: the Ypres salient is a good case in point. The Somme, in contrast, was quiet until the British began their pre-battle bombardment in June 1916. We are told that when it began a German grenadier put on his best uniform and went to see his company commander, begging him to stop the foolishness before somebody was hurt. Some units fought without respite: others slipped comfortably into a routine of live and let live, punctuated by ritualized patrol excursions. Sentries sometimes conversed, and front lines might be close enough for songs, carols, jests or enquiries to roll across no man's land. One German shouted: 'It is I, Fritz the bunmaker of London. What is the football news?' His adversaries were nonplussed to discover a fellow Chelsea supporter. ''E must be a damned good sort of sausage eater,' muttered one of them.

'RIDICULOUS PROXIMITY'

As the war went on the British army widened its hold on the front as it grew stronger. It moved southwards down the front, from a small sector around Ypres in late 1914 to the Somme a year later and the Oise in early 1918. This territory was in what Paul Fussell has called 'ridiculous proximity' to England. One officer 'had breakfasted in the trenches and dined in his club in London'; another, going up the line by train, told two comrades: 'Christ!… I was at *Chu Chin Chow* last night with my wife. Hard to believe, isn't it?' The rumble of the guns was easily audible in Kent, and the report of the mines exploded under Messines Ridge in 1917 could be heard in London. Newspapers arrived at the front only a day late: letters and parcels took two to four days. Officers' messes (and even well-found dugouts) sported copies of *Tatler* and *Punch*, although there was an understandable tendency for pictures of long-legged and flimsily clad beauties from *La Vie Parisienne* to find their way up on to walls. For the French, of course, the proximity was more striking and more poignant, as men went up the line through the ruins of a once-familiar town or even, in at least one documented case, died leading an attack into the family vineyard after savouring his last bottle of its produce.

CITIZENS OF THE FRONT

Contemporaries were aware that this counterfeit world, so close to the real one but somehow hideously malformed, swallowed a generation. Henri Barbusse, a French infantryman whose book *Le Feu* remains a classic, wrote of 'the compact mass of men who, for several seasons, have emptied France to concentrate in the north-east'. It was a great leveller, especially in the French and German armies, which had conscription from the outset. 'Schoolteachers are rifle company NCOs or medical orderlies,' wrote Barbusse. 'In the regiment, a Marist friar is a sergeant in the medical section; a tenor, the major's bicycle orderly; a lawyer, the colonel's secretary; a landlord, mess-corporal in headquarter company.'

The British regular army tended to mirror the social structure of Edwardian England, its officers drawn largely from traditional élites and its rank and file soldiers disproportionately representing the urban unemployed. But the volunteer New Armies, raised in response to Lord Kitchener's call to arms, were a far less accurate reflection, and thousands of well-educated men served in the ranks. The historian R. H. Tawney was a sergeant in a New Army battalion of the Manchester Regiment, and the writer H. H. Munro ('Saki') died as a lance-sergeant on the Somme. Conscription broke down even more traditional barriers, and in 1917–18 there were many middle-class, middle-aged men serving in the ranks. There is no easy correlation between rank and social class in the British army of the First World War. Regular sergeants in 1914 found themselves lieutenant-colonels by 1918: Regimental Quartermaster-Sergeant Fitzpatrick of the Royal Irish, who earned a Distinguished Conduct Medal by an act of remarkable bravery at Mons in 1914, may be the best-known example, but there are many others.

I know of at least two examples of the process in reverse. Harrow-educated Arthur Arnold Crow resigned his captaincy in the Loyal North Lancashire on account of ill-health in 1916. When he recovered he discovered that he could not regain his commission without giving up the chance of foreign service, so enlisted as a private in the Essex Regiment and was killed at Ypres in 1917. J. B. Osborne, invalided out as a lieutenant, joined the Argyll and Sutherland Highlanders and was killed as a private a month and a day before the war ended. He lies in Highland Cemetery at Le Cateau, and his headstone reminds us:

He that humbleth himself shall be exalted.

PEN AND SWORD

In the years that I have known the Western Front, the reputations of the men who commanded there have also been prone to exaltation and humiliation. Books on the war are enough to keep one busy for a lifetime. Not least among the hazards of life as a military historian is the sheer difficulty of logging the shells fired in a literary bombardment which shows little sign of abating. Of course this mass of literature has changed the way I think about the war, and does so still. And it goes deeper than that. Some authors are personal friends and others are professional adversaries, and not a few manage to be both. The best of them share the same passion, and are nerved by the need to find some hypothesis which makes sense – if any can – of the First World War. In *The Swordbearers* (1963), a book which stands the test of time remarkably well, Correlli Barnett pointed to the continuing fascination of the war, which goes:

> beyond the historical insights it gives. It is the fascination of events, of sentiments, as near as one's father's youth and yet as remote as the crusades; lances of the *Garde Ulanen* scratching the summer sky of 1914; the guns of Jellicoe's thirty-four capital ships firing the valedictory salute to British sea-power into the mists of Jutland; horizon blue and field grey; the Motherland; the Fatherland; *La Patrie*.

To begin with, there was certainly more humiliation than exaltation. Critics tended to blame what have been termed 'internal factors', primarily the incompetence of Haig, General Headquarters (GHQ) and senior British commanders, for the horror of the war. As a young man I was much influenced by A. J. P. Taylor's best-selling *The First World War* (1963) with its sharply honed laceration of commanders in general and those on the Western Front in particular. 'Third Ypres,' he tells us with characteristic directness, 'was the blindest slaughter of a blind war.' His mischievous captions drive the point home. Here is 'Sir John French in training for the retreat from Mons', and there 'Lord Kitchener with his keeper, Sir William Robertson'.

No less hard-hitting were Leon Wolff's *In Flanders Fields* (1963) and Alan Clark's *The Donkeys* (1963). The former, a poignant evocation of Passchendaele, concludes that the campaign was simply 'a caricature of war... unfairly and brutally conducted up to the highest level'. The latter, a study of the abortive offensives of 1915, concluded that most senior and middle-ranking officers were grossly incompetent, and that 'Haig, in particular, was an unhappy combination of ambition, obstinacy and megalomania'. The fact that its title, derived from 'Lions led by Donkeys', probably refers to a German judgement on French generals of the Franco-Prussian war of 1870–7, rather than to any comment on the First World War, seems not to have perturbed the author: the story is clearly too good to let that sort of detail get in its way. A 1962 *Spectator* article by Robert Kee sums up the genre, comparing the Western Front to a concentration camp in which 'millions of brave men' suffered 'in a hell comparable with nothing we know'. The war was, he declared, 'a gigantic swindle'.

It did not end there. Douglas Haig's reputation has been repeatedly assailed, perhaps most cleverly by Gerard de Groot in *Douglas Haig 1861–1928* (1988) and certainly most excessively by Denis Winter in *Haig's Command: A Reassessment* (1991). John Laffin's *British Butchers and Bunglers of World War One* (1988) takes as one of its sub-texts 'Incompetence, Callousness and Vanity', significantly an *Australian* subaltern's comment on the *British* high command, and an indication of another eddy in the critical current. He goes on to conclude that Haig's great equestrian statue on Whitehall is in exactly the right place: it stands facing the Cenotaph, which commemorates the servicemen killed in the war.

The opposing school of thought stressed external factors, including what Keith Simpson has termed 'pre-war British inexperience and lack of preparation, the problem of adapting to new technology, the fighting power of the German Army, restraints imposed by coalition warfare, and political interference'. For some time the principal defender of Haig, and through him Allied strategy on the Western Front, was the redoubtable John Terraine. The appearance of his *Douglas Haig: The Educated Soldier* in 1963 gave even me, then at an age when I was instinctively more likely to sympathize with the Donkeys thesis, pause for thought. He depicted a general who had thought seriously about his profession, was capable of what he termed 'grand scale imagination', and who recognized that the war on the Western Front was in essence a great continuous engagement which demanded the single-minded focusing of national resources, human and material. In successive works he has extended his argument, and has never flinched from assailing the 'cheap advantage' which he detects to be sought by the Donkeys school.

Terraine's efforts have brought him as many brickbats as bouquets, not least a deftly aimed missile from John Keegan, who accused him of 'trying to suggest that the generals who presided over the demolition of a whole British generation were somehow more respectable than idiots'. Some academic historians bewailed his reliance on well-worn sources and jeered at his extraordinary personal commitment to his cause. But there is a consistency to his case, as unyielding – and perhaps this is no accident – as Haig's devotion to his own task. This is summed up in an article written a year before *Douglas Haig*. 'Was the bloodbath on the Western Front inevitable?' he asks. 'Was there no other way? My own view will have become apparent by now: there was not.' The Germans were Britain's main enemy. They were in occupation of a huge swathe of territory belonging to France, Britain's major ally. They would leave neither voluntarily nor by negotiation, and the status quo was clearly unacceptable to the Allies. The British bore an increasingly heavy share of the war's burden, and eventually 'the task of engaging the main body of a main enemy in a continental war fell upon the British Army, for the only time in its history, and it carried out that task at very heavy cost with ultimately decisive effect'.

It was not really until the 1980s that a middle path could be trodden with much confidence. A generation of military historians, writing with wide access to a rich variety of source material, began to draw the internal and external arguments together. In *Fire-Power: British Army Weapons and Theories of War 1904–1945* (1982) Shelford Bidwell and Dominick Graham put the development of British tactics into a wider context. In his book *The Killing Ground* (1987) Tim Travers developed the internal factors to look more deeply at the British view of the nature of war and the personalized structure of its pre-war officer corps. Haig became the embodiment of the British army, warts and all. No less important was *Command on the Western Front* (1992), in which Robin Prior and Trevor Wilson examined the achievements of Sir Henry Rawlinson, divisional commander in 1914 and army commander 1916–18. The authors argued that historians who simply confined themselves to balancing internal versus external factors could not 'see the essential story at all'. At variance with some historians who have depicted the German army as such a wondrous organization that one might wonder why the shambolic British bothered to take the field at all, they go on to note 'the suicidal manner in which the German authorities squandered their irreplaceable infantry' in 1918. Finally, they observe that even at that late stage in the war:

> it was required of Rawlinson (as of Haig) to prescribe objectives and devise ways of operating which were not manifestly silly, and to provide a command structure that would facilitate his technical experts and his rank and file in accomplishing

these. That much Rawlinson achieved during the climactic stages of the First World War.

No reflection of the impact of other historians on this one would be complete without mention of Paddy Griffith, for many years a fellow-member of the Department of War Studies at Sandhurst in the 1970s, original thinker and convivial host. His *Battle Tactics of the Western Front: The British Army's Art of Attack 1916–18* characteristically broke new ground. It contrasts the 'amateurism, blundering and fumbling' of the first two years of the war with the battle-tested skills of 'the numerous army and corps HQs who knew how to win so many victories during 1917 and in the [war's last] Hundred Days'. This is a refreshing corrective to much of what had been written about the British army, although Dr Griffith, like one of his infantrymen seizing a fleeting tactical opportunity, sometimes takes his argument further than the supporting evidence will justify.

And of course there was always much more to the war's literature than the work of professional historians. I had read Siegfried Sassoon's *Memoirs of a Foxhunting Man*, *Memoirs of an Infantry Officer*, and *Sherston's Progress* and Robert Graves's *Goodbye to All That* before any scholarly book on the war, and was powerfully influenced by the literature of the 1920s and 1930s that mirrored so much of the war's poetry. Generals and their staffs were usually stupid and unfeeling; soldiers were decent, simple souls, martyred by the incompetence of the men who led them; the war itself was a ghastly reflection of what Wilfred Owen so tellingly called:

The old lie: *Dulce et decorum est / Pro patria mori.*

Even now, drawn back to my books as I work on this, I experience the same overwhelming sense of what Owen called 'the truth untold, the pity of war, the pity war distilled'. Any military historian worth his salt must recognize the risk that he will be 'beating his drum with the bones of the dead', and as far as the Western Front is concerned there are bones aplenty.

Yet there is another side to this. One did not need to be a psychopath to find some pleasure in the war. Sometimes it was the simple pleasure of celebrating survival. Ernst Junger, Germany's most decorated officer, thought that the war left most soldiers with two recurrent memories: one of its worst moments, the other 'when the bottle went round as madly and merrily as ever it did in times of peace'. There were moments when even battle had an insane rapture. At the beginning of the German offensive of March 1918 Junger and his comrades were 'mad and beyond reckoning; we had gone over the edge of the world into superhuman perspectives. Death had lost its meaning'. Malcolm Brown's *Imperial War Museum Book of the Somme*, based on first-hand accounts of the battle, includes Lieutenant Geoffrey Fildes's description of an attack, written shortly after the event. 'Those were sublime moments,' he wrote, 'for we were England upon the field of battle; conquerors offering to her yet further renown, so, with our bodies throbbing the *pas de charge*, we burst through fences, ditches and ruins to our goal.'

The front conferred its own sense of purpose, sometimes absent from civilian life. Graham Greenwell, who served in the infantry from first to last, admitted that 'I look back on the years 1914–1918 as among the happiest I have ever spent'. There were griefs and trials, but 'to be perfectly fit, to live among pleasant companions, to have responsibility and a clearly defined job – these are great compensations when one is very young'. Charles Carrington, another infantry officer, touched the very heart of the process that welded men together. 'We were banded together by a unity of experience that had shaken off every kind of illusion, and which was utterly unpretentious,' he wrote. 'The battalion was my home and my job, the only career I knew.' He resented what he saw as the post-war hijacking of all this. 'It appeared that dirt about the war was in demand... Every battle a defeat, every officer a nincompoop, every soldier a coward.'

The war has proved a fertile seam for film-makers, who have tended to find the Donkeys thesis most compelling, whether tragi-comically as in *Oh! What a Lovely War* or plain tragically as in *Regeneration*. On television Rowan Atkinson and Tony Robinson brought their own brand of humour to the front as Captain Blackadder and Private Baldrick. Such is the power of television that for tens of thousands of viewers Blackadder's aphorisms have become fact: the war's battles were indeed part of a long-running attempt to inch Field-Marshal Haig's drinks cabinet closer to Berlin. A well-turned line of script can sometimes carry more weight than all the scholarly footnotes in the world.

THE FRONT IN PERSPECTIVE

The Western Front presents a complex picture, whether analysed through the recollections of veterans or the work of historians. It also shuns being neatly slipped into its own historical pigeon-hole. For instance, trench warfare was not wholly surprising. Men had fought in trenches before, usually as part of siege warfare – which, in its way, the Western Front came to resemble. An English Civil War (1642–6) song includes the line 'Engineers in the trench, earth, earth uprearing'. Trenches figured in the American Civil War (1861–5) and, along with mines and barbed wire, were an even more common feature of the Russo-Japanese War (1904–5).

Nor was the front unique in terms of the suffering it caused. In the Second World War the Eastern Front imposed a far heavier cost in lives and, while it is impossible to compare human anguish in anything but the most superficial sense, the sheer misery of its battles equalled that of the Somme or Passchendaele. There were other theatres of the Second World War which, in their way, stand comparison with the Western Front in the First. John Ellis, whose work includes admirable studies of battle in the both wars, *Eye-Deep in Hell* for the First and *The Sharp End of War* for the Second, points to: 'The Kokoda Trail in New Guinea, flooded Dutch polders, the Hurtgen Forest and the Reichswald, an Arakan monsoon, frozen foxholes in the Ardennes and the Apennines, the beaches of Tarawa and the putrid slime of Okinawa' as examples of Second World War combat which paralleled the Western Front but somehow failed to grasp the popular imagination in the same way.

Yet the Western Front retains its particular fascination for the British. In part this is because it was the British army's dominating experience of the war. Most British soldiers who came under fire did so in France and Belgium. The fact that a higher proportion of men served in the front line in the First World War than in the Second meant that there was a sense of common experience to the men of 1914–18 that was denied to soldiers of the next generation. As John Ellis put it: 'For the public the First World War was the war in the trenches.' In part, too, it is because of the burden of casualties – Britain and her Empire lost almost a million dead, and most of them perished on the Western Front. The 'ridiculous proximity' of 1914–18 is a convenient proximity in the age of fast ferries, *Le Shuttle* and *Eurostar*. I can visit the Somme and be home in one long day. I recently filmed after lunch in a flooded trench near Ypres – discovered while a car-park was being built, and now buried under concrete – and supped at home. Lastly, there is the whole ineluctable poignancy of the Western Front. Every time I see it I am amazed afresh at what our grandfathers and great-grandfathers were asked to do: and how well they did it.

THE FRONT IN CONTEXT

Although, from the British, French and German viewpoints, the Western Front was the principal theatre of military operations during the First World War, it was not the only one. The war was a contest between two major alliances, with the Allies, chiefly Belgium, Britain, France, Italy, Serbia and latterly the United

States, facing the Central Powers – Germany, Austria-Hungary and their ally Turkey.

There was another major front in the East, where Germany and Austria-Hungary fought the Russians; and two theatres of war in the Middle East – in Egypt and in Mesopotamia (now Iraq). There was sporadic fighting too in Africa, where German colonies in Togoland and South-West Africa were swiftly overrun by Allied forces. Naturally, as military fortunes on both sides ebbed and flowed in these areas, operations in the Western Front were affected for good or bad – releasing more men and supplies or leeching them away. Similarly, the war at sea had its impact on the Western Front, the German submarine campaign trying to starve Britain out of the war; while the Allied blockade of Germany succeeded in restricting vital supplies.

In The War in Outline (page 239), I give a brief summary of the war as a whole, to clarify the strategic background against which the Western Front can best be understood.

THE WAY AHEAD

This book's six chapters examine the Western Front chronologically, from its waxing in the autumn of 1914 to its waning with the armistice of 11 November 1918. Each also focuses on a major theme. The first chapter looks at the ingredients, moral and material, of trench warfare, and describes how the front came into being. The second considers 1915, a year in which the British army in France expanded enormously and the government wrestled with the obdurate problem of feeding the hungry front with men and munitions. The French army and its defining battle, Verdun, are the subject of Chapter 3. Chapter 4 considers the Somme, not from the perhaps familiar viewpoint of the men who fought there, but from the standpoint of the British chain of command. The fifth chapter asks how in 1917, the year of the

French mutinies and Passchendaele, men coped with living and fighting on the Western Front. Finally, Chapter 6 examines attempts to break the front, from the British tank attack at Cambrai in November 1917, through the German offensives of spring and early summer of 1918, to the great Allied offensive of the last Hundred Days of the war.

MAKING THE
FRONT

THE ROAD TO WAR

Europe slid almost effortlessly into war in 1914. Although historians argue over whether the First World War was inevitable, a combination of factors – economic and colonial rivalry, lingering French resentment at the loss of her eastern provinces to Germany following the Franco-Prussian War of 1870–1, and a dangerously unstable system of alliances – certainly created a volatile mix, all too easily ignited. There is a similarly inconclusive debate over the degree of individual and national responsibility for the outbreak of war. It is safest to say that while there were warmongers on both sides, they were outnumbered by politicians and military leaders wrestling with problems quite beyond their resources: the events of July–August 1914 smacked more of calamity than conspiracy.

The spark that blew the old world apart came on 28 June, when Gavrilo Princip, a Bosnian Serb, shot the Archduke Franz Ferdinand, heir to the throne of Austria-Hungary, in Sarajevo, capital of the then recently annexed Austrian province of Bosnia-Herzegovina. Austria, confident of German support, sought to punish the Serbs and, when Serbia rejected an ultimatum designed to be unacceptable, duly declared war on her.

The Serbs had appealed to their Slavic brothers in Russia, who began a partial mobilization in an effort to deter the Austrians. Germany warned that she would answer a full Russian mobilization with one of her own. The Russians, undeterred but still hoping for a diplomatic solution, ordered full mobilization the following day. When Russia declined to cease her military preparations, Germany declared war on her on 1 August. France, Russia's ally, was asked to provide a guarantee of neutrality in a Russo-German war, and declined to do so: Germany accordingly declared war on her on 3 August.

Although Britain had no formal alliance with France, a series of informal staff talks had produced a plan to send an expeditionary force to France in the event of a German attack. Herbert Asquith's Liberal government hesitated briefly but, when German troops invaded Belgium, whose neutrality was guaranteed by a treaty to which Britain was among the signatories, Britain declared war on Germany on 4 August. German violation of Belgian neutrality was the ostensible cause of Britain's entry into the war, but Sir Edward Grey, the foreign secretary, argued that the Europe which would follow a German victory would be wholly hostile to British interests.

THE IMPACT OF CONSCRIPTION

Between the outbreak of war in August 1914 and the end of the First Battle of Ypres the following November, the Western Front was created. Its ingredients were twofold: physical and psychological. The physical components of the front can be traced to the French and Industrial Revolutions. The former had inspired the great *levée en masse* of the 1790s, which produced armies which were not merely huge but also politically inspired, with 'citizen-soldiers' and 'intelligent bayonets', imbued with patriotic fervour, surging out against the stately, pipeclayed armies of monarchical Europe. The latter not merely enabled these huge armies to be armed and equipped, but made possible the mass production of weapons of ever-increasing lethality.

The long peace which followed the Napoleonic wars saw

armies shrink in size, but it was Prussia's perfection of her system of universal conscription that played a major role in her victories over Austria in 1866 and France in 1870–1. Thereafter continental powers recognized that the efficient mobilisation of the nation's manhood was an essential component of military power. National policies varied, but in general the able-bodied young man could expect to be called up for two or three years' service after his eighteenth birthday. Thereafter he would be liable for recall: first as a regular reservist, fighting alongside his regular brother-in-arms, and later in a reserve formation with a less exacting task. One way or another, he would have a military service liability lasting for perhaps twenty years.

Many politicians argued that conscription did more than produce trained men: it also inculcated valuable social qualities, turning wild youngsters into steady, well-disciplined members of society. Middle-class sensibilities could be gratified by policies like the German 'One-year Volunteer' system, which enabled a well-educated young man to serve for only a year, live out of barracks and, all being well, pass to the reserve as an officer when his full-time service ended. In Germany, victory in 1870–1 and the growing militarism which followed it had helped elevate the army's place in society: it was said that the young officer was a god, the reserve officer a demigod. An elderly professor, offered the appointment of honorary privy councillor (which brought with it the title of Excellency) wistfully replied that what he really wanted was promotion from lieutenant to captain on the reserve.

There was not, however, universal support for conscription. In France and Germany alike the Left often complained of bullying NCOs, unjust discipline, needless hierarchical discrimination and pointless drill. There was also, especially in France, a growing distrust of the army's role in support of the civil power: in 1906 the Confederation Général de Travail (CGT), the principal working-class organization, decreed that 'antimilitarist and antipatriotic propaganda must become ever more intense and more audacious'.

The Left's suspicion of militarism cannot be wholly brushed aside. And, especially for France, the notion of the soldier as citizen too was to bring its own baggage to the Western Front. But the fact remains that in August 1914 conscription worked very much as its advocates had hoped. When call-up proclamations were read from town-halls and mobilization notices appeared on the walls, men duly did what was expected of them and reported for duty.

THE CALL TO ARMS

Some, especially the young, did it enthusiastically, and Berlin, Paris, Vienna and St Petersburg saw enormous popular enthusiasm for the war. The poet Charles Péguy wrote on 3 August that: 'Whoever failed to see Paris this morning and yesterday has seen nothing.' A German student was delighted to receive his orders: 'This morning I met a young lady I knew, and I was almost ashamed to let her see me in civilian clothes.' Another German, just turned sixteen, later wrote: 'It is impossible to convey to anyone nowadays the genuine enthusiasm that animated us all.' He did his best to volunteer only to find that all the choice regiments were already full. By the time he was old enough he feared the war would be over. Eventually a kindly major let him into a dragoon regiment. Luckier than most, he was wounded and captured a year later. Louis Barthas, a barrel-cooper (and militant socialist) from the wine-producing Minervois, heard a drum-roll in his village square announcing that the mobilization notice had been put up. It was, he wrote, 'the most terrible cataclysm which ever afflicted our humanity', but the announcement 'to my great astonishment, raised more enthusiasm than gloom'.

Most accounts of August 1914 emphasize this extraordinary excitement. They often fail to underline the darker side of mobilization. In a Breton village the order was greeted with 'a petrified dumbness. Not a voice applauded. Someone sobbed, once, and the crowd stirred, and everyone went their various ways home'. A French sergeant reported that the young peasants in his barrack-room were 'sick at heart'. Marc Bloch, history scholar and reserve infantry sergeant, travelled to a Parisian station in the back of a greengrocer's cart: the 'slightly acrid odour of cabbage and carrots will always bring back the emotions of the early morning depar-ture…' At the station, 'an aged, white-haired father made unavail-ing attempts to hold back his tears as he embraced an artillery officer'. Family men knew that they left hostages to fortune. Walter Bloem, a 46-year-old German novelist and drama critic called up as a captain with the 12th Brandenburg Grenadiers, enjoyed a last bottle of wine with his family and commented tellingly that 'the tear season' had begun.

BRITAIN AND HER ARMY

There was no conscription in Britain. Her geographical position had meant that she never ran the same risk of invasion as continen-tal powers, and her navy had long enjoyed primacy in national affection and defence funding. Her army, small by European stan-dards, was largely a colonial police force and could be kept near its established strength by voluntary enlistment. However, Britain had made heavy weather of dealing with the Boers in the South African War of 1899–1902, and the army that went to France in 1914 was a child of the thoroughgoing reform that followed the war.

Much of it was the work of R. B. Haldane, the formidable Göttingen-educated Scots lawyer who became secretary of state for war when the Liberals took power in late 1905. A general staff was created, and almost immediately embarked upon discussions with the French, at least in part in an effort to undermine the Admiralty's traditional primacy. The regular army was to produce an Expeditionary Force of six infantry divisions and a cavalry division. The nation's assorted non-regular forces – militia, volunteers and yeomanry – were reorganized into a Territorial Force of fourteen brigades of yeomanry cavalry and fourteen infantry divisions.

The Territorial Force trained part-time, helped by a small full-time cadre, and it was not expected to take the field until it had received six months' training after mobilization: even then it was not legally liable for overseas service. There were many regular officers, with the revered figure of Field-Marshal Lord Roberts prominent among them, who felt that the Territorials would never be much use, and who would have preferred conscription. However, despite the growth of anti-German sentiment and the suspicion that war was increasingly likely, old traditions died hard, and Haldane was right to recognize that, whatever the attractions of conscription to continental powers, most Britons found it repugnant.

THE FIREPOWER REVOLUTION

Mass armies, swept into being by conscription, were, then, one ingredient of the Western Front. Two others were the weaponry they carried – and the railways that carried them. During the eighteenth century armies imposed ever-greater standardization on weapons, which were increasingly produced by government arsenals, like Potsdam in Prussia or Charleville in France, or by large-scale contractors, rather than by shoals of artisans filing musket-locks here or casting brass butt-plates there. Although the huge armies raised during the Napoleonic Wars stretched national resources, making foreign purchase and capture useful sources of arms supply, soldiers were usually satisfactorily equipped with the muzzle-loading flintlock musket which was the characteristic weapon of the age.

From the mid-nineteenth century the pace of weapon development accelerated sharply. Breech-loading weapons became generally available, with the Prussian Dreyse 'needle-gun' leading the way: the Franco-Prussian War of 1870–1 was the first conflict in which the infantry on both sides carried breech-loaders. Moreover, these weapons were 'rifled' – spiral grooves in their barrel spinning the bullet, helping to give it greater range and accuracy. Black powder, which burnt slowly and gave off a dense, smelly smoke as it did so, was replaced from the 1880s by the more efficient smokeless powder. Soon infantry rifles used metallic cartridges, housed in a magazine below the breech or under the barrel, and loaded when the firer operated a turning bolt.

British regulars, products of an army which had taken the lessons of the Boer War to heart, were the most accomplished marksmen on the battlefields of 1914. With the .303 Short Magazine Lee-Enfield rifle in their hands, they were expected to hit a target 300 yards (273 metres) away fifteen times a minute, and many could double this rate of fire with almost no loss of accuracy. In both precision and rapidity of fire there was simply no comparison between the magazine rifles carried by European armies on the eve of the First World War and the muskets shouldered by their grandfathers.

Artillery also improved. In 1870–1 the German rifled breech-loading field-guns manufactured by Krupps of Essen dealt easily with muzzle-loading French weapons, and soon after the war the rifled breech-loaders were adopted by most major armies. Not only did the new explosives impel shells with greater efficiency than black powder, but they also increased their bursting effect: high explosive shells, filled with chemical compounds like the British lyddite, were not only effective against troops in field defences but also wreaked havoc on fortresses. In the Russo-Japanese War of 1904–5 Japanese heavy howitzers, their shells weighing 700lb (318kg), smashed the forts around the Russian fortress of Port Arthur. Engineers tried to keep pace with the new artillery by covering the stonework of old fortresses with earth and concrete, and taking their guns off unprotected ramparts and housing them instead in armoured cupolas, but it was a duel in which the gunner usually had the edge.

The new explosives also made shrapnel more effective. This air-burst shell had been invented by a British officer, Henry Shrapnel, during the Napoleonic Wars. By 1914 it had come of age. The shell, a hollow iron canister (still one of the most frequent finds on any First World War battlefield) contained round lead balls about the size of a finger-nail, with an explosive charge below them. The gun's detachment, using information provided by the forward observation officer, set the brass fuse to burst the shell at a given time after leaving the muzzle. Ideally it would explode above, and slightly in front of, its target: the shell acted like a stubby shotgun barrel and the balls shot out in front of it. A British medical officer remembered its effects:

> A young gunner subaltern was on his way up to observe a machine-gun position. Just as he got outside my door a shrapnel shell burst full in front of him. The poor fellow was brought in to me absolutely riddled. He lay in my arms until he died, shrieking in his agony and said he hoped I would excuse him for making such a noise as he really could not help it... he was a fine looking boy, not more than nineteen.

For centuries cannon had bounded back on firing, compelling their detachments to manhandle them back into position after each shot. In 1897 the French introduced the famous 75mm field-gun, the *soixante-quinze*, the first genuine quick-firer. Its ammunition was 'fixed', the shell fitting into a brass case, which made loading simple. When it was fired, most of the recoil was absorbed by hydraulic buffers: the layer, aiming the weapon, might need to make only a small adjustment before the next round was fired.

Gunners had long plied their trade using 'direct fire', engaging targets they could see. As infantry weapons improved so this became more risky, for a field-gun in the direct fire role was vulnerable to the fire of magazine rifles, as British artillerymen had found to their cost in South Africa. A metal shield on the gun gave some protection to its detachment, but was no real answer. 'Indirect fire', where guns were fired from behind cover at a target they could not see, their fire directed by an observer with a telephone, was the way ahead. Field guns were deployed about 20 yards (18 metres) apart, and, using their dial sights, a form of military theodolite called a director, and basic trigonometry, they were laid so that their lines of fire were parallel, and a target hit by one gun could be hit by all. Targets could be 'registered' by being hit, and their target information – the elevation and bearing required to hit them – was recorded, enabling gunners to bring down fire with the minimum of delay. Indirect fire was in its infancy in 1914, and in the first months of the war many gunner officers, by personal preference or tactical circumstance, found themselves using direct fire like their ancestors at Waterloo a century before.

The machine-gun had first been regarded by some armies as an artillery, rather than an infantry, weapon. In 1870–1 the French had treated their machine-gun, the Mitrailleuse, rather like a field gun, with the result that it was often knocked out by German artillery before it could do much damage to German infantry. The first machine-guns were often cumbersome, complicated and unreliable as their designers tried to solve the several problems connected with rapid fire. Most, like the Gatling and the Mitrailleuse, were multi-barrelled, but between 1883 and 1885 Hiram Maxim developed a weapon which used the force of the recoil to extract an empty case and push a new round into the weapon's chamber, making possible the single-barrelled machine-gun. A water-filled jacket fitted round the barrel to keep it cool, and ammunition was housed in fabric belts. The Maxim was adopted by Britain in 1888 and by Russia and Germany soon afterwards.

These machine-guns fired between 450 and 600 rounds a minute, and were well described as 'the concentrated essence of infantry'. They were not available in huge numbers in 1914. A British battalion had two, and a three-battalion German regiment six, contained in its machine-gun company. As the war went on, however, not only were these heavy machine-guns produced in ever-increasing numbers, but an assortment of lighter weapons, like the British Lewis and the German MG 08/15, were developed to increase infantry firepower.

WAR BY TIMETABLE

Technology did more than enable men to kill one another with greater facility. The military potential of the railway had been identified quickly. In 1840 the British moved a battalion by rail; six years later the Russians transported a corps of 14,500 men; and in 1859 the French sent an entire army, horse, foot and guns, to northern Italy by train for their campaign against the Austrians. Prussia, with her central position in Europe and the ever-present risk of war on two fronts, was especially well-placed to use the railway for military purposes, and not least among her reasons for success in the Austro-Prussian War of 1866 and the Franco-Prussian War of 1870–1 was the efficiency of the railway move to concentration areas.

After the Franco-Prussian War, staff officers across Europe studied the railway as if their lives depended on it – which, in a sense, they did. Moving troops to the frontier rapidly and efficiently was of fundamental importance: starting the process a day or two late might give the enemy an advantage which would prove decisive. The importance of railway timetables injected a note of desperate urgency into the events of July and August 1914. When, on 1 August, the Kaiser summoned General von Moltke, Chief of the German General Staff, and told him that the political situation demanded war only with Russia and not with France, Moltke replied that the plan to send the bulk of the army westwards by train was simply too complex to be altered. 'I answered His Majesty,' wrote Moltke, 'that this was impossible.' An appalled Kaiser, comparing Moltke with his uncle, architect of German victories in 1866 and 1870, snapped back: 'Your uncle would have given me a different answer.' And so he might, but in 1914 general staffs were rarely able to rise above the remorseless logic of the timetable.

THE CULT OF THE OFFENSIVE

The result of railway mobilization, universal conscription and the revolution in military technology was a weapon density unparalleled in the history of warfare: the material origins of the Western Front. Yet its psychological origins are no less important: all the weapons in the world would not produce stalemate unless the soldiers using them proved resolute. And European armies and the societies they served had spent much time and trouble ensuring that the young men who rattled off to war in August 1914 would indeed be resolute.

Offensive war plans ruled. Russia planned to advance into East Prussia. France proposed to launch Plan 17, an all-out attack into the lost provinces of Alsace and Lorraine. And Germany sought to execute a plan named after a previous Chief of the General Staff, Alfred von Schlieffen. Schlieffen had concluded that the huge size of Russia and her population made it possible to win only 'ordinary victories' in the east. Accordingly, if faced with the war on two fronts which the Franco-Russian entente made almost inevitable, he would leave a small force to check the Russians and throw the bulk of his armies against France. Because the French had fortified their common border with Germany – we shall see some of these fortifications loom large in Chapter 3 – he intended to send the strongest of his marching armies through Belgium, whence they would wheel down through France, the outer army passing west of Paris, to catch the French in a battle of encirclement somewhere in Champagne.

Moltke is often blamed for tinkering with Schlieffen's handiwork, but in truth the conditions which applied when the plan was new had changed by 1914. The Russians had embarked on serious military reform as a result of their defeat by Japan, and could no longer be relied upon to wait, supinely, while their French allies were dismembered. And in any event there were some aspects of the Schlieffen plan, not least the logistic problem of sustaining over a million men on the march, let alone in the campaign's decisive battle, which had never been properly addressed.

The plan was a gamble, its risk magnified by the violation of Belgian neutrality which would draw Britain into the war. If it did not produce a quick German victory, then Germany would find herself fighting the enormous human and material resources of Britain and her Empire. Indeed, one major reason for French interest in obtaining British support in August 1914 was not the tiny British Expeditionary Force (BEF) itself, but the fact that this was a promissory note for what might eventually be produced if, God forbid, the war was not over by Christmas.

These offensive plans were founded on the belief, held in slightly different forms by each of the combatant nations, that attack alone would produce decisive results. The British Field Service Regulations Part 1 of 1909 proclaimed: 'Decisive success in battle can be gained only by a vigorous offensive. Every commander who offers battle, therefore, must be prepared to assume the offensive sooner or later.' The French 1913 Regulations were even more extreme. 'The French army, returning to its traditions,' they decreed, 'henceforth knows no law but the offensive.'

But how were armies to relate their belief in the strategic imperative of the offensive to the ghastly reality, so vividly demonstrated in the Franco-Prussian and Boer Wars, that fire killed? It was certainly no simple task. Some theorists advocated the 'defensive offensive', a thrust into enemy territory with all the war-winning characteristics of the offensive, but whose attacking units actually fought defensive battles when they met the enemy. Others, like the clear-sighted Emile Mayer, writing just after the Boer War, predicted that the next European war would witness the collision of two human walls: each side would try to outflank the other until stopped by the sea or a neutral border. This sort of outcome was not merely the prediction of leftist politicians or military commentators. In 1906 Schlieffen himself warned:

> All along the line the corps will try, as in siege warfare, to
> come to grips with the enemy from position to position, day
> and night, advancing, digging in, advancing again, digging in
> again, etc., using every means of modern science to dislodge
> the enemy behind his cover.

At a British general staff conference in 1909 the future General Sir Aylmer Haldane observed that it was 'impossible to take a position which is well defended by machine-guns until these guns have been put out of action'.

Regulations reflected the evidence of the Transvaal battle-fields. The British, who had learnt their lessons the hard way, redrafted their infantry regulations to emphasize that fire must pave the way for the successful assault. The 1904 cavalry drillbook veered away from the charge altogether, and a preface by Lord Roberts decreed that 'the sword must henceforth be an adjunct to the rifle; and that cavalry soldiers must become expert rifle shots and be constantly trained to act dismounted'. In 1904 the French abandoned the shoulder-to-shoulder infantry tactics of the 1894 drillbook and replaced them with the more flexible use of fire and manoeuvre. They even went as far as contemplating the abolition of the *cuirassiers*, heavy cavalry equipped with breastplate and helmet, whose charge had helped decide Napoleonic battles but had been of diminishing efficacy ever since.

In the decade before the war the pendulum swung back. It did so partly because many European theorists maintained that wars elsewhere were special cases: in South Africa, for example, ranges were unusually long and visibility good. The British, ran the argument, were scarcely a proper European army and their Boer opponents were not soldiers at all, just warlike farmers. For Frenchmen and Germans, who were in any case out of sympathy with British aims in South Africa, it was temptingly easy to claim that the British had often failed to take Boer positions because they had not been determined enough. A French officer, General Langlois, coined the phrase 'acute transvaalitis', by which he meant 'abnormal dread of losses on the battlefield'. The British army was evidently infected by this, claimed its continental critics, and an army which was not would have pushed on through the dangerous zone of Boer rifle fire to win the battle.

The events of the Russo-Japanese War were used to support belief in the offensive. This time both combatants were recognizably first-rate armies: the Russians had a formidable reputation, and the Japanese had been trained by the Germans. Both sides had magazine rifles, breech-loading artillery, machine-guns and barbed wire. The Russians took up entrenched positions and lost: the Japanese attacked them and won. They did so by a mixture of careful preparation by their artillery and unstinted courage by their infantry. European observers were not slow to point up the 'lessons'. In Britain, Major General Edward Altham declared that the campaign in Manchuria, the region in north-west China contested by Russia and Japan:

> showed over and over again that the bayonet was in no sense an obsolete weapon and that fire alone could not always suffice to move from position a determined and well-disciplined enemy... The assault is of even more importance

than the attainment of fire mastery which antecedes it. It is the
supreme moment of the fight. Upon it the final issue depends.

His fellow-countryman General Sir Ian Hamilton declared that:

War is essentially the triumph, not of a chassepot [French
breech-loading rifle] over a needle-gun, not of a line of men
entrenched behind wire entanglements and fire-swept zones
over men exposing themselves in the open, but of one will
over a weaker will…

In France, General Joseph Joffre, appointed Chief of the General
Staff in 1911, linked belief in defensive doctrine to the lethargic
and politicized state of the French army generally, and welcomed
the fact that 'our young intellectual élite finally shook off the
malady… which had upset the military world and returned to a
more healthy conception of the general conditions prevailing in
war'. The influential Colonel de Grandmaison advocated 'a
conquering state of mind' and the need to 'cultivate with passion
everything that nears the stamp of the offensive spirit'. In doing so
he touched a popular nerve. The novelist Ernest Psichari wrote of
'a proud and violent army', and at the Sorbonne the philosopher
Henri Bergson spoke of *l'élan vital*: how better to demonstrate it
than to impose your will on the enemy in battle?

Even artists rallied to the cause. Among the works in the Paris
Salon of 1914 is one depicting a French dragoon looking east,
where a German *uhlan* (lancer) holds prisoner two maidens, embodiment of the lost provinces of Alsace and Lorraine. Around the
dragoon, uniformed spectres from the Franco-Prussian War – here
a *cuirassier*, there an Algerian *tirailleur* – rise to demand vengeance.

By 1914 the transformation was complete. The armies of
Europe went to war expecting heavy losses and intending to
impose their will-power upon hostile firepower. The 1907 edition
of British Cavalry Training set the tone. 'It must be accepted as a
principle,' it announced, 'that the rifle, effective as it is, cannot

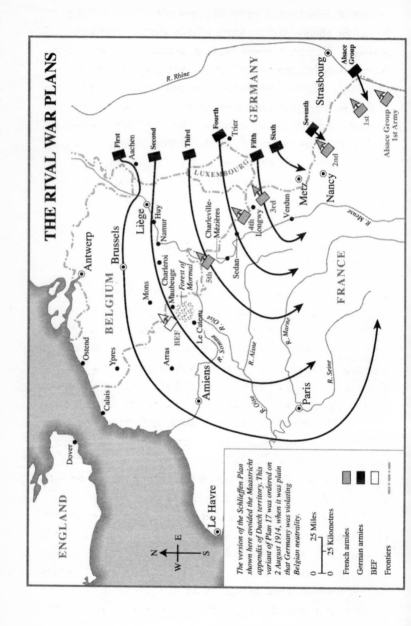

THE RIVAL WAR PLANS

ENGLAND

Dover

Le Havre

Calais

Ostend

Ypres

Antwerp

Brussels

BELGIUM

Mons

Arras

BEF

Amiens

Le Cateau

Maubeuge

Forest of Mormal

Charleroi

Namur

Huy

Liège

Paris

R. Seine

R. Oise

R. Somme

R. Aisne

R. Marne

5th

Sedan

Charleville-Mézières

4th

Longwy

3rd

Verdun

R. Meuse

Nancy

Metz

2nd

LUXEMBOURG

GERMANY

R. Rhine

First

Aachen

Second

Third

Fourth

Trier

Fifth

Sixth

Seventh

Strasbourg

Alsace Group

1st

Alsace Group
1st Army

FRANCE

N
W—E
S

0 _____ 25 Miles
0 _____ 25 Kilometres

The version of the Schlieffen Plan shown here avoided the Maastricht appendix of Dutch territory. This variant of Plan 17 was ordered on 2 August 1914, when it was plain that Germany was violating Belgian neutrality.

French armies

German armies

BEF

Frontiers

replace the effect produced by the speed of the horse, the magnetism of the charge, and the terror of cold steel.' 'Great victories,' wrote the German Colonel Wilhelm Balck, 'are nearly always accompanied by great losses.' And so, as Sir Michael Howard has so tellingly written, 'the casualty lists that a later generation was to find so horrifying were considered by contemporaries not an indication of military incompetence, but a measure of national resolve, of fitness to rank as a Great Power'. Many, particularly young regulars, had steeled themselves for the test. Lieutenant Alan Hanbury-Sparrow of the Royal Berkshires expected a short war with very heavy casualties: he told his parents that they must not expect to see him again.

THE OPENING MOVES

Early on the morning of 4 August troopers of General von der Marwitz's cavalry corps rode across the Belgian frontier about 70 miles (112 kilometres) east of Brussels. Behind them, detraining on the wide platforms of the frontier stations, were the leading elements of the three armies of the German right wing: Kluck's First, Bulow's Second and Hausen's Third. They were to move through the narrow gap between the hilly Ardennes to the south and the 'Maastricht appendix' of Dutch territory jutting down from the north, marching on into Belgium and then curling down into France. On their left, the Fourth and Fifth Armies formed up around Metz and Trier, and further south the Sixth and Seventh Armies held the bulk of Alsace and Lorraine.

It was the essence of Schlieffen's concept that the right wing should be kept strong. If the French attacked into Alsace-Lorraine they would do him a kindly favour, for the further they got the more certain would be their own defeat as the northern armies swung in behind them. Moltke, as we have already seen, was no gambler, and over the weeks that followed he was to dilute

Schlieffen's plan: first, by sending troops to the Eastern Front to shore up Germany's precarious position there; and second, by allowing the very capable Crown Prince Rupprecht of Bavaria, from 8 August in overall command of the Sixth and Seventh Armies, to counterattack, thus pushing the French out of a net that might have engulfed them.

Moltke's fatal hesitancy was, however, still a thing of the future when the Germans faced their first major challenge. The fortress of Liège, its twelve main forts encircling an old citadel, blocked the German avenue into Belgium. Initial attempts to take it failed, and although Major General Erich Ludendorff, fortuitously on the scene, managed to bluff his way into the citadel, the forts held out. But not for long: they were battered into submission by mighty Krupp 420mm siege howitzers, assisted by some Austrian-made 305mms. The Belgian commander, General Leman, was pulled unconscious from the wreckage of the last fort to fall.

The Belgian army retreated on Antwerp as German columns poured through Belgium. It was often a brutal passage. Footsore and frightened young soldiers reacted harshly to rumours of snipers, and their commanders sometimes used terror in an attempt to break the spirit of a nation whose resistance both surprised and irritated them. Allied propaganda was to make much of German atrocities in Belgium, and many of the stories were certainly overblown. Still, the episode helped harden the cement of the Western Front by persuading many Allied soldiers – and, no less to the point, their civilian friends or relatives – that theirs was indeed a hateful enemy.

The French commander-in-chief, Joseph Joffre, had established his headquarters (Grand Quartier Général – GQG) at Vitry-le-François on the stately River Marne, roughly equidistant between the headquarters of his five armies. He undoubtedly had some evidence of the scale of German preparations in the north. However, the French believed that if the Germans were able to extend well into Belgium it could only be by using reserve divisions in the front line, something the French, with their mistrust of reservists, would not countenance. Joffre's deputy, General de Castelnau, had previously greeted a sceptical regional commander and a local politician, concerned that there would be no troops left to defend the north-east, with the words: 'If they come as far as Lille, so much the better for us.' Just as Schlieffen had hoped that a French offensive into Alsace-Lorraine would make his own task easier, so the French believed that by extending far into Belgium the Germans could only weaken their own centre – where the French blow was to fall.

The French attack showed the early flare of a false dawn. The 1st and 2nd Armies advanced on Morhange and Sarrebourg, and Crown Prince Rupprecht's men obligingly gave ground before them: Sarrebourg fell on 18 August. But it could not last. The French infantry, in their long blue overcoats and red trousers, pushing on into broken ground unsuited for this sort of offensive, were cut to pieces by German machine-guns. German artillery, its fire directed by spotter aircraft, battered them mercilessly. Rupprecht, tired of defending against an enemy that was already losing momentum, begged Moltke to allow him to counter-attack, and Moltke weakly gave way.

What was called the Battle of the Frontiers raged from 20 to 24 August, and there could be no doubt that the French were the losers as the doctrine of *l'offensive à l'outrance* (the all-out offensive) died on the wooded slopes and open fields of northern Lorraine. Captain Charles de Gaulle (leader of the Free French a generation later) admitted that:

> The first shock was an immense surprise… Suddenly, the enemy's fire became precise and concentrated. Second by second the hail of bullets and the thunder of the shells grew stronger. Those who survived lay flat on the ground, amid the screaming wounded and the humble corpses. With affected

calm, the officers let themselves be killed standing up, some obstinate platoons stuck their bayonets in their rifles, bugles sounded the charge, isolated heroes made fantastic leaps, but all to no purpose. In an instant it had become clear that not all the courage in the world could withstand this fire.

The first month of the war cost Joffre 212,000 men, about 20 per cent of his mobilized strength and nearly 40 per cent of his regular officers. And there was little sign that the Germans could be stopped. Ferdinand Foch, commanding one of Joffre's corps in front of Nancy, held his ground with a tenacity which marked him out for rapid advancement, but elsewhere the view from Vitry was one of unrelieved gloom.

Things were especially bleak in the north. Charles Lanrezac, commanding the 5th Army on the French left, was a brilliant but acerbic officer who had the unfortunate distinction of being wise before the event. He warned Joffre that there were Germans in strength to his north, and asked to be allowed to edge round to face them, rather than attacking north-east alongside the 4th Army on his right. Joffre reassured him, but on 22 August Lanrezac's men were badly mauled around Charleroi by the German First and Second Armies, and on the 23rd he began to fall back.

ENTER THE BEF

Lanrezac's plight was of particular interest to the British Expeditionary Force (BEF), in position on his immediate left. Pre-war planners had assigned this post to the BEF for perfectly good reasons. It was relatively simple for the British to get there, moving by rail from their main port of entry at Le Havre to a concentration area in the triangle Maubeuge–Hirson–Le Cateau. As there was no certainty that they would actually arrive, as Britain's commitment to France could not be guaranteed, it seemed to the French that the left flank, where nothing much was to happen, was just the place for the BEF to go. But Schlieffen, as we have seen, had other ideas.

The BEF went to war about 100,000 strong, with a large cavalry division and four infantry divisions, 1st, 2nd, 3rd and 5th: 4th Division joined after the fighting had begun. In command was Field-Marshal Sir John French, a 62-year-old cavalryman who had made his reputation in the Boer War. His chief of staff, Sir Archibald Murray, was a charming but rather ineffectual officer who had made a bad recovery from a stomach wound received in South Africa. The real power on the staff was Henry Wilson, an ebullient francophile who had handled most of the pre-war negotiations with the French. The BEF's quartermaster-general, responsible for its supplies, was Sir William 'Wully' Robertson, a man of great common sense who had been commissioned from the ranks and advertised the fact by deliberately dropping his aitches.

The BEF formed two corps, each of two divisions. Sir Douglas Haig commanded I Corps. A dour Lowland Scot, Haig had been French's brigade-major (chief of staff) when French commanded the Aldershot cavalry brigade before the Boer War, and during it he served on French's staff. Their characters were very different. An officer who knew them both wrote that: 'French was a man who loved life, laughter and women, whereas Haig was… the dullest dog I ever had the happiness to meet.' French, who knew that he was not a natural staff officer, had a high regard for Haig, whose fluent prose gave form to some of French's airier conceptions. Haig was less impressed by French, writing: 'In my own heart I know that French is quite unfit for this great command at a time of crisis in our nation's history.' Although French had been on excellent terms with King Edward VII, whose amorous inclinations were similar to his own, he was less well-regarded by George V, who disapproved of the field-marshal's light-cavalry lifestyle. Haig, in contrast, was happily married to one of Queen

Mary's ladies-in-waiting, and his relations with the King were good enough for him to be able to disclose his reservations about Sir John before the campaign had started.

Sir James Grierson commanded II Corps. A capable but overweight officer, he joked that the medal ribbons on his well-filled chest commemorated many a hard-fought battle with knife and fork. A heart attack killed him in his train on the way to the concentration area. French wired Lord Kitchener, who had just taken over as secretary of state for war, asking for Sir Herbert Plumer as a replacement, but to his horror received Sir Horace Smith-Dorrien instead. The poor relations between the two men were a matter of common knowledge in the army, and Kitchener believed that French cherished 'great jealousy of and personal animosity towards' Smith-Dorrien. He seems to have made the appointment in the hope that Smith-Dorrien's sound professional judgement and robust moral courage would enable him to act as a sheet-anchor on the mercurial commander-in-chief. However, Smith-Dorrien was subject to occasional fits of uncontrollable rage which could make him difficult to work with, and it needed no deep knowledge of French's character to realize that he would be unlikely to forget that Smith-Dorrien had been foisted on him.

Before leaving England on 14 August Sir John French had been given written orders by Kitchener. These concentrate on the relationship between Sir John and the French, and in so doing go straight to the heart of the politics of the Western Front. 'The special motive of the force under your control,' wrote Kitchener,

> is to support and co-operate with the French army against our common enemies…
>
> It must be recognized from the outset that the numerical strength of the British force and its contingent reinforcement is strictly limited, and with this consideration kept steadily in view it will be obvious that the greatest care must be exercised towards a minimum of losses and wastage.

Therefore, while every effort must be made to coincide most sympathetically with the plans and wishes of our Ally, the gravest consideration will devolve upon you as to participation in forward movements where large bodies of French troops are not engaged...

I wish you distinctly to understand that your force is an entirely independent one and you will in no case come under the orders of any Allied general.

John Terraine observed that in these orders 'lay the germs of controversies that would bedevil the British Command throughout the war'. The relative strengths and capabilities of the French and British armies would change, as would the British government's attitude to 'losses and wastage'. From start to finish the war on the Western Front was fought by a coalition whose major partners had agendas, political and military, of their own: yet without that coalition there could be no Western Front – and no Allied victory.

Sir John French's confidence in that Allied victory was unbounded as he dined in Paris on 14 August, noting in his diary that 'the usual silly reports of French reverses' were 'all quite untrue'. He visited Joffre the following day, and on the 16th he went up to Rethel on the Aisne to meet Lanrezac. The latter was already preoccupied with reports of German forces moving round to his north, and the meeting was not a success. Sir John spoke bad French, and haltingly asked Lanrezac if he thought that the Germans proposed to cross the Meuse at Huy. 'Tell the marshal,' snapped Lanrezac, 'that in my opinion the Germans have merely gone to the Meuse to fish.'

The BEF began to move forward on the 21st, and on the night of the 22nd it halted with II Corps on its left, on the line of the Mons–Condé Canal, and I Corps on its right, in front of Maubeuge. Reports from the Royal Flying Corps and the cavalry confirmed that there were Germans to its front, and late on the 22nd Lieutenant Edward Spears, liaison officer with the 5th Army, told French that Lanrezac was in real trouble around Charleroi. If the BEF continued to advance as planned, it would risk being exposed and cut off.

MONS

Early on the morning of Sunday 23 August French spoke to his corps commanders, telling them something of his doubts and ordering them to be ready to move in either direction. He then set off for Valenciennes, on his left, to inspect his lines-of-communication troops who had just been converted into an infantry brigade. While he was away elements of Kluck's First Army collided with II Corps on the canal in front of Mons, and the British army fought its first battle of the war. By nightfall Smith-Dorrien had pulled back to an intermediate position south of Mons, and Haig had come up on his right. The action had cost the British just over 1600 men, but the Germans, whose attacking columns had been cruelly punished by British rifle fire, lost at least 5000 men and perhaps many more. Walter Bloem spent much of the day trying to close with an invisible enemy: his regiment, 12th Brandenburg Grenadiers, lost twenty-five officers and 500 men.

When he returned to his headquarters Sir John, buoyed up by the francophile optimism of Henry Wilson, at first hoped to hold his ground for another day, but around midnight he heard that Lanrezac had ordered a withdrawal and deduced that 3rd and 4th Armies were also falling back. He ordered a retreat, and Murray left it to the corps commanders to sort out the details for themselves. On the 24th I Corps, which had not been seriously engaged, broke away without difficulty. Smith-Dorrien moved 3rd Division, on his right, first: when it was clear he ordered 5th Division to pull back. The low ridge between the villages of Elouges and Audregnies was held by 5th Division's rearguard – a battalion each of Cheshires and Norfolks, with cavalry and gunner support. Orders to retire never reached the Cheshires, who were eventually overwhelmed: almost 2600 men were lost that day.

The 25th saw the two corps of the BEF separated by the Forest of Mormal, and that night they halted to its south, I Corps around Landrecies and II Corps west of Le Cateau. It was an eventful night. A party of Germans bumped into 4th Guards Brigade in Landrecies. Haig, whose headquarters was nearby, became uncharacteristically agitated, and told GHQ that he was under heavy attack. Smith-Dorrien, whose own rearguards were still on the road, was unable to help. Murray collapsed with the sheer strain of it all, and when Smith-Dorrien telephoned in the small hours to announce that he would not be able to withdraw as ordered because the Germans would be on top of him before he could move, French was not at his best. He sent a message which concluded: 'Although you are given a free hand as to method this telegram is not intended to convey the impression that I am not anxious for you to carry out the retirement and you must make every effort to do so.'

LE CATEAU

Smith-Dorrien hoped to hold his ground long enough to administer what he termed 'a stopping blow', checking the Germans and giving his own men a chance to resume the retreat uninterrupted. The 4th Division, which had just arrived, albeit incomplete, fought under his orders, prolonging his line to the west. Le Cateau was a much bigger battle than Mons. It began soon after dawn and, although Smith-Dorrien's men beat off frontal attacks with relative ease, the position of 14th Infantry Brigade, overlooking Le Cateau on the right of 5th Division, deteriorated rapidly, and 2nd Suffolks were eventually wiped out.

Early in the afternoon Smith-Dorrien felt that the moment had come to slip away, and ordered his divisional commanders to retire, starting with 5th Division on his right, followed by the 3rd Division, with 4th Division moving off last. There were inevitably some tragedies: a battalion of Gordon Highlanders did not receive the order, and held on till it was too late. Many of Smith-Dorrien's guns were fought right forward with the infantry, and when the time came to get them away their teams were shot down. In all, 7812 men and thirty-eight guns were lost. French's official dispatch paid tribute to Smith-Dorrien's 'rare and unusual coolness, intrepidity and determination', and most historians now agree that the controversial decision to stand and fight was indeed correct. Privately, however, French continued to blame him for disobeying orders, and believed that II Corps had suffered far more severely than was in fact the case.

THE RETREAT GOES ON

Colonel Huguet, French liaison officer with GHQ, certainly took a gloomy view, and reported that the British had lost the battle of Le Cateau and with it all cohesion. Franco-British relations cooled markedly on 26 August when French and Joffre met at St Quentin. Joffre discussed the creation of a new 6th Army on the Allied left, but French, whose staff had not yet told him of the scheme, was unimpressed. Relations thawed a little over lunch, when Joffre acknowledged that his plans had failed and expressed dissatisfaction with French's *bête noire,* Lanrezac.

The retreat went on, although the BEF was never in the same peril as before. In the days that followed Joffre showed his stature as a commander, dismissing the incompetent or unlucky (Lanrezac was soon replaced by Franchet d'Esperey, known to the British as 'Desperate Frankie'), sustaining the faint-hearted, cobbling together the 6th Army to bolster up his left, and always striving to keep Sir John up to the mark. As his grip tightened, so Moltke's weakened. His headquarters (Oberste Heeresleitung – OHL) had moved up to Luxembourg on 29 August, but Moltke was still far away from his marching armies. Joffre, in contrast, had himself whizzed between army headquarters by his chauffeur, one of France's leading racing drivers. He often listened in silence and said little, but somehow his calm, not often recognized as a gallic virtue, radiated through to his commanders. It was a time when this 'imperturbable calm and rough good sense' really counted.

The crisis came in early September. On the 1st, Sir John French was considering pulling the BEF out of the line altogether in order to refit but was summoned to meet Kitchener in the British Embassy in Paris. There were no witnesses to what was doubtless a difficult interview, though by its close Sir John was left in no doubt that the BEF's fate was inextricably linked to that of the French army. The French government left Paris the following day, leaving the cadaverous but tough General Joseph Galliéni, its military governor, with instructions to defend it to the last. It was an aviator from the Paris garrison who brought the first piece of really good news of the campaign. The German First Army, drawn eastwards by the nervousness of the neighbouring Second Army and not sustained on its course by a strong directing will from OHL, began to turn in front of Paris, offering a flank which could be attacked.

THE MARNE

The Battle of the Marne took place in sweltering heat along the lovely valley of the Marne. It was not decided by a single brilliant master-stroke or decisive breakthrough: ultimately the will of the commanders was no less important than that of the exhausted young men who actually did the fighting. Manoury's 6th Army, reinforced by troops from Paris sent out in taxi-cabs, struck at Kluck's flank. Although Kluck blocked the stroke, in doing so he opened a gap between First and Second Armies. The British, despite Joffre's desperate entreaty, were slow to exploit this, but Franchet d'Esperey pushed 5th Army forward, and on his right the new 9th Army, under Foch, also attacked.

Moltke, already wrestling with his moral responsibility for all the killing – his staff saw him weeping silently at dinner – was deeply worried, and sent out a trusted staff officer, Lieutenant-Colonel Hentsch, to visit the army commanders. It is not clear just how wide Hentsch's powers actually were, but a long journey in an uncomfortable car through the rear areas of fighting armies helped sap his resolve, and he was persuaded that retreat was the only answer. Moltke might yet have won: either on the Marne, where the battle still hung in the balance, or by switching resources to Rupprecht, who was close to a breakthrough further east. But he was a sick and beaten man: in his own defeat lay that of the armies he commanded. Not for nothing did the French hail 'The Miracle of the Marne'.

THE AISNE

Between 9 and 13 September the Germans fell back to the River Aisne, with the Allies close behind. The weather, blazing hot during August, broke, and the Allies reached the swollen river to discover the Germans securely dug in on the wooded spurs behind it. It speaks volumes for the skill of French's engineers that they managed to throw a number of bridges across the river, and for the valour of his infantry that they pressed their attacks with such courage towards unattainable objectives. It was soon evident that the Germans, with their preponderant artillery, were not to be shifted. Sir John noted in his diary that artillery was the dominant arm in this kind of battle, and told the King that: 'the *spade* will be as great a necessity as the rifle, and the heaviest types and cali-bres of artillery will be brought up on either side'.

THE RACE TO THE SEA

Deadlock on the Aisne induced both sides to feel for the open flank and to move troops northwards in what became known as 'the race to the sea'. Traditionally this sort of outflanking movement had often proved decisive, with the larger army able to lap round its opponent's flank and rear. In 1914, however, armies were too big, and the coast too close, for this to happen, and between September and October the trenchlines groped steadily northwards, across the uplands astride the Somme, in front of Arras, down into alluvial Flanders and on into the dunes of the North Sea.

The BEF moved north in early October. French felt that this would simplify his lines of communication and give him the best chance of acting against what he hoped to be the German flank, and on 13 October GHQ was established in the little town of St Omer. His army had already grown larger, with one more division sent out from England and another, initially sent out to support the Belgians at Antwerp, falling back to join the BEF just before Antwerp fell.

Foch had been sent up to command French forces in the north, and he encouraged Sir John in his belief that there was indeed a flank to be found around the small Belgian town of Ypres, and on 18–19 October he cracked the whip, urging his commanders to push on for Menin and turn the German flank. In the process they encountered powerful German forces intent on turning the Allied flank, and the First Battle of Ypres blazed out as Allied and German troops collided in the lush, low Flanders countryside.

THE FIRST BATTLE OF YPRES

It was soon clear that it was the Germans who were doing the attacking. On 31 October they came perilously close to breaking the British line, taking the village of Gheluvelt just as their shells hit the nearby château at Hooge, which housed two British divisional commanders, killing one and wounding the other. A counter-attack by a battalion of Worcesters stabilized the situation, but over the days that followed the fighting continued to be desperate. The cavalry corps, fighting dismounted with a skill which shamed many of those who had made jokes about 'donkeywallopers', held Messines Ridge, south of Ypres, and it was there that the London Scottish, the first of the many Territorial battalions to fight on the Western Front, went into a battle which cost it more than half its strength: thereafter there were fewer jests about 'Saturday night soldiers'. The battle reached its crisis on 11 November, when the Prussian Guard, coming on at a jogtrot through the mist, punched a hole repaired only by another stunning counter-attack, this time in Nonne Bosschen by the Oxfordshire and Buckinghamshire Light Infantry. Ypres was held, but at what a cost: the BEF had lost over 58,000 officers and men. In each of the battalions which fought on the Marne and at Ypres there remained, on average, only one officer and thirty men who had landed in August.

The First Battle of Ypres had also hit the Germans hard. Many of the students who had responded with such enthusiasm to the call to arms had perished. On 27 October Captain Rudolf Binding, a cavalry officer serving with a German infantry division, wrote:

> These young fellows we have, only just trained, are too helpless, especially when their officers have been killed. Our light infantry battalion, almost all Marburg students... have suffered terribly from enemy shellfire. In the next division, just such young souls, the intellectual flower of Germany, went singing into an attack on Langemarck [north of Ypres], just as vain and just as costly.

The Germans called the battle the *Kindermord zu Ypren* – the Massacre of the Innocents at Ypres.

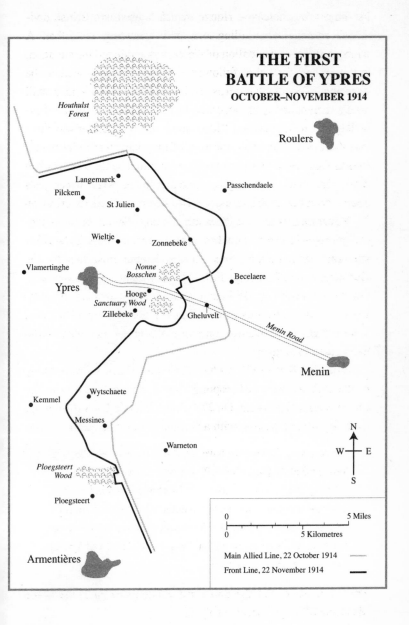

THE FIRST BATTLE OF YPRES
OCTOBER–NOVEMBER 1914

Houthulst Forest

Roulers

Langemarck

Pilckem

St Julien

Passchendaele

Wieltje

Zonnebeke

Nonne Bosschen

Vlamertinghe

Ypres

Hooge

Sanctuary Wood

Zillebeke

Becelaere

Gheluvelt

Menin Road

Menin

Kemmel

Wytschaete

Messines

Warneton

N
W —|— E
S

Ploegsteert Wood

Ploegsteert

Armentières

| 0 | | | | | 5 Miles |
| 0 | | | 5 Kilometres | | |

Main Allied Line, 22 October 1914 ....

Front Line, 22 November 1914 ▬▬▬▬

The Christmas overtones of this expression were not misplaced, for the battle died away with Christmas not far off. It was a miserable December, with rain giving way to freezing cold, as the soldiers on both sides settled down to the war's first winter. There had already been some instances of fraternization between the French and the Germans, and on 2 December Smith-Dorrien noted that there had been 'weird stories from the trenches' about Anglo-German fraternization, and decreed that such things would not go on in his corps. But somehow the human spirit was stronger than regulations, and there were a number of local truces that Christmas. They were small comfort to men who stood in trenches down in the Vosges, the chalk of Champagne, the mud of Flanders or the dunes of the coast, garrisoning a front that stretched from the Swiss border to the North Sea. The war had gone to earth.

FEEDING THE
FRONT

'WESTERNERS' AND 'EASTERNERS'

The New Year opened with a debate which was to become sharper as 1915 went on. While what were called 'westerners' maintained that the Western Front should continue to dominate British strategy, 'easterners' suggested that, as there was evident stalemate on the Western Front, the Allies should look elsewhere for a decision. The dispute was more complex than any simple outline suggests, and there were many whose views changed with tactical circumstances. But it was fundamentally important, for 1915 saw the character of Britain's commitment change. The old Regular army which had gone to the war in 1914 began to be replaced by the mass army which, ultimately, would win it in 1918. The chief task of British military and political leaders in 1915 was feeding the front with men and munitions. Yet the question remained: which front?

The year was only a day old when Sir John French received what he termed 'another incomprehensible letter' from his political master, Lord Kitchener, secretary of state for war. Kitchener told him that:

> The feeling here is gaining ground that, although it is essential to defend the line we now hold, troops over and above what is necessary for that service could better be employed elsewhere. The question *where* anything effective could be accomplished opens a large field and requires a good deal of study. What are the views of your staff?

Sir John was not pleased, for he already had firm views of his own. On 27 December 1914 he had visited Joffre at Chantilly and come to what he termed 'a complete understanding as to future plans'. The French would mount a two-pronged attack into the great German salient that bulged out malignantly towards Noyon, one thrust going in around Arras, in Artois, and the other in Champagne. The British, meanwhile, would take over the line between La Bassée and the coast as reinforcements arrived. French was hoping for a little more, as he had been encouraged by Winston Churchill, First Lord of the Admiralty, to mount an offensive along the Flanders coast, with the support of naval gunfire, in order to get the Germans out of the ports of Ostend and Zeebrugge. A gradual extension to the coast would delay this offensive.

The arrival of Kitchener's letter sharpened his concern, and made him increasingly anxious to push ahead with the coastal offensive, because doing so would help establish the primacy of the Western Front over the 'sideshows' which were being discussed in London. On 3 January he assured Kitchener that given sufficient men and munitions the German line could be broken. Attacking Turkey, Germany's ally, would simply 'play the German game... [and] draw off troops from the decisive spot, which is Germany herself'.

By January the issues which would dominate 1915, and echo far beyond it, had been clearly set out. There were those 'easterners' who, in Kitchener's words, were inclined to regard the Western Front as 'a fortress which cannot be taken by assault', and to look elsewhere for a decision. The 'eastern' solution was especially attractive to politicians like Churchill and David Lloyd George. On the other side of the debate were those who argued that there was no alternative to the Western Front. The bulk of the German Army was there, and the war could not be won unless it was beaten. Moreover, any British lack of commitment to the Western Front might weaken French resolve, and so imperil the very existence of the entente. Sir John French set out the case for the Western Front very clearly, and his successor Haig was to do the same.

French's note of 3 January highlighted the importance of men and munitions. The supply of both these commodities stood at the very forefront of British military policy. The 'westerners' argued that the war could be won only if they were sent to France and Belgium. However, doing so would result in Britain confronting her major adversary in the principal theatre of war, in a marked deviation of the practice of more than a century. Wellington had fought the French in Spain, a secondary theatre, with the navy at his back: most major battles of the Napoleonic wars had been left to Britain's continental allies. In the circumstances of 1915 the 'western' solution may well have been the only proper one: but, once adopted, it would commit the British army to the most obdurate test of its history.

RAISING NEW ARMIES

The war had already begun to transform the army. At the outbreak of war the regular army numbered almost 247,500 men, about a third of them stationed in India. There were, in addition, regular reservists, Territorials and colonial troops, most of them Indian, but the fact remained that this was not a force organized on a continental scale. Moreover, the regular army, the small special reserve intended to help bring it up to strength on mobilization, and the Territorial Force were all under-recruited, and comparatively few of the latter had accepted a voluntary liability to serve overseas. It was small wonder that Kitchener's August 1914 instructions to Sir John French had emphasized caution. Yet by November 1918 over 5,700,000 men had passed through the army, slightly over 22 per cent of the adult male population of the United Kingdom. 'The creation of the country's first mass citizen army,' writes Peter Simkins, 'was the product of a gigantic act of national improvisation which had considerable repercussions throughout British society.'

Kitchener had made his reputation overseas, first as commander-in-chief of the Egyptian army, at whose head he defeated the Dervishes at Omdurman in 1898; then as chief of staff to Roberts, and latterly commander-in-chief, in South Africa; and finally as commander-in-chief in India. In 1914 he was British Agent (effectively proconsul) in Egypt, and, fortuitously home on leave when war broke out, was appointed secretary of state for war, an unusual post for a field-marshal but one apparently justified by his towering status with the British public.

Kitchener's virtues and vices were, alike, on a grand scale. He believed that it would be a long war, and planned accordingly, with a breadth of vision few could equal. Despite his suggestion that there might be more fruitful theatres than the Western Front, he recognized the crucial importance of supporting the French. He was enormously hard-working and energetic. But he was not a team player, and needed only to see a settled organization in order to swing his boot through it. He had no knowledge of Whitehall, little regard for politicians, and increasingly became an isolated, rather forbidding figure.

On 7 August 1914 Kitchener published his appeal for his first 100,000 recruits, and his face, its unblinking gaze emphasizing that 'Your Country Needs You', glared down from the billboards. Recruiting soon became a flood, reaching 33,204 on 3 September, the highest ever attained on a single day. In the first eight weeks some 761,000 men joined the army. Kitchener had no time for the Territorials, calling them 'a town clerk's army', and raised his New Armies through the adjutant-general's branch at the War Office.

The great majority of them were infantry, and formed service battalions of country regiments. Kitchener was astute enough to harness local enthusiasm, and some of the most distinctive New

Army units were the Pals' Battalions, raised by mayors and corpo-
rations or recruiting committees of local industrialists and
magnates. Typical examples were 10th (Service) Battalion, the
Royal Fusiliers (the Stockbrokers Battalion); 16th North-umber-
land Fusiliers (the Newcastle Commercials); and 12th York and
Lancaster (the Sheffield City Battalion).

Raising the New Armies was one thing: training and equip-
ping them was quite another. During the first five months of the
war the Western Front had guzzled Britain's trained manpower,
and there was little enough left to train and command the New
Armies. Battalion Commanding Officers were very often retired
regulars, assisted, perhaps, by a young regular wounded at Mons
and a handful of pensioner NCOs. In some Pals' Battalions a
man's pre-war status was often reflected in his military rank, and
mill-owners commanded companies containing their workers: in
others there was a fierce pride in not taking a commission. In the
ranks of 23rd Royal Fusiliers (the Sportsmen's Battalion) there
were two England cricketers, the country's lightweight boxing
champion and a former lord mayor of Exeter.

There was far too little space in barracks for the New Armies.
A few units were housed in huts, but others lived in tented camps
while their huts were built, and discipline and health suffered. In
the winter of 1914 thousands of men were billeted on civilians,
which caused problems of its own. There were too few khaki
uniforms to go round, and 500,000 suits of blue serge were issued,
to the discontent of the recipients who feared that they resembled
postmen. Modern webbing equipment was in short supply, and
rifles were scarcer still: the Sheffield City Battalion received its
full quota a week before it went abroad.

Because all combatants had gone to war in the expectation of
a short conflict, all found themselves running short of artillery
ammunition in the autumn of 1914. During the two and a half
years of the Boer War the British fired 273,000 shells: between

15 August 1914 and 15 February 1915 the BEF fired a million. On a smaller scale, L Battery Royal Horse Artillery fired more shells on a single day, 24 August 1914, than it had in the Boer War. Shells were only part of the problem, for all armies had to provide that plethora of 'trench stores' – barbed wire, sandbags, duck-boards, picks and shovels – to build and maintain their defences. They also needed to produce the new weapons demanded by trench warfare, like flare pistols, light machine-guns and trench mortars.

Britain's problem was compounded because her army was expanding at a rapid rate, and she had to equip new soldiers as well as old. Kitchener observed that: 'The old-fashioned little British Army was such an infinitely small proportion of the world's demand that looking after its equipment was not much more difficult than buying a straw hat at Harrods. But now I am going to need greater quantities of many things than have ever been made before.' The supply of artillery ammunition had reached crisis-point by November 1914, and the British official history acknowledges that two of French's three corps had little more than enough ammunition for one day's battle, and the third had even less. Robertson told the master-general of the ordnance, responsible for ammunition supply, that it was a pity that his department had provided guns capable of firing ten rounds a minute if it took factories a day to produce these shells. In January 1915 he complained that there was a shortfall in delivery of 8000 4.5-inch howitzer rounds, and it was difficult to plan operations properly without knowing what ammunition would be available. For men in the trenches the effect was dispiriting: observation officers might call for fire, only to be told that already the day's allocation had been expended.

The provision of ammunition was an enormous problem. Existing factories, whether private or government-owned, were far too small to meet the demand, and there were too few tools and too few skilled workers. Contracts were placed with overseas suppliers, but their capacity, too, required time to surge. Sudden changes in requirements did not help: the BEF went to war with no high explosive shells for its field guns, because shrapnel had performed better in the Boer War, but immediately demanded them, forcing new production lines to be set up. And, in a mood where, in England, dachshunds were kicked and windows of German-owned shops smashed, the fact that the master-general of the ordnance was named Sir Stanley von Donop was an added difficulty.

NEUVE CHAPELLE

Joffre planned to launch his two-pronged offensive as soon as the weather improved, and Sir John intended to support it by putting in an attack of his own. The BEF had now been restructured into two armies: Haig's 1st Army in the south, opposite La Bassée, and Smith-Dorrien's 2nd in the Ypres salient. French considered attacking Messines Ridge, near Ypres, and Aubers Ridge, near La Basseé, and eventually decided on the latter, in Haig's view because 'he could never be sure of getting satisfactory results from SD, and... because my troops were better'.

Joffre emphasized that his offensive depended on the British relief of two of his corps north of Ypres, to which Sir John had agreed. Then, on 9 February, Sir John heard that the 29th Division – the last to contain mainly regular battalions – was to be sent to Salonica, in northern Greece, instead of France. Although he was to receive a Territorial division in its place, one could not 'carry out, with a Territorial Division, what I had proposed with a regular one'. Joffre was furious, and declared that because the British could not now relieve his troops as planned, the offensive was off. Sir John, undaunted, went ahead anyhow.

The attack was entrusted to Sir Henry Rawlinson's IV Corps,

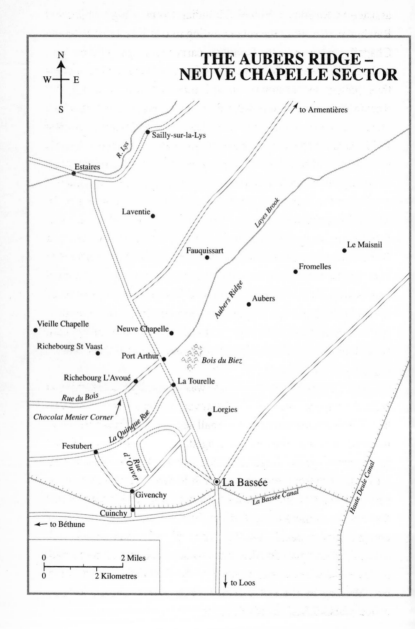

**THE AUBERS RIDGE –
NEUVE CHAPELLE SECTOR**

N
W E
S

to Armentières

R. Lys

Sailly-sur-la-Lys

Estaires

Loyes Brook

Laventie

Fauquissart

Le Maisnil

Fromelles

Aubers Ridge

Aubers

Vieille Chapelle

Neuve Chapelle

Bois du Biez

Richebourg St Vaast

Port Arthur

Richebourg L'Avoué

La Tourelle

Rue du Bois

Chocolat Menier Corner

Lorgies

La Quinque Rue

Festubert

Rue d'Ouver

La Bassée

Givenchy

La Bassée Canal

Cuinchy

Haute Deule Canal

to Béthune

0   2 Miles
0   2 Kilometres

to Loos

assisted by Sir James Willcocks's Indian Corps. Haig had ordered Rawlinson to capture the salient jutting into British lines at Neuve Chapelle, to 'surprise the Germans, carry them right off their legs, and push forward to the Aubers... ridge... and exploit the success thus gained by pushing forward mounted troops forthwith'. Rawlinson's preparations were meticulous. He concentrated 340 guns – as many as the whole BEF had taken to France in August 1914 – against the salient, representing one gun for every 6 yards (5.5 metres) of front attacked. He took great care that they registered targets only a few at a time so as not to alert the Germans.

When the bombardment began at 7.30 on the morning of 10 March its effect was stunning. 'The earth shook and the air was filled with the thunderous roar of the exploding shells', wrote a British officer. 'To the watching thousands the sight was a terrible one: amidst the cloud of smoke and dust they could see human bodies with earth and rock, portions of houses, and fragments of trench hurtling through the air.' The Germans had a single trench-line with a few machine-guns behind it and, because of the high water-table, trenches had high parapets and were easy to observe: the damage was severe.

The first wave of the attack was generally successful and Neuve Chapelle was taken. However, the late arrival of two howitzer batteries meant that a small section of German trench to its north was not effectively engaged, and its garrison included two machine-guns. These lacerated two of the attacking battalions, 1st Middlesex and 2nd Scottish Rifles. The latter's story is admirably told in John Baynes's book *Morale*. In it he notes that the Scots' Commanding Officer had left it to his company commanders to decide whether their officers would attack with swords that day: two decided that swords would indeed be carried. At least one officer wore a sword on the first day of the Somme, but this may be the last occasion when several British infantry officers brandished swords in battle.

If the sword was on its way out, the machine-gun had certainly arrived. When the undamaged trench was bombarded late in the morning, its garrison promptly surrendered. Captain G. C. Wynne describes how: 'one officer and sixty-three men of the 11th *Jäger* Battalion, came out from it… walking across the dead, estimated at about 1000, lying literally in rows, whom they had slain that morning…' The delay caused by this set-back, coupled with the great difficulty Rawlinson experienced in assessing what had actually happened at the front so as to issue purposeful orders (the rapidly emerging problem in such attacks) meant that the second phase of the attack, the advance on Aubers Ridge, was delayed.

Rawlinson's critics have suggested that Neuve Chapelle was a tragedy of wasted opportunity, and had the advance gone on without pause the British would have made significant gains. Another of the great truths about trench warfare was emerging: it was generally easier for the defender, whose reserves were not moving across a shell-torn battlefield, to compensate for his failure, than for the attacker, whose communications became more fragile by the minute, to reinforce his success. There were German reserves in position behind the broken line by 9.30 am, and in truth the prospect of a breakthrough, after the first hour of the attack, was never great.

By nightfall the British and Indian attackers had overrun the defences on a front of 4000 yards (3640 metres), penetrating to a maximum depth of 1000 yards (910 metres). The battle went on until the night of the 12th, but neither fresh British assaults nor a German counter-attack made much progress. French spoke warmly of 'the defeat of the enemy and the capture of his position'. but he had certainly expected more from the battle: it would show the French that they had an ally who knew his business, and demonstrate to Kitchener that feeding the Western Front was by no means pointless.

THE PROBLEM OF EXPLOITING SUCCESS

French had briefed his cavalry commanders personally. Rawlinson thought that their hopes that the cavalry would find an opportunity for effective action induced both French and Haig to prolong the battle longer than he himself thought wise. Mention of cavalry in the context of the Western Front still raises a guffaw, but the issue is more complex than it seems. Many commentators, including A. J. P. Taylor, who should have known better, have maintained that 'most British generals were cavalry men'. Both commanders-in-chief on the Western Front, French and Haig, were indeed cavalry officers. But by 1918, of seventeen corps commanders only one was a cavalryman, and of fifty-one divisional commanders, only five. As John Terraine has pointed out: 'The overwhelming majority of generals actually handling troops in battle came, as one might expect, from the arm which produced the majority of those troops: the infantry.'

The proportion of cavalry in the BEF dropped rapidly, from 9.28 per cent in September 1914 – a not unreasonable percentage for open warfare – to 3.88 a year later and 1.65 in March 1918. British cavalry were trained to fight dismounted as well as mounted – we have already seen them hold Messines Ridge with tenacity in the autumn of 1914 – and there remained times when they provided a mobile reserve, although the small establishment of cavalry units and the need to detail horse-holders meant that they generated less fire-power than comparable infantry formations.

For much of history the massed charge on the battlefield had been the most eye-catching of cavalry achievements. However, the pursuit after the battle, that converted a retreat into a rout, was often the finest achievement of the mounted arm. In 1914 exploitation remained a cavalry function, for there was, as yet, no other arm which could accomplish it. The proliferation of fire-power, not to mention the cluttered nature of the battlefield, meant that exploitation and pursuit were difficult to achieve. They were not impossible – as the brilliant action of the Canadian Cavalry Brigade, which advanced 8 miles (nearly 13 kilometres), killed many Germans, and captured 400 men and nearly 100 machine-guns at Cambrai in 1917, was to show. Yet there was, in essence, a technological gap which would be filled only by the development of the armoured car and the tank.

THE LESSONS OF NEUVE CHAPELLE

Neuve Chapelle raised several issues, the difficulty of injecting cavalry into the battle only one of them. It highlighted the problem of achieving effective command and control on the battlefield. If Rawlinson deployed killing-power which would have astonished the Duke of Wellington a century before, his communications had improved far less dramatically. The telephone was undeniably useful, but its wires were often cut by shellfire, and in an attack at this stage in the war the last links in the chain of command usually depended on runners toiling through the crater-fields.

The unlearned lesson of Neuve Chapelle concerned the artillery. Rawlinson achieved a higher concentration of guns per yard of front attacked than he would on the Somme a year later, and because he had little ammunition he fired it swiftly. In doing so he achieved not only what the Germans called 'the first real drum-fire [*Trommelfeur*] yet heard', but also surprise. Heavy fire, delivered rapidly and without warning, was to become a key ingredient of successful attacks towards the war's end: it made its unsung début at Neuve Chapelle.

Haig planned to try again elsewhere, but it soon became clear that there was insufficient ammunition to permit him to do so. French told Kitchener: 'Cessation of the forward movement is necessitated today by the fatigue of the troops, and, above all, by the want of ammunition.' He went on to observe that unless sufficient shells arrived, 'the offensive efforts of the army must be spasmodic and separated by a considerable interval of time. They cannot, therefore, lead to decisive results'.

Over the next two months the issue of ammunition supply rose to become a crisis which would help bring down the government. Sir John's approach to it was never wholly objective. He knew that some of Rawlinson's difficulties had more to do with command and control than with ammunition, but was reluctant to say so. This was partly to excuse failure, partly to safeguard his own position as commander-in-chief (he remained worried that Kitchener himself would bring the New Armies to France), and partly to maintain the primacy of the Western Front. Allied warships had already shelled Turkish positions on the Gallipoli peninsula, at the entrance to the Sea of Marmara on the sea route to Constantinople, and a landing would take place on 25 April. For much of 1915 the Gallipoli expedition competed with the Western Front for scarce resources, and the knowledge did little to calm the mercurial Sir John French.

THE SECOND BATTLE OF YPRES

Joffre, meanwhile, had resurrected his plans for an offensive, and yet again Sir John agreed to relieve the French north of Ypres. Gallipoli cast its shadow over planning, however, and Sir John was unable to discover if or when extra troops would arrive. Nevertheless, in early April the British took over almost 5 miles (8 kilometres) of French front to the north-east of Ypres, finding the trenches 'in a deplorable condition'. It was here that the Germans struck on the afternoon of 22 April, using gas for the first time. Their infantry went in behind a cloud of greenish-yellow chlorine, against which Allied troops in the sector had no effective protection. Within minutes men's eyes began to sting and their throats tightened. Soon they were fighting for breath, and the worst affected began to cough up blood.

It is not surprising that some French and British troops broke and ran: what is more astonishing is that some of the defenders held their ground. Private John Lynn of the Lancashire Fusiliers fired his machine-gun until the gas became too thick for him to see targets. Then he mounted it higher, on a stout fence-post where the gas was thinner, and fired long busts into German infantry until he collapsed, literally blue from the effects of gas; he died soon afterwards. The stand made by the Canadian Division, its flank around St Julien exposed by the attack, was a remarkable feat of arms and an early indication of the quality of Canadian troops.

The Germans were ill-prepared to capitalize on their success, and the front was soon stabilized closer to Ypres after a series of bloody attacks and counter-attacks that reflected little credit on the high command on either side. Sir John French was pressed to counter-attack by Joffre and Foch, but was unconvinced that his men had much chance of success and became increasingly critical of the French. Being allied to them once in a lifetime, he complained, was more than enough. Smith-Dorrien, whose 2nd Army held the sector, sensibly recommended pulling back to shorten the line. French, ever more mistrustful of Smith-Dorrien since Le Cateau, first put Sir Herbert Plumer, one of 2nd Army's corps commanders, in charge of operations at Ypres, and then, on 6 May, gave him command of 2nd Army. Wully Robertson had taken over as chief of staff from the exhausted Archie Murray in January, and he broke the news to Smith-Dorrien. ''Orace,' he said, 'you're for 'ome.' When Plumer proposed retiring to a shorter line, French promptly agreed.

If the handling of the battle does not show Sir John at his best, it does shed light on his increasingly impossible position. He knew, from liaison officers at Joffre's headquarters, that Kitchener had made it plain that he would be replaced if Joffre thought it wise. Thus failure to support the French, even when their plans were unrealistic, could bring him down. Kitchener had already told Asquith, in words with which many historians would agree, that French 'is not a really scientific soldier; a good capable leader in the field, but without adequate equipment and expert knowledge for the huge task of commanding 450,000 men'. Then on 31 March Kitchener warned him that:

> he considered Joffre and I were 'on our trial' – that if we showed within the next month or 5 weeks that we could really make 'substantial advances' then he would... always back us up with all the troops he could send. But if we failed it would be essential that the government should look for some other theatre of operations.

Lastly, the strain of command weighed heavily on him. In March he had told Lord Esher, who visited him at St Omer, that: 'It is a solemn thought that at my signal all these fine young fellows go to their death.' He believed firmly in the immortality of the soul, and thought that his room was '*thick* with the spirits of my dead friends'.

SPRING OFFENSIVE

On 8 May 1st Army attacked Aubers Ridge as an accompaniment to the French offensive further south in Artois. It was predestined to fail. As a result of Neuve Chapelle the Germans had been working like beavers on their defences, doubling or tripling the depth of their barbed wire, strengthening the front-line trenches and beginning work on a second trench a short distance behind it, with dug-outs for its garrison and communication trenches leading forwards, to form a much stronger first position. Much further back, a line of concrete machine-gun posts formed rallying-points in case the first position was broken. Over the months that followed this would become a second position in its own right, almost as strong as the first.

In their painstaking study of Rawlinson's command, Robin Prior and Trevor Wilson observe that British gunners were able to bombard this improved line with only one-fifth of the intensity of shells delivered at Neuve Chapelle. The plan for the infantry assault was complex: some battalions had to make a 45-degree turn, under fire, in no man's land. It is small wonder that the attack failed disastrously. The British and Indians lost 11,500 men, and the German regiments facing them reported losses of less than a thousand. The diary of the German 57th Regiment expressed its admiration for the magnificent courage with which the British had attacked, as well as surprise at the repetition of attacks in broad daylight once the first had failed.

THE SHELLS SCANDAL

French was appalled. He had watched the battle from the tower of a ruined church, and when he returned to his headquarters he found an order to send 22,000 shells to Gallipoli. Charles Repington, a retired officer and *Times* correspondent, was staying with him, and Repington's article of 14 May, with the headline 'Need for Shells: British attacks checked: Limited supply the cause: A Lesson from France', was, it later transpired, the result of collaboration between the two men.

French also sent two of his staff to London with the same documents which had been shown to Repington. They were passed to David Lloyd George, a member of Asquith's cabinet, and to the opposition leaders Balfour and Bonar Law. The government would have survived the 'shells scandal' had this been the only crisis facing it, but Lord Fisher had just resigned as First Sea Lord, and Asquith decided that the two events 'would, if duly exploited… in the House of Commons at this moment have had the most disastrous effect upon the general political and strategic situation…' He decided to form a coalition government, in which Lloyd George became minister of munitions. Kitchener stayed on at the War Office, although his reputation was damaged by a press campaign against him in which French was heavily implicated.

Lloyd George's ministry unquestionably made a difference, though perhaps this was not as profound as its many publicists were to suggest. The first consignment of munitions it ordered did not arrive till October 1915, and the much-reviled War Office had actually supervised a nineteen-fold increase in output in the first six months of the war. None the less, the ministry pressed ahead with energy, employing 'men of push and go', experienced businessmen who, as Lloyd George put it, could 'create and hustle along a gigantic new enterprise'.

By the spring of 1918, 61 per cent of the male industrial force was involved in war work. The number of women workers also grew: fewer than 100 worked at Woolwich arsenal in November 1916, but there were 22,000 six months later and 30,000 a year on. The social and political effects of this expansion were considerable, but represented less of a uniform advance towards women's rights than is sometimes supposed. Many women lost their jobs after the war, and the 1921 census showed that the proportion of 'gainfully employed females' was actually lower than it had been in 1911.

FRESH OFFENSIVES

Although, as the official verdict put it, Aubers Ridge had been 'a serious disappointment', the British continued attacking. On 16 May 1st Army tried again at Festubert, just south of Neuve Chapelle, this time after a deliberate three-day bombardment which embodied French's conviction, all too well justified in the light of Aubers Ridge, that 'it's simple murder to send infantry against these powerfully fortified entrenchments until they've been heavily hammered'. They were not hammered heavily enough: lack of shells saw to that. The bombardment seriously damaged the German trenches but left many machine-guns and dug-outs intact.

Three divisions attacked at night and daybreak, overrunning much of the front line but being held up by machine-guns which had survived the shelling, and isolated parties of Germans hanging on in shell-holes or sections of wrecked trench. The Germans eventually abandoned their first position and reinforced their second, but there was too little time and ammunition to engage this effectively, and although the British advanced a maximum of 1000 yards (910 metres) on a front of 3000 (2730 metres), it was for a cost of 16,500 men.

No sooner had Festubert ended than the British were again pressed to attack to divert German attention from an offensive of their own. Joffre initially suggested that Loos, at the southern end of the British sector, would be ideal, but the ground was unpromising and Haig gained permission to attack the Rue d'Ouvert at Givenchy, further north. Rawlinson was not convinced that Givenchy was much better, writing that: 'it will cost us many thousands of lives before we are in possession of the place unless we get an unlimited amount of ammunition to smash the place to pieces before we go in'. After a deliberate bombardment, with a slightly better ratio of guns to trench than at Aubers Ridge, IV Corps attacked, winning small lodgements which it could not hold when the supply of hand-grenades – one of the key weapons in this kind of fighting – faltered. Rawlinson was not surprised that the attack on the Rue d'Ouvert failed, and admitted that: 'A feeling exists that life is being thrown away on objectives which are not worth it… Are we not asking too much of our infantry?'

Rawlinson made no efforts to explain his uneasiness to his superiors, and with good reason. In July a 3rd Army was formed, and although Rawlinson was the senior corps commander he was not given command, which went instead to Sir Charles Monro. He suggested in his diary that he could not 'expect fair treatment with Sir John and old Robertson' against him. He was quite right. French had already come close to sacking him, and wrote the following year that: 'No one trusts or believes in Rawlinson.' This drew Rawlinson closer to Haig, the only real candidate for supreme command if French fell.

ALLIED PLANS

French and Joffre met at Chantilly on 24 June and gave a ringing vote of confidence in the Western Front. A passive defence in the west, they argued, would be 'a bad strategy, unfair to Russia, Serbia and Italy, and therefore wholly inadmissible'. They were united in their opposition to the Gallipoli venture, and urged that all available British troops should be sent to France. Another series of conferences in July, attended by the principal Allied leaders, established broad agreement that there should be a major offensive on the Western Front. Joffre soon revealed that, unoriginally, he proposed to attack in Artois, with the French 10th Army around Vimy supported by the BEF to its north, while another major assault was delivered in Champagne. Cavalry, and infantry in motor-buses, would exploit the breakthrough, whose final objective lay beyond the Belgian frontier.

Joffre was anxious for the BEF to attack on his immediate left, around Loos, into the area taken over by Haig's 1st Army in June. Haig was initially inclined to think that the sector offered good prospects for an attack, but soon changed his mind. On 23 June he reported to French that the ground was hopeless: the Germans were securely dug into an industrial landscape of mining suburbs, slag-heaps and pitheads. On 12 July French went up to Notre Dame de Lorette, a piece of commanding ground near Vimy Ridge (now crowned by a cemetery and ossuary housing many of the French soldiers who had died taking it), to see for himself. He too was not favourably impressed, for the terrain was 'covered with all the features of a closely inhabited flourishing mining district...' The only advantage was that artillery fire could be directed against it from high ground in Allied hands. Yet this was not enough. On 20 July he told a liaison officer with Joffre's headquarters that the most he could do would be to launch diversionary attacks and soon, prompted no doubt by Haig and Robertson, he decided against these too. He was quite firm, declaring that: 'we should not be helping the French by throwing away thousands of lives knocking our heads against a brick wall'.

Sir John could not hold his ground. Joffre leant hard on him in August, earnestly requesting his support, and, when Sir John replied that he would attack chiefly with artillery, Joffre demanded instead 'a large and powerful attack... executed with the hope of success and carried through to the end'. French gloomily told Haig that 'we must have big losses in order to achieve any result', but privately suspected that success was impossible. Then Kitchener threw his weight into the balance. The Russians had just lost Warsaw and were in full retreat. Sir John was bidden to attack 'and do our utmost to help the French, even though, by doing so, we suffered very heavy losses indeed'. In the face of this unequivocal order, GHQ and 1st Army set about planning the battle. Perhaps because it was the only way out of his moral quandary, Sir John's confidence improved, and a visitor to GHQ in late August found his staff 'quite optimistic'.

A German officer had prophesied that his own side's use of gas at Second Ypres would earn Germany widespread criticism, but, having expressed their moral outrage, her enemies would follow suit. He was perfectly correct, for having condemned 'that damnable gas' Sir John immediately demanded a retaliatory capacity. By early September there was confidence that lavish use of gas would make a real difference at Loos. Rawlinson was less sure, noting presciently that 'we are not very good at these improvisations'.

LOOS

Haig's outline plan was simple enough. His I and IV Corps would attack between the distinctive double slag-heap south of Loos and the La Bassée Canal, while his two other corps made diversionary attacks. Once the German first position was broken, the General Reserve, Lieutenant-General Haking's IX Corps and the cavalry, would pass through the gap. Haking's corps was dangerously untried. Its headquarters was newly formed and its staff largely inexperienced, and although the Guards Division was built on a nucleus of well-trained men, its two New Army divisions, 21st and 24th, had never fought before: some of their units, indeed, arrived in France as the preparations reached their climax. Archie Murray had written from London to tell French that the New Armies were not really what they would term soldiers. Their artillery was 'an unknown quantity' (scarcely surprising, given its shortage of guns, ammunition and range-space) and the infantry was not well enough trained to go straight into the line. However, endless route marches meant that it was very fit, and would do well if it could be thrown in once the battle was won.

French and Haig disagreed profoundly about the positioning of IX Corps. French believed that it would not be needed until the battle's second day and could therefore be kept well behind the front, where he, as commander-in-chief, could commit it as required. French was an avid fan of Napoleon, and his handling of the reserve was very much in the Napoleonic tradition. Haig, however, argued that he would need the reserve much more quickly, stressing that he would have no spare troops and: 'The whole plan of operations of the 1st Army is based on the assumption that the troops of the General Reserve will be close at hand…'

French remained obdurate. His opponents were to suggest that this was because he wanted to initiate the decisive blow himself. It is, however, more likely that his initial fears about the battle had not fully subsided. If he put IX Corps at Haig's disposal from the outset, there was always the risk that Haig would commit it to battle come what may: French wanted to be sure that the gap really was there before Haking's green troops were shoved into it. Haig was not at all pleased that the General Reserve was being held back, and wrote that it was 'impossible to discuss military problems with an unreasoning brain of this kind'.

Rawlinson, for his part, had misgivings about even the first phase of the battle. The Germans had been working hard on their second position, some 2500–3000 yards (2275–2730 metres) behind the first, so that field guns used to bombard the first position would have to be moved forward in order to have the range to hit it, and situated on a reverse slope (behind the crest-line of low ridges) so that it could not be seen from British trenches. Rawlinson noted that this second position was now fully protected by barbed wire, and was convinced that simply capturing the first position would be a real achievement. His dependence on Haig precluded him from raising his concerns, and at Loos in 1915, just as at the Somme a year later, there was no meeting of minds between Rawlinson and his immediate superior.

The attack was preceded by a bombardment, going on for four days, in which 533 guns fired more than a quarter of a million shells. But because the front was so wide – this was the biggest offensive in the British army's history to date – the ratio of guns to yard of front was far lower than at Neuve Chapelle. However, the attack was not wholly reliant on the shelling, for it was hoped that the 5100 cylinders containing about 140 tons of chlorine would have a profound effect. Most German soldiers had primitive gas masks, but the gas release would persist far longer than these would retain even their marginal effectiveness: even the

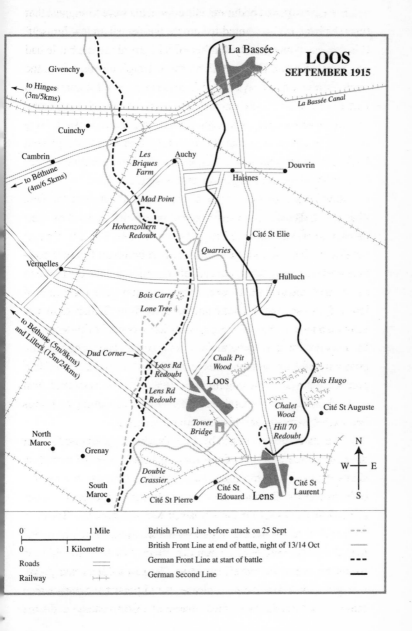

LOOS
SEPTEMBER 1915

La Bassée

La Bassée Canal

Givenchy

to Hinges
(3m/5kms)

Cuinchy

Cambrin

to Béthune
(4m/6.5kms)

Les
Briques
Farm

Auchy

Douvrin

Haisnes

Mad Point

Hohenzollern
Redoubt

Cité St Elie

Quarries

Vermelles

Hulluch

Bois Carré

Lone Tree

to Béthune (5m/8kms)
and Lillers (15m/24kms)

Dud Corner

Loos Rd
Redoubt

Chalk Pit
Wood

Bois Hugo

Lens Rd
Redoubt

Loos

Chalet
Wood

Cité St Auguste

Tower
Bridge

Hill 70
Redoubt

North
Maroc

Grenay

N

W   E

S

South
Maroc

Double
Crassier

Cité St
Edouard

Cité St
Laurent

Cité St Pierre

Lens

0		1 Mile
0		1 Kilometre

Roads

Railway

British Front Line before attack on 25 Sept   - - -

British Front Line at end of battle, night of 13/14 Oct

German Front Line at start of battle   - - -

German Second Line

better gas-masks issued to machine-gunners would be unable to cope. Smoke was to be added to the gas-cloud to confuse the Germans, and shrapnel would sweep their trenches when the gas was released and the defenders would be likely to man their parapets. Manhandling the heavy cylinders into front-line trenches was back-breaking, and connecting them to release pipes, one vertical and one horizontal, was difficult work in poor light with cross-threaded nuts, jammed joints and spanners that sometimes broke or failed to fit. None the less, by dawn on 25 September the 1400 men of the gas companies had done a better job than either their own inexperience or the inherent difficulty of their task implied, and were ready to launch what the high command insisted on calling 'the accessory'.

There remained one problem. Successful use of gas relied on wind strong enough to carry it to the German lines but not so strong that it blew the gas cloud apart. Haig spoke to his meteorologist, Captain Gold, early that morning. Then, in the garden of his château at Hinges, he asked his senior aide-de-camp, Lieutenant-Colonel Alan Fletcher, to light a cigarette. The smoke drifted gently towards the German lines and the leaves on the poplar trees rustled encouragingly. It was barely adequate but, aware that without gas only a much smaller-scale attack would be possible, Haig gave the order to launch the gas.

The gas behaved erratically. In the south it spread straight into Loos valley, where it lingered among the German trenches. Further north, it drifted obliquely between the trench-lines, and some of it blew back into the British trenches, causing some of the confusion perhaps too vividly described by Robert Graves in *Goodbye to All That*. During the whole battle there were 2632 British gas casualties, of whom only seven died, so stories about wholesale slaughter of friendly troops by gas are simply not true. Nevertheless, the British respirator, known as 'the goggle-eyed booger with the tit', which consisted of cloth impregnated with chemicals with two eye-pieces and a rubber mouthpiece, was no adjunct to effective fighting, and because the gas hung about in trenches, shell-holes and pockets in the ground men either had to wear them when no gas seemed evident or to do as most did and unmask in sheer frustration and take their chances.

The battle went well in the south where IV Corps attacked. The Territorials of 47th London Division took the southern part of Loos, and another Territorial division, 15th Scottish, poured through Loos itself, encouraged by the shriek of the pipes as several pipers risked the gas to play their comrades into battle. North of the Hulluch–Vermelles road, which bisects the battle-field, I Corps was less fortunate. As we have seen, the gas was less effective here, but 7th and 9th Divisions made some progress, entering the Quarries just north of the road and establishing a foothold on the Hohenzollern Redoubt, a strongpoint which dominated much of the northern sector.

The infantry attacked at 6.30 a.m., and half an hour later Haig sent an officer by car to French's forward command post at Lillers to announce that progress was good and to urge that IX Corps should be ready to move. At 9.30 he reported that his own reserves were committed and asked for IX Corps to be put under his command. French visited him just after 11.00 and agreed to put Haking's two New Army divisions at his disposal, driving off to give Haking the news in person. At 1.20 Haking phoned to announce that his two divisions were now under Haig's command and were on their way up. He added ominously that there were serious delays on the road.

The divisions had been on the march since early on the 24th, under rain coming down in stair-rods and along cobbled roads congested with the traffic in 1st Army's rear. There was some less than meticulous staff-work: one brigade commander was not allowed to take his men through Béthune because he lacked the correct pass, so had to march round it. Most of the advancing troops managed to eat once on the 25th: it was the last meal for all too many of them.

The Germans were also moving up reserves. Even on the first day their second position was held so strongly that an attack on it would have been difficult, but by dawn on the 26th it was more strongly held than the first line had been at the beginning of the battle and, to make matters worse, it had scarcely been touched by the British artillery.

It was not until the afternoon of the 26th that Haking's men advanced between Loos and the Hulluch–Vermelles road. They presented an impressive sight: German observers saw what seemed to be ten columns of extended lines of infantry, coming on as if on parade. Consternation turned to amazement, for there was no covering fire, and: 'A target was offered to us such as had never been seen before, nor even thought possible.' The machine-guns opened fire at 1500 yards (1365 metres) and, although men fell in their hundreds, the survivors pushed on. 'Never had machine-guns had such straightforward work to do, nor done it so effectively,' recounted one German regimental history. 'With barrels burning hot and swimming in oil, they traversed to and fro along the enemy's ranks unceasingly: one machine-gun alone fired 12,500 rounds that afternoon.' Some of the attackers actually got as far as the German wire but: 'Confronted by this impenetrable obstacle, the survivors turned and began to retire.' The two divisions lost over 8000 killed and wounded.

The battle sputtered on for several more days. The Guards Division went into action to stabilize the situation, and in the fighting north of Loos Rudyard Kipling's only son John, a lieutenant in the Irish Guards, was reported missing, believed killed. The British lost over 43,000 men, including three major-generals, and the Germans less than half as many. The French 10th Army's attack on the right fared no better.

HAIG TAKES COMMAND

After the battle came the recriminations. French's position which was weak before Loos, was now untenable. Robertson, in London to assist the War Office, discussed his replacement with the King and Asquith. Haig had long been convinced that French should go, and now told Rawlinson that he should have been replaced after Mons. When the King came to France in October Haig made it clear that 'the C-in-C was a source of great weakness to the army', adding that he personally was prepared to serve in any capacity. There was a bitter dispute between GHQ and 1st Army over the mishandling of the reserves, and Haig ensured that the relevant papers were sent to the King. Asquith decided to replace French, and when attempts to persuade Sir John to resign failed, his old friend Walter Long, now a junior minister, phoned to say that he would have to go.

French suggested that Robertson should replace him, but everyone, Robertson included, recognized that his talents lay on the staff. He had, in any case, been earmarked for the post of Chief of the Imperial General Staff. French went the rounds making his farewells. Foch cried, and Joffre lamented: 'If they do things like that, how can we hope to win the war?' On 18 December French met Haig, who was to succeed him. It was a painful interview. French had by now discovered what had been afoot. Both men were stiff and formal: one of French's staff saw that Haig never for a moment unbent, and another officer recalled that Sir John was 'very bitter against Haig'.

Haig had been in office for ten days when he received his own set of instructions from Lord Kitchener. These informed him that:

> The defeat of the enemy by the combined Allied Armies must always be regarded as the primary object for which British troops were sent to France, and to achieve that end, the closest co-operation of combined Allied Armies must always be

regarded as the prime object for which British troops were sent to France.

He did his best to establish cordial relations with the French, inviting the head of their liaison team at GHQ to attend his daily staff conference. An inter-Allied conference at Chantilly in early December had concluded that decisive results would only be achieved if the Allies mounted co-ordinated attacks on the principal (Western, Eastern and Italian) fronts.

Robertson, now indeed Chief of the Imperial General Staff (CIGS), passed on these conclusions to Haig, amplified with views of his own. Gallipoli would be evacuated, and every effort would now be concentrated on the Western front, where the Allies were to mount a spring offensive. Despite the miseries of 1915 – that sterile year – the British Army in France, increasingly well fed with men and munitions, was stronger and better-equipped than ever before. It remained to be seen what use the new commander-in-chief would make of it.

HOLDING THE
FRONT

FRANCE AND THE WAR

Most of the Western Front cut through French soil. The great city of Lille and the mining belt around it lay behind the German lines, and the nose of the huge salient bulging out into France was as close to Paris as Canterbury is to London. Georges Clemenceau, the brilliant radical politician who became premier in 1917, reminded his parliamentary audience, speech after speech, that: 'The Germans are still at Noyon.' For part of the war Paris was within range of German superguns tucked into forests north of the Aisne: the Ecole des Mines, on the eastern edge of the Luxembourg gardens in Paris, still bears the scars of shellfire from the siege of Paris in 1870–71 and shelling in 1918.

Tens of thousands of French soldiers came from towns and villages behind the German lines, and their miseries were sharpened by the knowledge that their homes were occupied. A broad swathe of French territory was ravaged by the war, sometimes accidentally, but sometimes – especially before the German withdrawal to the Hindenburg Line in 1917 – deliberately. In 1914 thousands of refugees from the advancing Germans found themselves on the wrong side of the lines when the front solidified.

Many Frenchmen were shot, imprisoned or deported for resisting the Germans, but many, in this war as in the next, came to a working accommodation with the occupier. It was often difficult, especially in rural communities housing German soldiers who were themselves often countrymen, to preserve a necessary hostility. The war could not stand in the way of human nature. When French armies followed up the German retreat to the Hindenburg Line some soldiers, as Edward Spears, a British liaison officer observed, went home to discover a flaxen-haired babe or pregnant wife. Many somehow managed to take this most poignant consequence of occupation in their stride, for they knew that nights were long and yearning deep.

Although the rumble of the guns could be heard in southern England, and prowling aircraft, airships and warships sometimes brought death and destruction to Britain, the Channel provided a barrier between Britain and the war that was both physical and psychological. There was no such barrier in France: the line between the *Zone des Armées*, under military control, and the remainder of France was simply a line on the map. While French soldiers endured the sufferings of the front line and the dismal conditions in camps behind it, they knew that there was a world of theatres, cafés and restaurants not far away. It was a world they seldom glimpsed and never sympathized with. The *embusqué*, the shirker, with a soft job, clean fingernails and another man's wife, was the target of deep hatred reflected in the trench newspapers which provide such a valuable understanding of the way the French soldier thought.

RED TROUSERS, WHITE GLOVES

Armies are, among other things, symbols of national culture, reflecting a nation's political and social structure and illuminated by its history. The French army of the First World War was coloured by the Franco-Prussian War of 1870–1 and the political instabilities which followed it. In the summer and early autumn of 1870 the armies of the Emperor Napoleon III, nephew of a greater emperor, were destroyed by a German coalition under Prussian leadership in what was little less than a lightning war.

The Germans besieged and bombarded Paris and, in the provinces, fought a war of increasing bitterness against the Armies of National Defence, a hotch-potch of forces cobbled together by the government which had succeeded the fallen Empire. The war was concluded on humiliating terms which included the loss of France's eastern provinces of Alsace and Lorraine. Government troops then took Paris from Communard insurgents in a brutal war which was to have a lasting impact on French politics. The Third Republic was established, with its president and bicameral legislature, and survived a sickly infancy menaced by royalist pretenders or flamboyant soldiers.

The French army entered a Golden Age after the war. Charles de Gaulle described the 'exceptional prestige' enjoyed by the officer:

> In the garrison, everyone treats him with respect. Tradespeople extend him credit. He is at the centre of every activity. People admire his bearing. Women are favourably disposed. Families would be glad to have as a son-in-law this 'man of honour' who, as they say, has a future, or at any rate a pension for later on.

It was a period characterized by the work of two of France's greatest military artists, Edouard Detaille and Alphonse de Neuville. Both specialized in historical paintings, with the wasted gallantry of the Franco-Prussian as a recurring theme. And they looked ahead as well as back. In 1888 Detaille carried off the Salon's medal of honour with *Le Rêve* (the dream), a work that was both realistic and allegorical. The officers and men of a French regiment on autumn manoeuvres sleep, rolled in their blankets: in the skies above, the warriors of old France lead the way to future glory.

French politicians had rarely agreed about the army. The Right traditionally preferred professional soldiers, or at least conscripts who served for so long as to be regulars in all but name, to short-service conscripts. The latter might prove unreliable in terms of political crisis, and go home having become all too familiar with the use of arms. The Left, in contrast, was suspicious of hired praetorians, and during the Franco-Prussian War reverted to the old Jacobin tradition which fused universal conscription and Republicanism.

The likelihood of a new war against Germany helped bring politicians together. In 1872 the National Assembly agreed on universal conscription, decreed that the army's peacetime organization would mirror that of war, and established officer and NCO cadres which would permit the army to double on mobilization. The army itself set about learning the lessons of 1870–1. A Staff College was created in 1875 and a proper general staff established in 1890. The swashbucklers of the Second Empire were replaced by a new generation of officers who read books and subscribed to professional journals. The sons of old noble families rediscovered the profession of arms. Weapons and equipment were comprehensively reformed. Forts arose on the bleak uplands overlooking the new frontier as engineers began to cast the framework of the future battlefield. Although political debate went on, there was widespread realization that the army must be kept out of political quarrels.

Clashes between troops and strikers started to tarnish the gilt. In 1894 the Dreyfus affair broke, driving a wedge between army and nation. Captain Alfred Dreyfus, a Jewish officer serving on the general staff, was accused of spying for Germany, convicted after a questionable trial and imprisoned for life on Devil's Island in French Guyana. Doubts arose about his guilt, and in January 1989 Emile Zola published an article accusing the army of supporting the conviction of an innocent man. The nation was divided, some seeing the conviction as the embodiment of everything authoritarian and arbitrary, others claiming that the army's honour was being besmirched by Jews and radicals.

Dreyfus was retried, found guilty 'with extenuating circumstances', and eventually cleared altogether, but the damage was enormous. The affair, coupled with other scandals, encouraged young men to turn away from military careers. The number of candidates for St-Cyr – broadly the French equivalent of Sandhurst or West Point – fell in 1897 from 1920 to 871 in 1911, and over a similar period the number of NCOs who chose to re-enlist fell from 72,000 to 41,000. With its prestige diminished, the army had few attractions: pay was poor and promotion slow. A colonel described how the most able officers became majors between the ages of forty-four and forty-nine, and thereafter it was a race between promotion and compulsory retirement.

THE TWO ARMIES

Some officers turned their backs on the burgeoning gloom of metropolitan France by soldiering in the colonies, where initiative might be richly rewarded and the bonds linking officers and men were closer. There were in effect two armies, a metropolitan army of yawning barrack-rooms and jammed promotion lists, and a colonial army of dash and enterprise. The two were not on comfortable terms. Joseph Galliéni, governor of Paris in 1914, had turned down high command, fearing that the metropolitan army would not accept him. He tapped his button, with its marine infantry anchor, remarking: 'It is a question of buttons.' Joffre was a colonial sapper, and at least part of his messianic devotion to the offensive came from a desire to galvanize the metropolitan army into much-needed activity.

In 1905 military service was fixed at two years, loopholes through which the privileged had escaped were blocked up, and a total liability of twenty-five years was established. But in practice reservists were called for training less and less frequently, and the mistrust of regular officers for the reserves grew more marked. In

1913 the disparity between the French and German armies encouraged parliament to increase army pay and make it easier for warrant officers (confusingly called *adjutants* in French) to gain commissions, and after heated debate military service was extended to three years.

FRANCE GOES TO WAR

When France mobilized in 1914 her army bore the scars of the previous two decades. She had 2500 automatic weapons against the German army's 4500, and only 3800 75mm field guns compared with the 6000 77mms in the German army. She was also pitifully short of heavier weapons. Emphasis on the offensive encouraged officers to regard the 75mm as 'God the Father, God the Son and God the Holy Ghost': it would have been nice, said one cynic, to have seen it surrounded by a few saints of heavier metal. True, there had been a marked revival of moral values in the years immediately before the war, and a student wrote that: 'It is in the life of the camps and under fire that we will experience the supreme flowering of the French forces that dwell with us.'

On 31 July 1914 the graduating class of St Cyr swore to go into battle in parade uniform, with plume and white gloves. Many of them did so, and even in 1916 a French officer saw a comrade, some distance away, lying dead, his gloves flecks of white against his blue greatcoat. The officer who inspired the oath was luckier than many of his comrades: he lived till April 1915. The French army had suffered 955,000 casualties by December 1914, and in the next year it lost an appalling 1,430,000. The Champagne offensive of September 1915 cost 145,000 men. One general warned President Poincaré that the army could not go on like this: 'the instrument of victory is being broken in our hands'. In all, France was to lose almost a million and a half men, nearly half as many again as the 947,000 fatalities suffered by Britain and her Empire.

MILITARY POLITICS

There are strong political currents in almost any army, and in the French army they ran deep. There were complaints that the army was run by 'generals from the Jesuit warrens', like Castelnau, Joffre's assistant in 1915–16: a lay member of a religious order, he was known as *'le capucin botté'*, the fighting friar. In contrast, there was General Sarrail, commanding the 3rd Army in 1914, with a reputation for confirmed Republicanism. One broadsheet proclaimed that: 'If General Joffre was unavailable for a period of two weeks and if supreme command were entrusted to General Sarrail, there can be no doubt that the Germans would be chased from the national territory.' In late 1915 Sarrail was sent off to command the expedition to Salonica, and the need to keep him in a position suited to his political status became a powerful reason for not closing down a front that was widely regarded as a pointless sideshow.

Joffre himself had not had an easy time. He was characteristically modest about the Marne, declaring that he was not certain who had won it, but knew who would have been blamed for losing it. In September 1914 he replaced one-third of the French command. Generals were posted to the southern town of Limoges to await further orders, or *limogé*. In popular parlance they came unstuck *(dégommé)*, a word the British plundered to produce 'degummed'. His offensives in 1915 failed largely because of lack of materials but, at the close of the year, as we have seen, he was anticipating a new offensive in 1916, which, it was subsequently agreed, would be mounted where the British and French armies joined, on the River Somme.

GERMAN PLANS

War is nothing if not two-sided, and it was never wise, in either world war, to assume that the Germans would behave as expected.

General Erich Falkenhayn had replaced the broken Moltke as Chief of the General Staff in September 1914 at the early age of fifty-three. He was, on the face of things, a surprising choice, originating in the thrifty junker squirearchy of East Prussia and enjoying a decidedly average career until attracting royal attention, and with it rapid promotion, just before the war. A biographer dubbed him 'the lonely general', and his hard face and punishing lifestyle both testified to a single-minded strength of purpose.

It is still hard to fathom the man and the real logic behind the part he played in the events of 1916. The received wisdom is clear enough. In December 1916 Falkenhayn wrote a memorandum reviewing the progress of the war to date. France, he believed, was weakened almost to the limit of her endurance, and Russia had lost her offensive power. Britain remained the arch-enemy, but she was hard to reach. She could scarcely be invaded, and defeats in Egypt or Mesopotamia would not bring about her collapse. Attacking her armies in Flanders was impossible because of the state of the ground – a telling analysis. Launching unrestricted submarine warfare against her maritime lifelines might work, even at the risk of drawing America into the war, but it would take too long. He concluded that Germany's only chance of victory was to knock 'England's best sword', the French army, from her hand. Then he went to the dark heart of the matter:

> Within our reach behind the French sector of the Western Front there are objectives for the retention of which the French General Staff would be compelled to throw in every man they have. If they do so the forces of France will bleed to death – as there can be no question of a voluntary withdrawal – whether we reach our goal or not. If they do not do so, and we reach our objectives, the moral effect on France will be enormous. For an operation limited to a narrow front, Germany will not be compelled to spend herself as completely.

He believed that there were two such objectives: Belfort, so bravely defended in 1870–1 that it had been retained by France at the peace, and Verdun. Preference, he argued, should be given to Verdun.

Although Alistair Horne's *The Price of Glory* was published as long ago as 1962 it remains one of the best works on the subject, and stands not least among its author's remarkable achievements. Its assessment that the Falkenhayn memorandum made military history because it was the first time any great commander had proposed to vanquish an enemy by bleeding him to death seems grimly fitting. We cannot, unfortunately, be absolutely sure that it is correct. There is no trace of the Falkenhayn memorandum in the archives: the only version we have is the general's own, contained in his autobiography. Falkenhayn is believed to have visited the Kaiser at Potsdam some time between 15 and 22 December 1915, but the Kaiser's memoirs are silent on the point.

The possibilities continue to perplex historians. It may be that there was indeed a memorandum, all copies of which vanished so comprehensively that they were not available to the authors of the German Official History between the wars. It may be that there was never a memorandum as such, but that the views expressed in Falkenhayn's memoirs accurately summed up his mood at the time. Lastly, there is the possibility that Falkenhayn attacked at Verdun with the intention of taking the town, possibly hoping that by doing so he would unbalance the Allied armies on the Western Front and open the way for a successful offensive further west. By the time he wrote his memoirs it was all too evident that Verdun had not fallen, and the argument that he had never meant to take the town but simply planned to use it to sap the strength of the French army was a convenient justification after the event for a lost and bloody battle.

VERDUN

Another factor complicates the question: the status of Verdun itself. Alistair Horne accurately describes it in 1916 as 'a sleepy, duller-than-average French provincial town, unassumingly modest about its noble past and strangely insouciant about the future'. Virodunum to the Romans, Verdun lies inside a ring of hills, the Meuse heights. It owed its military importance to its position, where the main road from Metz to Paris crossed the gentle River Meuse. To its east lies the boggy Woevre Plain, with the River Moselle and the great fortress city of Metz on its eastern edge. To its west stands the forest of the Argonne, with the open plains of Champagne beyond them. An invader advancing from the east needed to take Verdun before pushing through the defiles of the Argonne and debouching into Champagne, where he could manoeuvre more freely.

It is small wonder that Verdun's history was martial. It was sacked by Attila the Hun in 455, and in 843 Charlemagne's heirs signed the Treaty of Verdun which divided his empire among them. One received 'Lothar's kingdom', Lothari Regnum in Latin and hence Lothringen in German and Lorraine in French. Lorraine became, as Verdun's historian Alain Denizot puts it, 'a stake in the game between France and the Germanic Holy Roman Empire'. Between 925 and 1552 it was under German control. Its bishop, supported by the citizens, offered Verdun to France in 1552, and Henry II's occupation of the town was formally recognized in 1648 by the Treaty of Westphalia, which ended the Thirty Years War.

Fortifications surround the town like the rings of an onion. There are some medieval survivals, like the crenellated Porte Chaussée, grinning out across the Meuse, but most date from the seventeenth century. Jean Errard de Bar le Duc transformed the Abbey of St-Vanne into a citadel in 1624, and Sebastien de Vauban, the most distinguished military engineer of his age, built the ramparts, bastions and ravelins which still mark the town-scape. Verdun was taken by the Prussians in 1792 – its governor committed suicide rather than surrender – but was soon recaptured. During the Napoleonic wars it housed British internees and prisoners of war: officers were allowed to live in relative comfort provided they did not attempt to escape. Correspondence in the charming Musée de la Princerie testifies to the fact that their presence was not wholly unwelcome. A citizen asked the Minister of Marine to allow a British midshipman to marry his daughter. She had become very fond of him and was expecting their second child, and so, suggested the bourgeois, it would be as well to regularize the relationship.

FORTIFYING THE FRONTIER

Verdun was taken by the Prussians on 8 November 1870 and was not returned to France until September 1873. With much of Lorraine lost, the new Franco-German border ran across the Woevre Plain, only a day's march from Verdun, and the town was incorporated into the frontier defences laid out by General Séré de Rivières. A belt of fortifications ran from Verdun down the Meuse to Bourlemont. Another network of forts defended the confluence of Meuthe and Moselle around Toul. South of this lay the Charmes gap, into which it was hoped that an incautious enemy might venture for a mauling, and then more fortifications stood on the upper Moselle, from Epinal to Belfort and Montbéliard. North of Verdun, another ring of forts encircled Maubeuge.

From above the forts looked like broad arrow-heads, their points facing the enemy. Originally they mounted heavy guns on a flat fighting platform, the *terreplein*, with a stout rampart in front and masonry shelters between them. A deep, wide ditch, faced with stonework, surrounded each fort, with defences in it to enable the garrison to deal with enemy infantry who got so far.

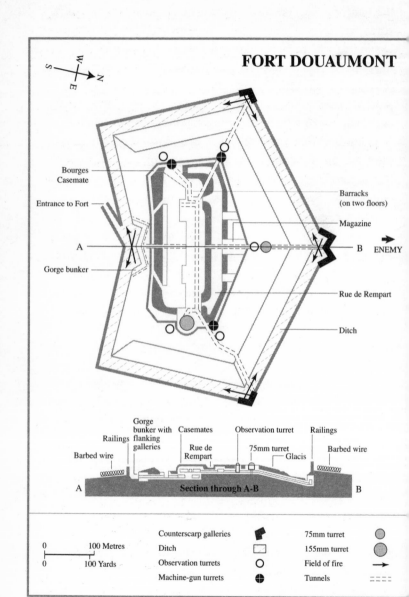

FORT DOUAUMONT

Bourges Casemate

Entrance to Fort

A

Gorge bunker

Barracks (on two floors)

Magazine

B ENEMY

Rue de Rempart

Ditch

Gorge bunker with flanking galleries

Railings

Barbed wire

Casemates

Rue de Rempart

Observation turret

75mm turret

Glacis

Railings

Barbed wire

A **Section through A-B** B

0 — 100 Metres	
0 — 100 Yards	

Counterscarp galleries

Ditch

Observation turrets

Machine-gun turrets

75mm turret

155mm turret

Field of fire

Tunnels

ABOVE The misery of Passchendaele, 1917. The dreadful conditions, the result of the worst weather in memory and bombardments which destroyed the drainage system, made the battle a byword for the horror of the Western Front.

RIGHT The recruiting drive, 6 August 1914. Children accompany recruits down Whitehall. They are marching, ironically, towards the site where the Cenotaph now stands.

ABOVE A German 1908 pattern machine-gun with water-cooled barrel clearly visible. The Germans adopted steel helmets in 1916.

LEFT General Joseph Joffre, flanked by Castelnau, his deputy (left), and Pau (right), who lost a hand in 1870 and was recalled from retirement to command the Army of Alsace.

RIGHT Field-Marshal Sir John French, commander of the BEF till 1915. The mercurial French had made his reputation in the Boer War and was out of his depth on the Western Front.

BELOW Ancient and modern. The commanding officer of 1st Cameronians (centre) confers with his mounted adjutant at Le Cateau, 26 August 1914.

ABOVE The tide turns. A company of Cameronians crossing a
pontoon bridge, manned by Royal Engineers, over the Marne
at La Ferté sous Jouarre, 10 September 1914.

ABOVE The genesis of trench warfare. Men of 2nd
Scots Guards in a shallow, hastily-dug trench,
near Ypres, in October 1914.

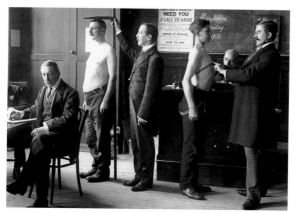

LEFT New recruits' medicals. Thousands rejected for service early in the war were called up later as medical standards fell.

ABOVE Neuve Chapelle, March 1916. Breastworks were built up because the wet ground made entrenchment difficult. German shells are bursting behind the British front line to prevent troops coming up.

RIGHT General Sir Douglas Haig, taciturn, reserved and single-minded, became Commander-in-Chief of the BEF in December 1915.

LEFT Women munitions workers in the shell-filling factory at Chilwell near Nottingham. The wood-block floor was designed to prevent sparks, but there were several explosions, one of which gutted this building: it was rebuilt immediately.

BELOW Argyll and Sutherland Highlanders wearing the primitive gas protection issued in May 1915. Although gas masks were improved by the time of Loos, they were still uncomfortable and constricting.

ABOVE A French 75mm field-gun showing the barrel at full recoil after firing. France was pitifully short of modern heavy guns.

ABOVE The Crown Prince of Prussia, commander of the German Fifth Army, talking to soldiers near Verdun. His men began the battle wearing the spiked helmet, but adopted the coal-scuttle helmet as it went on.

ABOVE An apparently un-posed photograph shows French infantry attacking through barbed wire in the face of shellfire.

ABOVE Generals Pétain (left) and Joffre.

RIGHT A French soldier is buried on Hill 304.

ABOVE The real price of glory: human remains at Verdun.

Stout iron railings with sharp tips ringed the enemy side of the ditch, with a thick belt of barbed wire beyond them. Beneath the *terreplein* lurked barracks, kitchens and hospitals.

By 1916 there were three layers of forts round Verdun. Forts Belleville, St-Michel and Belrupt secured the high ground close to the town. An intermediate ring, including Souville, Tavannes, Moulainville and Rozelier, protected the right bank of the Meuse, with Bois Bourrus, Marre and Vacherauville among the forts on the left bank. In front of this second line stood Douaumont, strongest of Verdun's forts, securing the long ridge that dominates a large part of the right bank, with the lesser Vaux to its east. Smaller *ouvrages* (defence works) and detached batteries helped fill gaps and strengthened likely approaches.

The forts were initially built of stonework about 5 feet (1.5 metres) thick, covered by up to 16 feet (5 metres) of earth. The development of high explosive rendered them obsolete at a stroke. Guns on the surface were vulnerable, and the stone and earth layers were too thin to sustain direct hits. Unfortunately, the public mood had begun to swing away from military expenditure, and there were insufficient funds available to update all Séré de Rivières's work.

However, such was the importance of Verdun that most of its defences were modernized. A shell of concrete up to 8 feet (2.5 metres) thick encased the forts, with about 13 feet (4 metres) of earth on top of it, and a layer of sand, to absorb the shock of explosions, between the concrete and the original stonework. Heavy guns were placed in armoured turrets on top of the forts, with 75mm pieces in concrete flanking defences called Bourges casemates. Steel observation cupolas and machine-gun turrets speckled the forts. The number of guns they mounted dropped dramatically: the mighty Douaumont had only a single turreted 155mm, two 75mms in another turret, and another pair in a Bourges casemate.

Part of the reason for this apparent weakness was the belief that a single turreted piece, its gunners protected and ammunition supply assured, was worth a battery in open field. There was also a growing suspicion that despite all the expensive improvements, forts would remain vulnerable to high explosive, and might best be used as centres of resistance, providing observation posts and shelters for the defending infantry, rather than strongpoints in their own right.

The events of August 1914 seemed to confirm this gloomy prognosis. The Liège forts, for all their armoured cupolas and gallant defenders, were demolished by German heavy howitzers. In France, Fort Manonviller, built to command the Paris–Saverne railway line, was hit by 17,000 shells and surrendered: the fumes of the explosions made the place untenable. Joffre ordered that as many guns as possible should be withdrawn from forts and sent off to the field armies. Although the 75mms in Bourges casemates could indeed be modified for field service, the stubby, turret-mounted 155mm and 75mm could not, and so they stayed on. He added that if the Germans attempted to surround Verdun, the town should not be held: the defenders should withdraw to the left bank and defend that. By 1916 the Verdun forts were held by skeleton garrisons, men whose advanced age and low rank testified to the sadly diminished status of these concrete monsters.

PROPHETS OF GLOOM

The town's military governor, General Herr, warned that his defences were weak. His views were echoed, though much more forcefully, by one of the army's mavericks, Emile Driant. Born in 1855, Driant was an infantry officer who had married the daughter of General Georges Boulanger, minister of war in 1886–7. This might have proved a wise move in an army which quipped that there were three routes to promotion – seniority, selection and

son-in-law. Unfortunately for Driant, Boulanger, the classic political general, became the figurehead for a variety of anti-German
political groups and was eventually exiled. Driant's career, already
damaged by this association, was ruined when he protested at the
keeping of dossiers on 'clerical' officers.

He retired to write futuristic (and anti-British) works under
the pen-name of Captain Danrit, and was elected to the Chamber
of Deputies. Recalled from the reserve in 1914, in 1915 he was a
lieutenant-colonel commanding two *chasseur* battalions on the
Verdun front. *Chasseurs* had much in common with rifle regiments in the British army or *Jäger* in the German. They prided
themselves on their marksmanship, and on tenacity which sprang
in part from a greater degree of independence and initiative than
was allowed to their comrades in line regiments.

Driant's men held the Bois des Caures, on the right bank of
the Meuse and on the very chin of the French-held salient,
formed by the defences of Verdun, which jutted into German
lines. Like his superior, General Herr, Driant had a low opinion
of the state of defensive preparation at Verdun but, unlike Herr,
he had powerful friends. On 22 August 1915 he wrote to Paul
Deschanel, President of the Chamber of Deputies and an old
personal friend, warning of 'a sledge-hammer blow... on the line
Verdun–Nancy... If our first line is carried by a massive attack,
our second line is inadequate and we are not succeeding in establishing it; lack of workers, and I add: lack of barbed wire'. This
warning was passed on to the minister of war, now General
Galliéni, saviour of Paris in 1914, who sent a delegation to
Verdun. This reported that all was indeed not well on the Meuse
Front, and Galliéni duly forwarded a copy to Joffre, asking for his
comments. They were barely printable.

'I cannot be a party,' thundered Joffre, 'to soldiers under my
command bringing before the Government, by channels other than
the hierarchic channel, complaints or protests concerning the

execution of my orders.' There were no grounds for Driant's concern. The Germans would not attack Verdun. And that was that.

The massive attack predicted by Driant was, as we have seen, exactly what the Germans had in mind. Yet, given the neglected state of the town's defences and the French headquarters' orders that Verdun was on no account to be surrounded, how certain could Falkenhayn be that it would indeed be held to the last drop of French blood? The truth is that there was no certainty to it at all. Most of Verdun's significance to France stems from its role in 1916. Falkenhayn was painfully aware, when he wrote his memoirs, that he had indeed managed to touch something deep and primal in the French psyche. He cannot have been sure of this before the event, and this must strengthen the arguments of those who doubt the reliability of Falkenhayn's version of events. He may indeed have sought an attritional battle, and found the Verdun salient, where superior German artillery could be applied to a weak defence, an appropriate spot for it. Yet there is every chance that if the strength of French resistance astonished both France and her allies, it surprised Falkenhayn too.

THE ELEVENTH HOUR

The instrument of Falkenhayn's attack was the German Fifth Army, commanded by the Kaiser's son Wilhelm, Crown Prince of Prussia, which had come close to taking Verdun in 1914. The Crown Prince's Chief of Staff, General Schmidt von Knobelsdorf, enjoyed a close relationship with Falkenhayn and, in the months that followed, helped ensure that the Crown Prince did what Falkenhayn expected of him. In late December 1915 and early January 1916, however, Knobelsdorf found his loyalties strained as it became clear that Falkenhayn was not quite sure what he expected. Both the Crown Prince and his Chief of Staff wanted to attack on the left and right banks simultaneously. Falkenhayn maintained that there were insufficient troops for this, because a reserve must be kept to meet Allied attacks elsewhere. Indeed, these ripostes, he argued, might 'bring movement into the war once again'. Once they were repulsed, then more men could be used against Verdun. Crown Prince Rupprecht of Bavaria, an accomplished professional soldier commanding the German Sixth Army, suggested that Falkenhayn 'was himself not clear as to what he really wanted, and was waiting for a stroke of luck that would lead to a favourable solution'.

Little was left to luck in German preparations. New narrow-gauge railway lines were laid to enable the mountains of material needed for the attack to be brought to the front. Artillery ammunition had pride of place, for it was the essence of German plans that their gunners should make out a cheque which the infantry would simply present for payment. Over 1200 guns were to be used on an attack frontage of 12 miles (19 kilometres). They ranged from giant 420mm howitzers, whose shells weighed over a ton apiece, long-barrelled 380mm naval guns, stocky Austrian 305mms, and on down through the 210mm, 150mm and 130mm guns to numerous short-ranged trench-mortars, heavy and light, to scores of 77mms, work-horse of the field artillery. Targets were meticulously allocated: the heavy howitzers would take on the forts, naval guns would reach out into and beyond Verdun, and other guns, howitzers and mortars would deal with French batteries, trench lines and communications. They had two and a half million shells available for the first week of battle.

The experience of 1915 showed that attacking infantry were at their most vulnerable when the defender's artillery-fire fell on crammed jumping-off trenches, whose crowded state in any case drew attention to what was to come. The Germans averted this problem by constructing numerous *Stollen*, large, deep dug-outs in which the attacking infantry was to await zero hour. The assault was initially scheduled for 12 February, but the atrocious weather led to its postponement, much to the discomfort of waiting troops in the *Stollen*, many of them knee-deep in water.

Lastly, the Germans paid special attention to the air. All combatants had used aircraft for reconnaissance at the beginning of the war, and soon artillery-spotting became a major task. It was a small step from harassing the enemy's observers to shooting at them, initially with a variety of weapons, private and official. In June 1915 the Fokker Eindekker single-seat fighter appeared at the front, pointing the way ahead: a mechanical interrupter gear enabled machine-guns fitted to the fuselage to fire through the propeller's arc.

In early 1916 the Germans concentrated the bulk of their aircraft at Verdun. Fighter patrols denied French reconnaissance aircraft access to German territory, observation balloons and aircraft spotted for the artillery, and two-seaters attacked road and rail junctions with bombs, dropping 4500lb (2043kg) in the first few days of the offensive. It was the first time in military history that air superiority had paved the way for an attack, but it was certainly not to be the last. Falkenhayn had christened the battle Operation Gericht – tribunal, judgement-place, or even scaffold. As the short February days went by, the executioner prepared to drop the trap. Despite careful German precautions, the French were aware that an attack was coming. Prisoners admitted that something serious was in the wind. The occasional aircraft got through the German net and came back with news of dreadful preparation. And down in the chilly Bois des Caures, Emile Driant's *chasseurs* could hear the rumble of ammunition wagons.

THE ATTACK BEGINS

Early on the morning of 21 February a 380mm naval gun opened the bombardment, its shell spinning high over chalk and woodland to burst in the bishop's palace at Verdun. It had been aimed at one of the Meuse bridges. Though a near miss at a range of nearly 20 miles (32 kilometres) was not bad shooting, the damage was seized upon by Allied propagandists as another example of Hunnish behaviour. The main bombardment began three hours later, beating upon the French positions like a metal flail wielded by some demented giant. In the Bois des Caures, Driant had wisely abandoned a defence based on continuous lines of trenches for a series of dug-outs and bunkers, many of them made of concrete, consisting of small outposts, bigger *grandes gardes*, and even larger redoubts. Branches were lopped off, whole trees uprooted, and men were buried alive by direct hits on their bunkers. When the fire slackened towards midday and the survivors emerged to man the wreckage of their defences, German artillery observers brought fresh fire to bear on centres of activity. Elsewhere, across the whole of the Verdun front, the story was the same. Forward positions were methodically ploughed by shells, and a continuous barrage falling behind them boxed them off from support. Heavy guns and howitzers hit French batteries with a mixture of gas and high explosive: by mid-day the Germans estimated that only one gun per battery was still in action.

The infantry went forward at 4.00 p.m.. The Germans were still wearing the pre-war spiked helmet, its fabric cover bearing a stencilled regimental number: the 'coal-scuttle' steel helmet would appear while the battle was in progress. Spikes had been unscrewed to prevent them snagging trees or undergrowth, and the attackers wore white armbands so as to identify one another in the dangerous gloaming. Two of the three attacking corps heeded 5th Army's instructions that only strong fighting patrols were to advance that day, identifying breaches in the defences through which the main assault would pour on the 22nd. General von Zwehl's VII Reserve Corps, attacking the Bois d'Haumont, north-west of the Bois des Caures, was less cautious, and its assault

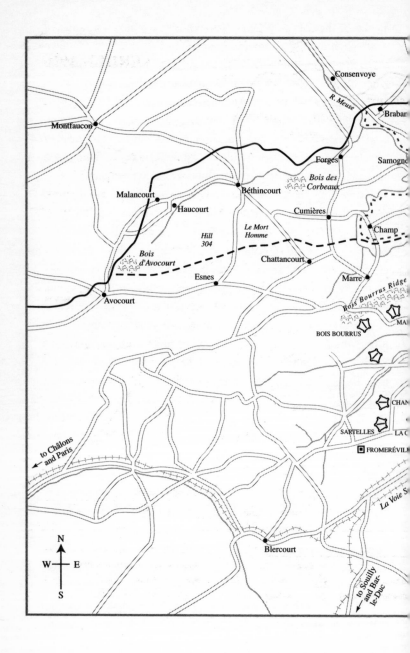

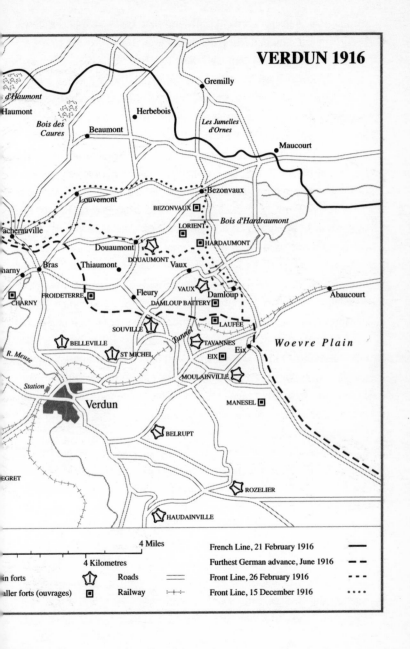

VERDUN 1916

d'Haumont

Haumont

Bois des Caures

Gremilly

Herbebois

Les Jumelles d'Ornes

Beaumont

Maucourt

Louvemont

Bezonvaux

BEZONVAUX

Bois d'Hardraumont

LORIENT

acherauville

HARDAUMONT

Douaumont

DOUAUMONT

Vaux

Bras

Thiaumont

narny

FROIDETERRE

Fleury

VAUX

Damloup

Abaucourt

CHARNY

DAMLOUP BATTERY

SOUVILLE

LAUFÉE

Woevre Plain

BELLEVILLE

Tunnel

TAVANNES

Eix

R. Meuse

ST MICHEL

EIX

MOULAINVILLE

Station

Verdun

MANESEL

BELRUPT

EGRET

ROZELIER

HAUDAINVILLE

4 Miles

4 Kilometres

French Line, 21 February 1916

Furthest German advance, June 1916

Front Line, 26 February 1916

Front Line, 15 December 1916

n forts

Roads

aller forts (ouvrages)

Railway

troops bounded forwards, confident that there would be few Frenchmen in any condition to resist them.

The Bois d'Haumont fell quickly, but elsewhere German gains did not live up to their expectations. Although perhaps less than half of Driant's men had escaped death or injury, the survivors defended the remnants of the Bois des Caures with a grim tenacity, and XVIII Corps, attacking that sector, made little progress. The surprising thing about the bombardment was not the enormous physical damage it caused, but the extraordinary ability of men to live though it and somehow fight back.

On the 22nd the French, true to a doctrine that still insisted that ground lost should be retaken as soon as possible, put in local counter-attacks that were usually shot to pieces but sometimes, against all the odds, bought an hour or two. However, assisted as always by their crushing artillery, and a fresh horror, the flamethrower, against strongpoints, the Germans took the village of Haumont, and, late in the afternoon, at last drove Driant's men out of the Bois des Caures. Driant himself was killed as he withdrew. Even in a battle as large and impersonal as Verdun the inspirational quality of valiant men made a difference, and Emile Driant, as physically brave in action as he was morally courageous out of it, had thrown the first substantial piece of grit into the German machine.

On the 23rd the defence was badly shaken by a sequence of order and disorder which led to the abandonment of Brabant, on the Meuse. The villages of Haumont and Herbebois, held with remarkable determination, were eventually taken, and Samogneux, too, fell after a ghastly misunderstanding in which newly arrived French 155mm guns broke the back of a gallant French defence. On the 24th the Germans pushed right through the intermediate line sited by General de Castelnau, Joffre's deputy, when he visited Verdun the previous month. The battle had already crippled the 51st and 72nd Divisions of General Chrétien's XXX Corps, and when he flung in the North Africans of the 37th Division in an effort to patch the broken line it rapidly disintegrated. The leading elements of General Balfourier's fresh XX Corps were on their way, but combatants on both sides sensed that Verdun would fall before they reached it. The Crown Prince was to write that 'the way was open to us', and lamented that, by not pressing on at all costs, the Germans missed the psychological moment. And a French general admitted: 'Even were I Napoleon, I could not save the army from this disaster.'

PÉTAIN TAKES COMMAND

A mixture of sound French decisions and serious German mistakes was to achieve more than Napoleon. On the evening of the 23rd General Langle de Cary, commanding Army Group Centre and as such Herr's immediate superior, telephoned Joffre in his headquarters at Chantilly, seeking permission to give up the ground he held east of Verdun. Joffre was non-committal, but before long Castelnau arrived, on the first of two visits, to warn him just how serious the situation was. We cannot be certain what happened in Joffre's quarters in the Villa Poiret that night: one version has the great man roused from bed in his nightshirt, but we do know that two key decisions were made. The first was that the 2nd Army, currently in reserve, would be sent to Verdun to hold the left bank. The second was that Castelnau would go to Verdun to see things for himself.

It was one of those moments in the war when much would depend on the line taken by a visiting staff officer. In 1914, Moltke's emissary Lieutenant Colonel Hentsch had allowed the pessimism of those at the front to infect him. On 25 February 1916, however, Castelnau showed himself a man of sterner stuff. Sustained alike by heartfelt patriotism, deep religious belief, and the knowledge that three of his sons had already died for France,

Castelnau left Chantilly not long after midnight. He was at Langle de Cary's headquarters at Avize before dawn, instilling calm there and telephoning ahead to warn poor Herr that if he gave up any more ground 'the consequences would be very grave for him'. Soon afterwards he was with Herr in person, and at 3.30 that afternoon he telephoned GQG. Verdun could be held. Pétain should defend the right bank as well as the left, advised by the unlucky Herr until the latter could be gently sacked.

General Philippe Pétain's night was rather different. In 1914 he was an infantry colonel with unfashionable views on firepower and, at fifty-eight, close to retirement. The war transformed his fortunes. He commanded a brigade during the retreat, and was promoted *général de brigade* and given a division in late August. An elderly spinster kindly prised some stars for his cuffs from a dead relative's uniform. He added another star soon enough, and the autumn saw him *général de division* and a corps commander. In May 1915 his corps attacked Souchez, below Vimy Ridge, capturing 3000 prisoners and advancing 2 miles (3.2 kilometres). It was lightning war by that year's dismal standards, and that summer, he was sent off to command 2nd Army.

Pétain was unmarried at the time, but was as adept in the courts of Venus as on the field of Mars. On the night of 24–5 February his trusted aide de camp Alain de Serrigny eventually tracked him down to the Hotel Terminus at the Gare du Nord. Outside the general's room, awaiting the attentions of the boot-boy, were a pair of large field-boots and a tiny pair of lady's shoes. Serrigny knocked, and Pétain eventually appeared, listened impassively to the news, and announced that they would set off for Chantilly in the morning. Meanwhile, the night imposed its own duties.

After pausing briefly at Chantilly, Pétain and Serrigny set off for Verdun. It was a difficult journey in appalling weather, and once they had left Bar-le-Duc to drive up the single road connecting Verdun with the outside world they could average only 2 miles

(3.2 kilometres) an hour. The flotsam of defeat swept past in the other direction: civilian refugees with a few pathetic belongings on their carts, ambulances full of wounded, and the debris of broken regiments: one lieutenant, staggering back with a handful of survivors, saw tears glistening in the big general's eyes. Herr's headquarters at Dugny was so chaotic that Pétain could not stand it, and retraced his steps to the village of Souilly on the Bar-le-Duc road. There he met Castelnau, who gave him a written order to hold both banks of the Meuse, and to take command at midnight. Pétain had one piece of news for him, obtained at Herr's headquarters: Fort Douaumont had fallen.

THE FALL OF FORT DOUAUMONT

There could be no better evidence of the uneasy relationship between the Verdun forts and the commanders of the formations holding the ground on which they stood than General Chrétien's repulse from Douaumont. He had attempted to visit it in early February, only to be told by the fort's custodian, an elderly warrant officer called Chenot, that he opened the gates only to the governor of Verdun. This anomaly persisted, with the forts answering direct to General Herr rather than to the generals whose troops surrounded them.

It was not until early on the 25th that divisional commanders were told to maintain garrisons in the forts in their sectors. Chrétien, about to hand over the sector to Balfourier, assured him that the order had been passed on, and Balfourier, exhausted after his long approach march, took him at his word. In the event, nothing had been done and, at a crucial stage in the battle, with the German attack gaining momentum and French defensive responsibilities being reorganized, Douaumont had a tiny garrison.

Chenot commanded six regular and fifty-seven Territorial gunners; Private Meyer, responsible for the maintenance of the fort's oil lamps; and an engineer sergeant sent there to prepare demolitions in case the fort had to be abandoned. On the afternoon of the 25th the fort, despite having sustained some damage from shelling by 420mms in February 1915 and during the bombardments accompanying the attack, was in good order, and its 155mm turret was firing away steadily at a distant target, given to it some time before. Most of the garrison was in the bowels of the fort, listening to a lecture.

While Chenot's men went about their duties, the crack 24th Brandenburg Regiment advanced towards Douaumont Ridge, with its 2nd Battalion on its right, 3rd on the left and 1st in reserve. The preparatory barrage had failed to materialize, and so the regiment advanced anyhow, scattering some French and making excellent progress. The 24-year-old Sergeant Kunze, with his section of pioneers, was on the left of the 2nd Battalion, and had been told to deal with obstacles in the path of the advance. After a brisk action against defenders in trenches, Kunze found himself under the lee of the fort. His men cut through the already damaged barbed wire around it, and got as far as the iron railings edging the ditch. Kunze was blown into the ditch by a shell which landed nearby, and his men followed him down. Ordering them to make a human pyramid, he scrambled up on their backs, pushed back the ditch-defence cannon protruding from an embrasure, and entered.

All but two of his men declined to follow Kunze into the fort but, wandering about the gloomy and unfamiliar corridors, he eventually found his way to the 155mm turret and detained the gunners. Then, after managing to lock up the lecturer and his audience, he found a well-stocked mess-room and wolfed down a good meal. The gun came back to life when a relief crew arrived, much to Kunze's chagrin. However, by now two officers from the Brandenburgers, Captain Haupt and Lieutenant Radtke, had also managed to enter the fort. At the head of different parties, both had climbed from the moat on to the fort's superstructure. They eventually made contact with one another and with Kunze: Haupt took command, and by about 4.30 p.m., Douaumont was firmly in German hands.

Another Brandenburg officer, Lieutenant von Brandis, entered the fort after Haupt and Radtke, but, detailed to take the news back to regimental headquarters, appears to have been over-generous with the truth and received one of the two Pour le Mérite, Germany's highest decoration, awarded for the action. He later wrote a best-selling book, The *Stormers of Douaumont*, in which his own role lost nothing in the telling. The other decoration went to Haupt. Kunze received nothing, and it was not until the 1930s, when he was serving as a police constable, that he read accounts of the capture and realized the part he had played. He wrote to his old commanding officer, who investigated the case. Kunze's claims were indeed justified and, although it was a little too late for the Pour le Mérite, he was given accelerated promotion to inspector.

Despite their propagandists' attempts to minimize its public and international impact, the loss of Douaumont was an appalling blow to the French. It was followed by something approaching panic in Verdun, and the shaken commander of 37th Division pulled right back off the Douaumont Ridge. Had the Germans not been over-cautious there is little doubt that Verdun would have fallen.

THE FRENCH HOLD FAST

But if the German command faltered, the French did not. Pétain telephoned his senior officers to tell them that he was in command, but awoke on the 26th shaking with pneumonia. Using his trusted staff officers as intermediaries, Pétain managed to gather the reins of battle into his hands. The whole of XX Corps was now at the front and two more corps were on their way. Commanders were told to conserve their strength and hold their ground: no more wild counter-attacks. And above all Pétain made it clear that this was a gunners' war. He began his telephone conversations by asking his commanders: 'What have your batteries been doing?' The Germans felt the effect almost immediately. Fresh batteries were tucked in behind the ridges on the left bank and raked the gullies around Douaumont with their fire.

Men, guns and ammunition could reach Verdun only via a little road from Bar-le-Duc and the narrow-gauge railway running alongside it. The task seemed impossible, for soon there were half a million men and 170,000 animals to be fed. However, Major Richard, responsible for transport, divided the road into six sectors, each with its repair crews and teams of engineers. Vehicles were commandeered all across France: the price of vegetables in Paris doubled in consequence. As the weather worsened, all available Territorials were set to road-mending, men working almost shoulder-to-shoulder. During the week beginning 28 February more than 25,000 tons of supplies and 190,000 men reached Verdun, and when the road was running at full capacity in June one vehicle passed a given point every fourteen seconds. In defiance of pre-war staff tables, the road maintained an army fighting at the highest intensity, and without it all that courage, determination and suffering would have been in vain. This unremarkable provincial road richly deserved the title still proudly marked on the kilometre stones that measure its length: La Voie Sacrée, the Sacred Way.

THE LEFT BANK

Close as the Germans had come to taking Verdun, there could now be no escaping the fact that they had been checked. In early March they tried a major change of plan, sending the fresh VI Reserve Corps into action on the left bank – something which Falkenhayn's critics argued should have been done from the very start. The ground there was dominated by a long, irregular ridge, with Hill 304 at its western end, and the Mort Homme (dead man), its sinister name reflecting, perhaps, some grim tale from the Middle Ages, at its eastern end. Important though these crests were – for guns behind them could enfilade German lines on the left bank – they were but one rung of a ladder. Behind them, firmly held by its intact forts, lay Bois Bourrus Ridge. As it was, the German attack was too weak and too poorly prepared to succeed, and an attempt at a co-ordinated attack on the right bank fared no better. However, as March squelched into April the Germans maintained their pressure on the left bank, taking Malancourt, Haucourt and Béthincourt.

On 9 April the Germans mounted a major offensive on both banks simultaneously, with General von Mudra commanding on the right bank and General von Gallwitz on the left. This time there was ample artillery support – the Germans fired seventeen train-loads of artillery ammunition – but the French, too, were well-prepared and the battle see-sawed to and fro below the crests of the Mort Homme and Hill 304. On 3 May the Germans concentrated 500 guns against the ridge, and attacked after two days of concentrated fire which sent up a pillar of smoke 2500 feet (750 metres) high. They took Hill 304, and then, after another bombardment which, in the Crown Prince's words, left the Mort Homme flaming like a volcano, they took that too. By the end of May the whole ridge was in their hands. Yet Bois Bourrus was still intact, and the burden of losses, which had favoured the Germans early in the battle, now seemed almost even.

THE PITY OF WAR

Many of the war's great battles had their own terrible distinctions. The fruitless heroism of the Battle of the Frontiers; the wasted hopes of the first day on the Somme; the mud of Passchendaele.

But there was something peculiarly dreadful about Verdun. The front was so narrow (it is less than 15 miles – 24 kilometres – as the shell flies, from Hill 304 in the west to Damloup in the east) and the concentration of men and shells so great that many combatants remembered a battle which epitomized the impotence of the individual in the face of shellfire.

Men might be killed instantly, but without apparent damage, by concussion; blown to tatters by direct hits; cut up as if by some malicious butcher; crippled by flying fragments of their comrades' bodies, or shocked into babbling incoherence by a capricious hit which left them unscathed among the remnants of their friends. A French Jesuit, Sergeant Paul Dubrulle, summed up the great anguish of the combatants on both sides:

> To die from a bullet seems nothing; parts of our being remain intact; but to be dismembered, torn to pieces, reduced to pulp, this is a fear that the flesh cannot support and which is fundamentally the great suffering of the bombardment...

Evidence of death was all too abundant. Bodies hacked apart as men dug with pick and shovel; splintered trees turned to gibbets, heavy with dismembered limbs; glistening ropes of entrails. One French officer wrote feelingly of a 'small compass where one cannot possibly distinguish if the mud were flesh or the flesh were mud'.

A soldier recalled walking happily out into the sunshine, only to be confronted by a new shell-hole.

> At the bottom, in the freshly turned earth, five bodies were spread, but in such a regular manner that you could see that the shell had burst in the middle of this little knot of men to send one in each direction, so that these poor bodies formed the five branches of some macabre review. The violence of the explosion had pushed them deep into the earth: three were almost completely driven into the lips of the crater, stuffed in

like rags. The arm of one of these crushed bodies stuck straight up out of the clay: the hand was intact, and an aluminium ring encircled a finger.

After a storm of shellfire, another man found 'nothing but a head in a red puddle, a few bits of limb in a shell-hole and nameless scraps plastered to the parapet. That was all that remained here of our poor comrade'.

Simply living in this blighted landscape wore men out. That common enemy, mud, was everywhere, as a soldier described in a trench newspaper.

> It has rained since morning, one of those winter rains which nothing keeps out: cold, fine, eternal. The front-line trench is an earth-coloured brook… Water, mud. You stick in it, you slip down, dragged by some irresistible force. The molecules of the stuff open up at first, but then you feel them come back, sticking together with a tenacity that nothing prevails against… Here the mud is obsessive. It is everywhere, under your feet, under your hands, under your body as you stretch out… it sticks to your clothes, penetrates right to your skin, and soils everything…

THE AIR BATTLE

High above the front the rival pilots fought it out, envied by many who raised their eyes from the squalor of the battlefield. Aircrew enjoyed flying pay, dry quarters, the prospect of rapid decoration, and a public adulation which not all found to their taste. And to earn it they climbed, muffled in fur and leather, into wood and fabric aircraft whose handling characteristics made them sometimes scarcely less lethal than enemy guns. When hit, they might be faced with the agonizing decision of staying in the doomed aircraft as burning petrol torched back into the cockpit, or jumping without a parachute to a different kind of death.

Some pilots hated the act of killing, but others, perhaps with comrades to avenge, felt a wild joy at the moment of victory. Albert Deullin put 25 rounds into a Fokker at a range of less than 30 feet (about 10 metres), and recalled: 'The fellow was so riddled that vaporized blood sprayed on my cowling, windscreen, cap and goggles. Naturally, the descent from 2600 metres [8500 feet] was delicious to contemplate.'

The Germans had begun the air battle with numbers and technology on their side, but the French quickly concentrated their own air power at Verdun. That spring the Nieuport fighter arrived but, even before that, the pilots of the élite *Group des Cigognes* (Storks) had already made their appearance, with the legendary Jean Navarre shooting down two German aircraft over Fort Douaumont the day after its fall. Georges Guynemer, France's ace of aces, who was to amass fifty-four victories before disappearing above the Ypres salient in 1917, shot down twenty-one aircraft in 1916, including a triple kill in March. American volunteer pilots, forerunners of what was to become the Lafayette Squadron, were also on the scene, and Kiffin Rockwell opened their tally with a kill on his first combat sortie.

Like the fighting on the ground, the war in the air ebbed and flowed. The German ace Oswald Boelcke developed the *Jagdstaffel* (hunting squadron) whose co-ordinated tactics might have spelt disaster for the more gladiatorial French had Boelcke not been grounded in June on the news of the death of Max Immelmann: the Kaiser felt that Germany could not risk losing two aces so swiftly. Thereafter the skies above Verdun remained French, and as their lines were pounded by guns directed by spotter aircraft, it was German soldiers who paid the price.

COMMAND DECISIONS

German commanders, less than unanimous about the battle even in February, bickered on. Mudra, thoroughly pessimistic about German prospects, was sacked in late April, but not before the Crown Prince had caught his mood and decided that the attack ought to be discontinued: 'although we had more than once changed our methods of attack, a decisive success at Verdun could only be assured at the price of heavy sacrifices, out of all proportion to the desired gains'. Unfortunately the Crown Prince was not a free agent, and lack of experience left him at a marked disadvantage in the debate. The 'oak hard' Knobelsdorf, his chief of staff, remained committed to the offensive, and replaced Mudra with the aggressive General von Lochow. Even Falkenhayn wavered, but after a series of meetings in May it was decided, against all the Crown Prince's instincts, to press on.

The French were scarcely more unanimous. For all Pétain's chilly exterior, the sacrifices made by his men moved him deeply, and the experience of standing on the steps of the town hall at Souilly on the Voie Sacrée, watching fresh troops going up the line and decimated survivors lurching back, never left him. At his insistence the French rotated divisions through Verdun, relieving them before they were exhausted: the Germans, in contrast, kept the same divisions and replaced casualties as necessary. Each system had its strengths and weaknesses. French troops were often fresher, but the dreadful experience of Verdun was spread across the whole army, and it became harder and harder for Joffre to harbour reserves for the great Allied offensive due that summer. The flood of fresh troops depressed German soldiers, but encouraged Knobelsdorf to believe that he was steadily wearing down the French army. His own system was depressing for front-line soldiers, who saw the effect of the battle on their own units and calculated that there were only two ways out of Verdun: the stretcher or the grave. Small wonder that they called it 'The Mill on the Meuse': a mill that ground men, not corn.

Pétain's dogged caution, which Joffre had found so valuable in February and March, became increasingly unpopular at GQG. Yet Joffre could not sack the man of the hour without imperilling his own position. The solution was to kick him upstairs. On 19 April Pétain was told that he would replace Langle de Cary in command of Army Group Centre. His place would be taken by General Robert Nivelle, a 58-year-old artillery officer whose rise had been scarcely less meteoric than Pétain's own. Cultured and eloquent – he was as fluent in the tongue of his English mother as he was in French – Nivelle charmed generals and politicians alike. He was powerfully influenced by two men: Colonel d'Alenson, head of his personal staff who was dying of tuberculosis and committed to winning the war before he perished, and by Charles Mangin, who commanded one of his divisions.

On 22 May Mangin attacked Fort Douaumont after a savage bombardment, which included some 370mm howitzers. Despite an accurate barrage on their jumping-off trenches the French infantry surged on across the fort's superstructure and for a time it looked as if they had secured it. But their grip was never firm: the Germans leeched troops into the fort from the north, and they surged up from beneath the attackers. The French were dislodged on the 24th, and the failure bruised that morale which Pétain had done do much to foster.

THE FALL OF FORT VAUX

On 1 June the Germans began their biggest assault on the right bank since the beginning of the battle. Five divisions attacked with the aim of capturing Fort Vaux and then pushing on to the ridge crowned by Fort Souville, the French command post, from which Verdun itself was visible. Little Vaux had already been attacked without success, but in the process its single 75mm turret, prepared for demolition, had been destroyed when a German shell exploded the charge. Its commander, the 49-year-old Major Sylvain-Eugène Raynal, who arrived at the fort on 24 May, had already been so badly wounded that he walked with the aid of a stick. Raynal estimated that shells hit the fort at the rate of 1500 to 2000 an hour on 1 June, and on the 2nd German infantry attacked. They lost men to the ditch-defence machine-guns, but when one jammed the Germans were able to break into the north-east gallery. Captain Tabourot, Raynal's second-in-command, delayed them until he was mortally wounded. The other ditch-defence position fell later, leaving the Germans in possession of the fort's superstructure.

Raynal, however, had used the time to good effect, and sandbag barricades had been prepared along the tunnels connecting the galleries to the main body of the fort. Over the days that followed the French defended the galleries yard by yard. The Germans would blow up a barricade, killing its defenders, only to find another, as bravely held, behind it. Raynal recalled that 'through the loopholes they poured flame and gas, which gave off an intolerable smell and gripped our throats'. His men fought on in gas-masks.

Contact with Fort Souville was maintained by signal lamp, runner and pigeon. Raynal's last bird, carrying a message demanding relief, died delivering its message and was decorated for the feat. In the end it was lack of water that finished Vaux. The gauge on the fort's water-tank was faulty, and men were reduced to drinking their own urine or licking moisture from the walls. Counter-attacks petered out short of the fort, and on 7 June Raynal flashed his last message to Souville, and told his survivors that it was all over: they must surrender. 'They understood,' he wrote, 'and together in one shout we repeated the last message which my instrument had just sent off: "*Vive la France!*"' He was taken before the Crown Prince, who noticed that he had lost his sword, and presented him with the weapon taken from another French officer. A chivalrous gesture on a barbarous field.

THE BATTLE'S CLIMAX

Elsewhere the Germans made steady progress despite dismal weather, and that second week in June saw Verdun in greater peril than at any time since February. Nevertheless it was saved, not simply by the courage of French soldiers, but by the fact that the members of both contending coalitions had obligations, and both France's major allies, under tremendous pressure to distract the Germans from Verdun, honoured theirs.

On 4 June the Russian General Brusilov attacked the Austrians in distant Galicia. Nearly half a million Austrians were captured, and for a moment it seemed as if the Eastern Front would collapse altogether: Falkenhayn sent three divisions eastwards. And there were clear signs that the British were preparing to attack on the Somme. Falkenhayn hesitated, and in the time that it took him to order the Crown Prince to try again, Nivelle re-established his line.

The last major German attack was launched on 23 June after a bombardment in which a new gas, specially designed to penetrate French respirators, played a lethal part. It came within inches of success, taking Fleury and lapping right up against Fort Souville. But on 1 July the British began their long-awaited offensive, and almost everyone – save the oak-hard Knobelsdorf – realized that Verdun could not remain the focus of German attention. It speaks volumes for his persuasive powers that he managed to persuade Falkenhayn to authorize one last attack. It failed, but not before a handful of Germans, briefly on top of Fort Souville, glimpsed the sunlight glinting off the Meuse in Verdun.

Knobelsdorf was one of the casualties of German failure, and was shunted off on 23 August to command a corps on the Eastern

Front. Falkenhayn was not far behind him. He had predicted that Romania could not enter the war on the Allied side until the harvest was safely in, and when she joined the war on 27 August Falkenhayn's position was untenable. He resigned, and was replaced by the formidable combination of Field Marshal Paul von Hindenburg and General Erich Ludendorff, who had made their reputation on the Eastern Front.

THE RECAPTURE OF FORT DOUAUMONT

There were dramas still to be played out at Verdun. On 24 October Nivelle and Mangin retook Fort Douaumont in a meticulously planned operation that left nothing to chance. The sector was boxed off by an impenetrable barrage while batteries methodically raked over the ground around the fort. So unnerving was the impact of French heavy guns that the fort's garrison withdrew to the comparative safety of shell-holes outside, and when the French entered the fort they found it almost unoccupied.

The recapture of Douaumont set the seal on Nivelle's reputation, and when old Joffre was promoted marshal of France and appointed to a meaningless advisory post in December it was Nivelle who vaulted over the heads of the army group commanders to replace him. 'We have the formula,' announced Nivelle, 'our experience is conclusive. Our method has proved itself. Victory is certain. I give you my assurance...' What had been done at Douaumont could, he asserted, be done on a much larger scale. He was peddling victory, and it was a seller's market.

THE PRICE OF GLORY

Even now we cannot be sure what Verdun meant in human terms. Some French and German authorities suggest that Alistair Horne's estimate of casualties is too high, but it cannot be lightly dismissed.

He suggests that the French lost 377,231 killed, wounded and missing, and the Germans roughly 337,000. At least 700,000, and for 1916 alone: rather more than half the total casualties suffered by Britain and her Empire in the Second World War. Nine villages, which had stood on those uplands for a thousand years, were destroyed and never rebuilt. Woods and field were so polluted by metal, high explosive and bodies that they were beyond cultivation. Declared *zones rouges*, red zones, they were cloaked in conifers and left to the recuperative powers of nature.

Some of the soldiers who died there were buried in military cemeteries, but the bodies of thousands could not be identified, or had lost all physical integrity. A temporary wooden ossuary was established to house their bones and, thanks to the efforts of Canon Noel and Monseigneur Ginisty, Bishop of Verdun, a permanent structure was begun on Douaumont crest in 1920 and inaugurated twelve years later. It contains the bones of around 130,000 unknown soldiers, French and German.

The psychological impact of the battle cut deeper than its physical wounds. 'If the French succeeded in holding Verdun,' wrote Philip Guedalla, 'they had lost something far more irreplaceable upon the naked slopes above a town of no particular significance.' French soldiers had fought a defensive battle summed up by Pétain's ringing order of the day: '*Ils ne passeront pas*' – They shall not pass. They had made extraordinary sacrifices. But there was less spring in their step, less glint in their eyes: theirs was an army running out of patience with its leaders.

COMMANDING THE
FRONT

RED TABS AND DUG-OUTS

Somehow it is hard to like First World War generals. In so many of their photographs they seem comfortable, secure and well-breakfasted. Their uniform doesn't help. Breeched, booted and spurred, they ride or stride their way about a world of châteaux and staff conferences. There is an age-old tension between the man on horseback and the man on foot: when mounted it is hard not to look, very literally, down on those below. On the Western Front polished leather and tailored whipcord conveyed a message which muddy folk in khaki serge did not always welcome, and at the end of the twentieth century it is hard to see behind the sepia image, foot flexed on château doorstep, chest quilted in medal ribbons. It is small wonder that one veteran was to write that all officers above the rank of lieutenant-colonel should have been strangled at birth. Small wonder, too, that the general has been embodied in popular entertainment from *Oh! What a Lovely War* to *Blackadder* as the deadly buffoon, the cheery old card with the heart of flint.

The historical debate on British generals has, as I explained in the Introduction, now reached a remarkable maturity. While there are still historians who resolutely defend the thesis that British soldiers were indeed lions led by donkeys, the majority takes a more balanced view, admitting that generals were called upon to solve military problems of staggering complexity. Yet the scholarly debate has scarcely touched popular consciousness: to the ordinary man on the street, the generals of the First World War remain damned beyond hope of reprieve. This chapter is concerned with the British high command in 1916, the year of the Somme, but begins by looking at generals and their staffs more widely, for it is only by understanding who they were and how they worked that we can begin to make sense of what they did.

The British army distinguished between units, lieutenant-colonels' commands like infantry battalions or cavalry regiments, and formations, which were collections of units and which varied in size from the tiny brigade to the mighty army. A unit had its CO, Commanding Officer: a formation its GOC, General Officer Commanding. During the First World War there were four grades of general officer. Armies were commanded by a general. He would have an indeterminate number of corps at his disposal, the precise number depending on the importance of his army's task. In July 1916 Rawlinson's 4th Army had five corps: 3rd Army, its northern neighbour, only three. A corps, with a lieutenant-general at its head, normally comprised three infantry divisions, and had its own integral artillery and engineer support.

Divisions, commanded by major-generals, contained three brigades, again with artillery and engineers. Their detailed establishment changed as the war went on, and numbers fluctuated as casualties were incurred and replacements arrived. In 1914 a division fielded a little over 18,000 officers and men, but by 1918 might, even without exceptionally bad luck, find itself half this size. While divisions were often shifted between corps, they tended to retain the same units within them, and to have a character which might survive repeated misfortune or the vagaries of a personnel system which, by design and accident, increasingly mingled regulars, Territorials, New Army men and, from early 1916, conscripts. The brigade, with a brigadier-general at its head, was the smallest of the formations, and the only one not to contain a mix of all arms. Until the winter of 1917 the infantry brigade contained four battalions, but thereafter manpower shortages reduced this to three.

Simply glancing at our GOC, as he genially asked us whether mail arrived promptly, or more curtly suggested that a haircut would not come amiss, might actually tell us little about him. He would be unlucky not to have medal ribbons from the South African War or a colonial campaign or two. Were he a general, lieutenant-general, or rising star among the major-generals, he would have a knighthood, or at least the companionate of an order of chivalry like the Bath or St Michael and St George.

His badges of rank would tell us only what he was at the moment. There were three sorts of rank in the army. Substantive (permanent) rank, of which an officer could be deprived only by due process; temporary or local rank, given him for the duration of a particular appointment; and brevet rank, given as a reward for good service but not entitling its holder to employment in that particular grade. To take an extreme example: in 1908 W. H. Manning was inspector-general of the King's African Rifles. He was a substantive captain, a brevet lieutenant colonel and local brigadier general: at the time the latter grade was not a substantive rank in any event. The commanding officers of the units under his command were all substantive captains but local lieutenant-colonels.

On the Western Front generals might well find themselves 'acting up', in the case of brigadier-generals by several ranks. Many brigadier-generals were camouflaged majors, and even some substantive captains commanded brigades. Substantive promotion took time to catch up with temporary rank, and its arrival – betokening pay, status and pension which would not evaporate at the end of the war – was often very welcome. On 29 December 1916 Rawlinson heard that he had at last been promoted to the substantive rank of general, and wrote: 'From

Capt. to Full Genl in 17 years is not bad going after being in 3 Form at Eton too so there is hope for everyone.' Hubert Gough was less fortunate: when he was sacked as commander of 5th Army in 1918 he was only a temporary general, and had to revert to his substantive rank of lieutenant-general.

We have already seen how the British army expanded dramatically during the war. In the process it developed an enormous appetite for generals and staff officers. On the Western Front alone in 1914 it had one army headquarters, two corps and seven divisions. By mid-1916 there were five armies, 18 corps and about 50 divisions. In addition, special staffs, such as artillery and engineer staffs, had proliferated. The *Army List*, which catalogues all the army's officers, is not always an accurate guide to temporary rank and shows us only part of the iceberg, suggests that between 1914 and 1918 the number of major-generals and above had doubled.

This fountain of promotion played most freely upon pre-war regulars. Australians, Canadians and New Zealanders were different in this respect because their pre-war regular establishment was so tiny and tradition of citizen-soldiering so strong as to make it easier for non-regulars to become generals. Indeed, one of the war's outstanding successes was Lieutenant-General Sir John Monash, ANZAC corps commander in 1918, who was a civil engineer by profession. In the British army, however, the moderately competent regular could expect advancement. In 1918 nine substantive Royal Artillery lieutenant-colonels were temporary major-generals, another seventy-seven were brigadier-generals, and among the fortunate majors was temporary Brigadier-General Ironside, a future field-marshal. Three of the five lieutenant-colonels in the Grenadier Guards were brigadier-generals.

Some generals were promoted on the basis of previous success. Among the divisional commanders in 1916 were Maxse, Davies and Ingouville-Williams – the first an outstanding trainer of troops, the third killed on the Somme – given divisions after commanding brigades in 1914. Others were retired regulars 'dug out' of retirement. The fact that Biddulph was sixty-one did not prevent his commanding a division very competently, and Bryan Mahon, brought back at the age of fifty-two, later went on to be GOC in Ireland. Broadwood, a retired lieutenant-general, was brought back, unusually, in a temporary rank junior to his retired rank, and died of wounds as a major-general commanding the 57th Division in June 1917. Most of the new brigadier-generals needed in 1914–15 were dug-outs – retired lieutenant-colonels were well placed – and the rest had made their reputations as COs in 1914.

A few non-regulars entered the charmed circle: in 1917 the Earl of Derby, then secretary of state for war, told the House of Lords that four Territorials had commanded divisions and fifty-two brigades. However, this included officers who had held these appointments on a temporary basis. The Territorial general was a rare beast, and the 1918 *Army List* shows only six Territorial brigadier-generals. The regular army's control of key staff appointments was just as marked: only three Territorials held the post of GSO (General Staff Officer) Grade 1, a key figure at large formation headquarters.

None of this is particularly surprising, nor would it necessarily have been easy to have organized matters very differently. But it did mean that the field from which generals and their staff were selected was very narrow. As there had been no pre-war emphasis on training officers to step up in rank when war came, many generals, like the men they commanded, were learning on the job.

Promoted regulars and dug-outs alike brought with them much that was admirable. But they also often brought characteristics which chimed discordantly with the largest citizen army Britain had ever seen. We must beware of what can only be generalizations, but the British high command reflected the loyalties of the pre-war army, where the bonds of experience shared (or personal antipathies aroused) in the same intake at Staff College or on the same campaign endured for years. Peacetime rings of influence rippled on into the war, and the private papers of almost any senior officer testify to cronyism which might make many real politicians blush. There were also many generals who were more brave than imaginative; found it hard to tolerate opposition, even when it was loyal and constructive; and equated the quality of advice with the rank of the adviser.

They were often prepared to hazard their lives, but sometimes less prepared to risk their jobs. Their motives here were by no means wholly dishonourable. Of course rank, pay and the prospect of decoration cannot be ignored. Yet among letters and diaries there is frequent reference to their desire to be where it mattered, doing a job that counted. Losing the confidence of one's immediate superior, rightly or wrongly, was often fatal. French never forgave Smith-Dorrien – 'wordy, windy and unintelligible' – for making his stand at Le Cateau. Rawlinson blamed Davies (8th Division) for errors at Neuve Chapelle. Davies, inches from dismissal, produced a dossier in his own defence. This persuaded French that Rawlinson should be sent home instead. Haig intervened, and although Rawlinson was saved it was made clear that further attempts to blame subordinates would see him relieved of his command. It was also clear that Rawlinson owed his survival to Haig, a point of no little importance in the story that follows. A débâcle at St Eloi, south of Ypres, cost Alderson command of the Canadian Corps in May 1916, and among the generals degummed on the Somme were Montagu-Stuart-Wortley (46th Division), Philipps (38th Division), Ryecroft (32nd Division) and Barter (47th Division).

Generals often fell between the hammer of a hard-driving superior and the anvil of the battlefield. Brigadier-General F. M. Carleton, a dug-out who had left the army in 1908, was recalled in 1914 and commanded a battalion before being appointed temporary brigadier-general in June 1916: he was relieved of command of 98th Infantry Brigade on the Somme. 'I want no sympathy,' he told his wife, 'nor do I want to see anyone...' His complaint was a common one: he had been sacked because his men had failed to achieve the impossible. 'The men had been fighting for nearly six weeks, and had suffered enormous casualties,' he wrote. 'They were done to a turn. We were ordered to do something which was a physical impossibility... I have been sacrificed to the ambitions of an unscrupulous general.' The likes of Carleton were in an agonizing position. If they tried to do the impossible and failed, the butcher's bill would at least testify to the scale of their effort. If, recognizing the impossible, they objected or made a token attempt, they risked being branded as 'sticky', the badge of professional suicide.

THE GILDED STAFF

Music-hall comics of the time joked that 'if bread is the staff of life, the life of the staff is one long loaf'. Philip Gibbs, the best-known British war correspondent, was scarcely less scathing. 'Within their close corporation,' he wrote of the staff,

> there were rivalries, intrigues, perjuries and treacheries like those of a medieval court... They worked late into the night. That is to say, they went back to their offices after dining at mess... and kept their lights burning, and smoked more cigarettes, and rang each other up on the telephone with futile questions...

Needless to say, things did not look the same from behind the staff officer's desk. Memoirs and diaries testify to cripplingly long days – it was not unknown for officers at GHQ to collapse at their paperwork. Brigadier-General John Charteris wrote: 'There are few, if any, officers who do not do a fourteen-hour day, and who are not to be found at work far into the night.' And a staff job was often a mixed blessing. In 1916 Alan Hanbury-Sparrow told his mother that:

> I am feeling most frightfully homesick for my regiment and bitterly repent the day when my selfishness urged me to go onto the staff... My conscience pricks me most horribly as I know I am far more useful with them than here.

Charteris spoke for many when he said that: 'Perhaps the hardest thing of all is that we cannot share the dangers we send others to endure.' Many staff officers repeatedly sought employment at the front, only to be told that they were too valuable to be released. Charteris lost his job in December 1917 and asked to go to the front. When told that Haig wanted to keep him on at GHQ as deputy inspector-general of transport, he wrote: 'It is a disappointment, but is softened by the verdict of the doctors that in any case they could not have passed me as fit for front-line work.'

Nor were senior officers immune from personal risk. No fewer than fifty-eight generals were killed, or died of wounds received, on the Western Front. Of the first six divisions sent to France, three had their commanders killed and one wounded. Three divisional commanders, Capper (7th Division), Thesiger (9th Division) and Wing (12th Division), were killed at Loos in 1915. Haig's chief of staff at 1st Army, Johnny Gough (whose brother Hubert was to command 5th Army), was mortally wounded by a sniper while visiting his old battalion at the front. At least twice as many were wounded, many of them seriously. Big, brave Tom Bridges lost a leg commanding a division at Passchendaele: he had characteristically set off across the mud while it was 'raining old iron'.

There was bitter personal grief, too, for so many officers from military families. Walter Congreve, commanding XIII Corps on the Somme, was in the middle of a difficult attack when he was told that his son Billy had been killed. He paused, said, 'He was a good soldier,' and carried on with the battle. Edmund Allenby was commanding in Palestine when he heard that his boy Michael, a gunner officer, had died of wounds at the age of nineteen. Outwardly a hard man, he asked for no sympathy, but the level of his sorrow is marked by a letter whose strong, careful script is blotched by tears.

Corps and army headquarters would normally be found about 8–15 miles (13–24 kilometres) from the front line. Châteaux, a term which covers a broad band from manor houses to stately homes, were a logical choice for accommodation, for while the main house could often hold the general and most of his staff, servants' quarters and outbuildings could accommodate drivers, cooks and grooms. There was also space within the grounds for temporary buildings, like those erected in the grounds of 1st Army's HQ at Hinges château in 1915 to house the intelligence staff.

Staff officers manned the main headquarters branches. At their head came the chief of staff, whose rank varied according to the level of his headquarters: a lieutenant-general at GHQ, major-general at army, brigadier-general at corps, lieutenant-colonel at division and major at brigade. The G (General Staff) Branch was responsible for all operational matters, developed plans and orders on the commander's behalf, was responsible for the acquisition and collation of intelligence and co-ordinated staff work. The A (Adjutant-General's) Branch oversaw appointments, promotions and discipline, while the Q (Quartermaster-General's) Staff dealt with supply and accommodation. Artillery and engineer staffs dealt with their own specialisms, and as the war went on the artillery staff grew in importance: by 1916 there was a Major-General Royal Artillery at each army headquarters and an artillery adviser (from June Major-General Noel Birch) at GHQ.

All officers on the general staff, including aides de camp to generals, wore red tabs on their collars. In addition, coloured armbands bearing a variety of symbols showed the branch to which an officer belonged. These signs, intended to be part-honorific and part-helpful, were often wholly irritating. There were jokes about 'the red badge of funk', as well as unflattering doggerel:

> *He had red tabs upon his chest and even on his under-vest.*
> *He had the Military Cross and rode about upon a hoss.*

There is an age-old friction between those at the sharp end of war and those in safer jobs behind them, and relations between the staff and the men they commanded were often brittle. Again, there are no universal truths. Charles Carrington came close to finding one, suggesting that hostility was very much a matter of perception. Front-liners resented:

> the bloody munitions workers at home who were earning high wages and seducing your girl-friend; number four platoon in the next trench who made such a noise that they woke up the enemy gunners... and, of course, the staff who could conveniently be blamed for everything.

He acknowledged that 'my colonel, brigadier and divisional commander were men I could respect', and added: 'While every man in my company knew Brigadier Sladen and General Fanshawe by sight I doubt if one in ten knew the corps commander's name.'

W. N. Nicholson, with wide experience of a divisional headquarters, thought the real break-point came between division and corps: 'Lord Cavan [XIV Corps] was one of the rare corps commanders who was known by name to more than divisional commanders.' He pointed out that senior officers were not universally unpopular. The men liked 'Daddy' Plumer of 2nd Army because 'he doesn't see red; and he looks after us'. Nicholson felt that Haig's problem was partly presentational. In 1918 the commander-in-chief visited his division.

It was the first time that any man present had seen the commander-in-chief. A man can issue orders till he's blue in the face; he can write – and the best of his orders and letters will be criticized. But if he'll come and let his soldiers see him, they'll do anything he asks them.

Such was this presentational problem that, soon after the war, the rank of brigadier-general was abolished so that there would be fewer generals. It was briefly replaced by the untidy hybrid colonel-commandant, and then by simple brigadier. Red tabs disappeared from all officers below full colonel. Second World War commanders remembered the damage done by the remoteness of their predecessors, and many cultivated a more personal style of command.

PLANS AND PREPARATIONS

From December 1915 the British commander-in-chief was Douglas Haig, then a general but promoted to field-marshal, the highest rank in the army, a year later. His headquarters moved to Montreuil-sur-Mer, a pleasant Picardy town from which the sea had long receded, in April 1916. He had attempted to translate his staff from 1st Army direct to GHQ, but his chief of staff, Major-General Butler, was considered too junior, and instead Haig took Lieutenant-General Sir Launcelot Kiggell. John Terraine, Haig's most acute defender, observed that 'Kiggell never was, nor aspired to be, more than a mouthpiece for Haig.' He adds that 'a distinct weakness of Haig's period of command is a lack of forceful and energetic personality at his side until the last months of the War, when Sir Herbert Lawrence joined him [as Kiggell's replacement]'.

Haig had been left in no doubt, by Kitchener's instructions of December 1915, that the defeat of the Germans by 'the closest co-operation of French and British as a united army' was to be his objective. The Chantilly conference of early December had set out

THE EVE OF THE SOMME, 1916
THE BATTLE FRONT OF THE BEF, 30 JUNE 1916

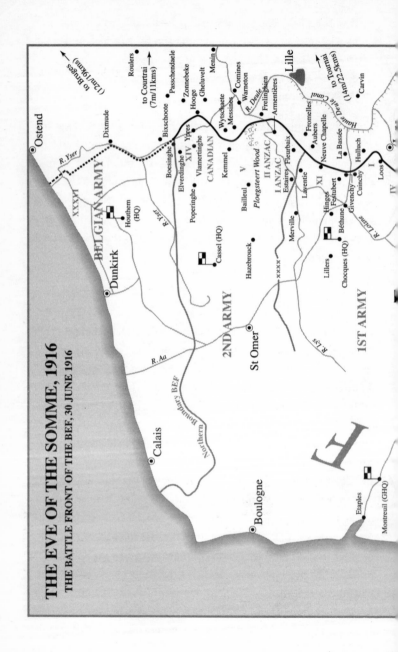

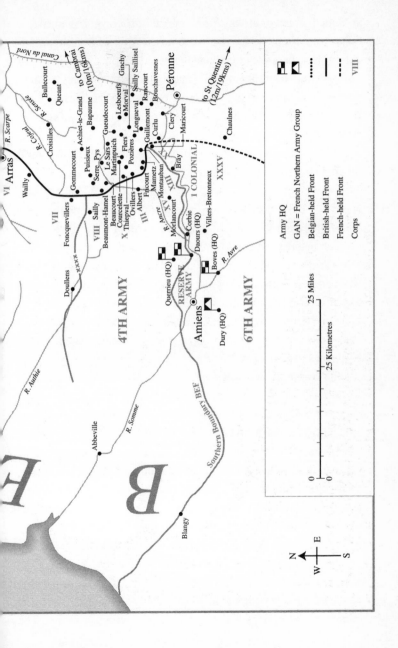

an Allied strategy, in which a combined offensive was to play a major role. Haig had his doubts about the level of French participation even before the Germans attacked Verdun, writing on 14 January that he thought the French unlikely to stand another winter's war, and so 'the war must be won by the forces of the British Empire'. This being so, he was reluctant to hazard his army in the 'wearing-down fights' of which Joffre had spoken: he argued that there would be little merit in fighting such battles until the main offensive was imminent.

On 14 February he met Joffre at Chantilly. Although Haig could not agree to relieve the French 10th Army, currently sandwiched between the British 1st and 3rd Armies around Arras, the two commanders-in-chief were able to agree on a combined offensive astride the Somme, with a target date of 1 July. Haig then told Rawlinson, designated to command the new 4th Army, to consider how this offensive might best be handled. But at the same time he ordered Plumer, commanding 2nd Army in Flanders, to plan for operations there, in an area where the German communications bottleneck presented an attractive target. At this early stage we can see the contradictions inherent in the choice of the Somme as a battlefield. There were no significant tactical objectives close behind it, and advance of even 30 miles (50 kilometres) would not strike a fatal blow. A much smaller advance from Ypres, however, would seize the railheads upon which the northern wing of German armies depended. Sir James Edmonds, the official historian, complained that, this being the case, 'the Somme offensive had no strategic object except attrition'. That the Somme became a battle of attrition there is, as we will see, little doubt. But in early 1916 Haig saw it as something more: a potential breakthrough.

As soon as news of Verdun broke Haig agreed to relieve the 10th Army, and on 28 February he saw Joffre 'to shake him by the hand and place myself and my troops at his disposition'. Over the coming months Haig had to balance conflicting priorities. The

French urged him to attack as soon as possible to take the weight off them: given the importance of maintaining the alliance these demands could scarcely be ignored. But on the other hand Haig was all too well aware of the real state of his army, writing: 'I have not got an Army in France really, but a collection of divisions untrained for the Field. The actual fighting army will be evolved from them.'

There were sound reasons for delaying the offensive until the New Army divisions were better prepared, but sounder reasons for not imperilling the alliance. On 26 May Haig entertained Joffre in his modest château at Beaurepaire, near Montreuil. When he suggested that his army might not be ready to attack till August Joffre declared that 'the French army would cease to exist if we did nothing till then'. Haig, an abstemious man, noted that:

> They are, indeed, difficult Allies to deal with! But there is no
> doubt that the nearest way to the hearts of many of them,
> including the 'Generalissimo', is down their throats, and some
> 1840 brandy had a surprisingly soothing effect.

Rawlinson's newly formed 4th Army took over the right of the British line, about 20 miles (30 kilometres) of chalk downland from Foncquevillers in the north to Maricourt, just short of the meandering Somme, in the south. The Albert–Bapaume road slashed obliquely across its main feature, a long, irregular ridge running from Thiepval to Ginchy. Rawlinson himself took up residence in the delightful Château de Querrieu, about 12 miles (19 kilometres) behind the front. He thought it 'capital country in which to undertake an offensive when we get a sufficiency of artillery'.

It had previously been a quiet sector, and German defences, prepared at leisure, were very strong. There were two completed systems, with a third in preparation. The first, composed of several lines of battle and communication trenches, incorporated fortified villages like Serre, Thiepval, La Boisselle and Fricourt.

The lie of the land made it immensely strong, for the villages enabled their defenders to bring flanking fire to bear on the sections of line between them. The second line was a mile or two behind the first, and both this distance and the intervening ridges meant that an attack on the second line would have to be distinct from the assault on the first. The firm chalk was ideally suited to the construction of deep dug-outs. The Germans had built many, some of them 30 feet (9 metres) deep and impervious to direct hits by all but the heaviest guns. These were no surprise to the British, who had already captured one near Touvent Farm.

Rawlinson and his chief of staff, Major-General A. A. Montgomery, developed their plan in March. It embodied what Rawlinson called 'bite and hold', and was based on the mathematical calculation of the front that could be attacked by his troops and the 200 heavy pieces available to support them. He concluded that he should be able to seize the German first line on a front of 20,000 yards (18,200 metres) and then, in two distinct attacks, push on to take the German second line. Rawlinson knew that Haig was unlikely to welcome the plan, and wrote on 4 April that he had heard that the commander-in-chief favoured wider objectives 'with the chance of breaking the German line'.

Here Rawlinson was perfectly correct. Haig declared that the methodical bombardment favoured by Rawlinson would forfeit surprise, and complained that the whole scheme was far too cautious. He favoured a more ambitious attack behind a short hurricane bombardment. The serious flaws in Haig's proposal, not least the difficulty of dealing with German barbed-wire and strongpoints with a short bombardment, and bringing cavalry through to exploit the break-in, were apparent to Rawlinson. However, he declared himself 'quite game to try although it does involve considerable risks'. He told Haig as much, but added that he would do as he was told, and expected instructions in due course.

Haig eventually conceded that a deliberate bombardment would be necessary, but could not be deflected from his confidence in an ambitious attack, which would break the German line and allow Lieutenant-General Sir Hubert Gough's Reserve Army, then consisting largely of cavalry, to be pushed through the gap. Rawlinson never shared this enthusiasm. He warned his corps commanders that, despite the commander-in-chief's views on the subject, 'I had better make it quite clear that it may not be possible to break the enemy's line and push cavalry through at the first rush.' While on the whole he was 'pretty confident of success', he expected that it would come only after heavy fighting, and expected 10,000 wounded a day, hardly an index of a clean break-through.

This was not the message conveyed to the soldiers of 4th Army. Brigadier-General Gordon of 8th Brigade was expounding official orthodoxy when he told his men that they could 'slope arms, light up your pipes and cigarettes, and march all the way to Pozières before meeting any live Germans'. In the week before the attack British gunners fired a million and a half shells. The 18-pounders concentrated on the wire and trenches while heavier pieces hit German strongpoints and reached out to strike batteries. When the attack started, a creeping barrage – which was a new concept developed by Major-General C. E. D. Budworth, Rawlinson's Major-General Royal Artillery – would move ahead of the infantry. Tunnels had been dug beneath German strongpoints, and chambers hollowed out and packed with explosives: these nineteen mines were to be exploded shortly before zero hour.

The expectation was that the shelling and mines between them would cut the wire, destroy or neutralize the first garrison of the first position, and cripple the German artillery's prepared response. The infantry was to advance at a walk, in extended lines, carrying full kit, in the belief that it was occupying ground already conquered by artillery. Rawlinson was well aware of the importance of the bombardment, and postponed the attack from 29 June to 1 July to give his gunners more time. Yet although the bombardment was dreadful for the Germans – the rats in some dugouts went mad and scrambled up the walls, where they were killed with spades – and conversely inspiring to the British, it failed to accomplish what was expected of it. The shelling of an exceptionally strong section of front was proportionately about half as heavy as that of the far flimsier defences at Neuve Chapelle. The French, attacking on both sides of the Somme on the British right, had double the ratio of heavy guns per yard of front. About one-third of the shells fired failed to explode because of faulty fuses or shot-out gun barrels which meant that shells tipped over and over in flight. Inexperienced artillery observers, and there were many in the New Armies, often moved sections of German wire but failed to cut it.

The interrogation of prisoners produced conflicting views of the state of German defences. Some said that dugouts offered complete protection: others that they were being destroyed. Some patrols reported that the wire was cut: others found it intact. While Haig was convinced that the wire was indeed cut, Rawlinson was less confident, and was not 'quite satisfied that all the wire has been thoroughly well cut'. There was enough doubt in the efficacy of the bombardment for a private soldier, Rifleman Percy Jones, to write: 'I do not see how the stiffest bombardment is going to kill them all. Nor do I see how the whole of the enemy's artillery is going to be silenced.'

Rawlinson, as we have seen, had his own misgivings about the attack, some of which were shared by corps commanders. Yet 4th Army specifically warned that: 'All criticism by subordinates... of orders received from superior authority will, in the end, recoil on the heads of the critics.' The plan had become sacrosanct: and even those who successfully deviated from it kept their intentions secret. Had Rawlinson been more morally robust, and the decision process less constrained by status, he might have argued his case more vigorously. As it was, he made what Robin Prior and Trevor Wilson call 'an unhappy act of obeisance to Haig's authority', with the consequence that the result of 1 July 1916 was less 'an unforeseeable misfortune… [and] more in the nature of a fore-gone conclusion'.

THE FIRST DAY

The first day of the battle is marvellously chronicled by Martin Middlebrook's *The First Day on the Somme*, which remains one of the best books written on the war. In the south, Water Congreve's XIII Corps had taken its objectives, thanks partly to the fact that French gunners, anxious to avoid their own infantry being taken in the flank by intact positions on their left, had added their own fire to that of British guns. Henry Horne's XV Corps had made fair progress, taking Mametz and getting so close to Fricourt that the Germans gave it up next day. But further north the results were grievously disappointing. William Pulteney's III, Thomas Morland's X and Aylmer Hunter-Weston's VII Corps had achieved few lasting gains. There had been some short-lived successes: the inimitable 36th Ulster Division, attacking north of Thiepval, had overrun the German first line but, with the defences of Thiepval intact behind their right shoulders, the Ulstermen could not be supported.

The British army had lost 57,470 officers and men, 19,240 of them killed and 2152 missing, on what remains its bloodiest day. Unusually in a war in which artillery was the major killer, about 60 per cent of these casualties were caused by machine-gun fire. The Germans, sheltering in dugouts, emerged as the barrage lifted to fire into the massed ranks in front of them, and their batteries came to life to drop a curtain of shell-fire across no man's land. Their official account observed that:

> The training of the infantry was clearly behind that of the
> German; the superficially trained British were particularly

clumsy in the movement of large masses… The strong, usually young, and well armed British soldier followed his officers blindly, and the officers, active and personally brave, went ahead of their men in battle with great courage. But owing to insufficient training, they were not skilful in action.

The British official historian admitted that this appeared to be fair comment.

DEVELOPING THE BATTLE

Although the initial casualty reports that reached Rawlinson were optimistically inaccurate, even the real numbers could scarcely have deterred him, for the attack's operational imperative remained unaltered. On the night of 1 July he set out his vision for the next phase of the battle: 4th Army would hold on to what it had gained, and make fresh efforts to secure the many front-line strong points where it had failed. This was a novel reversal of the principle of reinforcing success, and did not commend itself to Haig when he visited Querrieu on the 2nd. He gave Gough command of the two northern corps, VIII and X, and told Rawlinson to renew the attack in the south, where he had already made progress. Joffre demurred, perhaps fearing that operations in the south would leech away French resources too, but Haig, rightly this time, was adamant.

On 3 July attacks on Ovillers and Thiepval failed, and XV Corps could not exploit a promising attack at Contalmaison. That night XV Corps reached the southern edge of Mametz Wood, lying between the two German positions, and XIII Corps cleared Bernafay Wood, on the British right. Before he could attack the German second position Rawlinson had to secure Mametz Wood, and it was not until 12 July that he did so, after grim fighting which sadly mauled the New Army's 39th (Welsh) Division, whose composition owed much to the influence of David Lloyd George. In less that a fortnight 4th Army lost some 25,000 men securing the start-line for the assault on the second position. What is noteworthy is that these battles were fought without overall direction from Querrieu. For example, when XV Corps attacked Mametz Wood on 7 July, the artillery of XIII Corps remained silent. Attacks on one sector were disrupted by unsuppressed fire from another, and there was no attempt at cohesive action across the whole of 4th Army's front.

Yet Rawlinson was not idle. He and his staff were considering the problem of the German second line, leering down at them from the Longueval Ridge. Rawlinson proposed a night attack, and was only able to persuade Haig that the troops were well enough trained for this when Horne and Congreve, his remaining corps commanders, firmly assured GHQ that the plan was indeed feasible. Night attacks were no novelty, and often raised as many problems as they overcame. Forming up and negotiating the wire could be difficult, although the laying of miles of white tape helped men keep direction. Machine-guns firing on fixed lines, and artillery engaging registered targets were as deadly by day as night. The Germans were amply provided with illuminating flares, and, like any defender in a night battle, knew their ground while the British did not.

Of course darkness did afford some shelter to the attacker, and contributed to the shock of a surprise assault. But what really made the 14 July night attack work was the fact that Rawlinson's gunners were engaging about 6000 yards (5460 metres) of front as opposed to the 22,000 yards (20,000 metres) of 1 July, and that trench systems behind the front attacked on 14 July were no more than another 12,000 yards (11,000 metres). Although Haig's allocation of part of the old 4th Army to Gough had reduced the number of guns available to Rawlinson, in essence he had two-thirds as many guns with which to demolish one-eighteenth of the length of trench. There was steady bombardment on 11–13 July, and at 3.20 on the morning of the 14th a five-minute blizzard of fire preceded

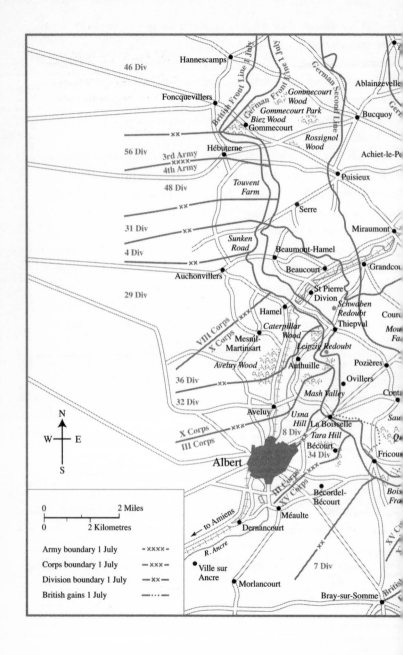

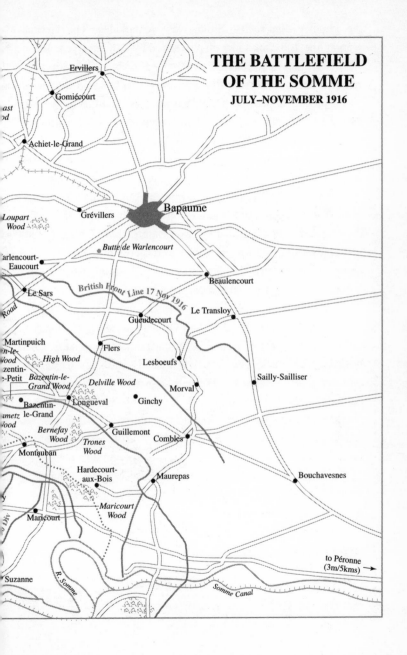

THE BATTLEFIELD OF THE SOMME
JULY–NOVEMBER 1916

Ervillers

Gomiécourt

ast
od

Achiet-le-Grand

Loupart
Wood

Grévillers

Bapaume

Butte de Warlencourt

arlencourt-
Eaucourt

British Front Line 17 Nov 1916

Beaulencourt

Le Sars

Road

Gueudecourt

Le Transloy

Martinpuich

n-le-
Wood

High Wood

Flers

Lesboeufs

Sailly-Sailliser

zentin-
-Petit

Bazentin-le-
Grand Wood

Delville Wood

Morval

Bazentin-
le-Grand

Longueval

Ginchy

ametz
Wood

Bernefay
Wood

Trones
Wood

Guillemont

Combles

Montauban

Hardecourt-
aux-Bois

Maurepas

Bouchavesnes

Maricourt
Wood

Maricourt

Suzanne

R. Somme

to Péronne
(3m/5kms) →

Somme Canal

the infantry attack. Its results were remarkable. The German second line, trenches and wire pulverized by a shelling proportionately five times heavier than that which fell before 1 July, was overrun on a broad front from Bazentin-le-Petit to Longeuval.

It proved impossible to exploit success. Getting the cavalry forward across slippery ground and deep trenches was a problem in itself and, despite Royal Flying Corps reports that High Wood was empty, it was in fact laced with trenches and German reserves were on hand. The battle was less a tragedy of missed opportunities than a successful instance of bite and hold: which, of course, is what Rawlinson had favoured from the start. However, the fact that the Germans remained in possession of both Delville Wood and High Wood enabled them to slip reserves over the crest-line behind them to turn the new line into a position it would take Rawlinson's men two bitter months to break.

On Rawlinson's left Gough's men made steady progress, taking La Boisselle on 7 July and Ovillers on the 16th. Pozières, on the Albert–Bapaume road at the heart of the German second position, was attacked by the newly arrived Australians on 23 July, and over the next two weeks the village was smashed to pieces as they fought their way through it. They were masters of it on 7 August, but at what a cost. Three Australian divisions lost almost 23,000 men, and with them their faith in British leadership. 'If Australians wish to trace their modern suspicion and resentment of the British to a date and a place,' writes the Australian historian Peter Charlton, 'then July–August 1916 and the ruined village of Pozières are useful points of departure.'

SUMMER STALEMATE

It was an atrocious summer, with rain turning the shattered woods and charnel villages into a stinking slough as the British and German armies slogged it out on the uplands. It is important to grasp the significance of these 'forgotten battles' that defined the real character of so much of the Somme fighting. At this stage in the war German doctrine emphasized the importance of immediate recovery of lost ground. On 2 July Falkenhayn visited General von Below, whose Second Army held the Somme front, and emphasized that 'the first principle in position warfare must be to yield not one foot of ground, and if it be lost to retake it by immediate counter-attack, even to the use of the last man'. Below immediately passed these instructions on to his troops, with the result that British and French attacks were almost always followed by German counter-attacks. Terraine castigated historians who portrayed the Somme as British troops rising from their trenches to be mown down: it ought, he pointed out, to be set beside an image of German troops doing precisely the same thing.

Nor is this all. One of the consequences of Falkenhayn's prior commitment to Verdun had been the concentration of German artillery in that sector, and it was not easy to disengage guns for use elsewhere. As the Somme ground on, so Allied artillery preponderance became more marked and the squat triangle of tortured earth with Bapaume at its apex was dominated by the gun. One of the less than fair consequences of the British army's regimental system, with its emphasis on county regiments – most now gone for ever – was a tendency to undervalue the contribution made by the Royal Artillery. The remarkable improvement in artillery technique was an important legacy of the Somme. It is natural enough for a British audience to reflect on what German guns were doing to its grandfathers and great-grandfathers, and easy to forget what it was like on the other side of the hill. Between 15 July and 14 September British gunners fired 6.5 million shells, and the Royal Flying Corps' superiority over the battlefield meant that much of this fire was very well controlled.

Lieutenant Ernst Junger, who was to become Germany's most decorated officer, described the artillery landscape.

> The sunken road now appeared as nothing but a series of enor-
> mous shell-holes filled with pieces of uniform, weapons and
> dead bodies. The ground all round, as far as the eye could see,
> was ploughed by shells... Among the living lay the dead. As
> we dug ourselves in we found them in layers stacked one on
> top of the other. One company after another had been shoved
> into the drum-fire and steadily annihilated.

The German army was extraordinarily resolute. Junger recalled
being led forward to the front line through the village of Sailly-
Saillisel one night in late August by a guide who was beyond hope
and beyond fear. Nothing was left but supreme, superhuman indif-
ference. 'They attack every day,' he said. 'But they can't get
through. Everyone knows it is life and death.'

Yet by now there were cracks in this splendid edifice. A
German regimental history described these days as 'the worst in the
War'. On 10 September a reservist told his family: 'You can form
no idea what the poor soldiers have to go through here in this place
and how cruelly and uselessly men are sacrificed: it is awful.' In
August Sergeant Frederick Oehme, an ex-law student, described
Martinpuich, once 'a pretty place', as 'a region of horror and
despair. *'Lasciate ogni speranza'* – Abandon hope – are the words
over the portals of hell in Dante's *Divine Comedy*. I kept thinking of
them as we tore through the village.' He was killed on 25 October.

What is at issue is not the terrible damage that this fighting
did to the contending armies, but whether the British could have
inflicted this damage on the Germans at less cost to themselves.
There were too many small-scale operations, with the same objectives being attacked, time and time again, by too few soldiers
behind too light a barrage. Lack of progress coupled with heavy
casualties – 4th Army lost about 82,000 men during this period –
led to growing disquiet in the British government, and on 29 July
Robertson warned Haig that 'the powers that be' were becoming
more restive. This induced Haig to give firmer direction to

Rawlinson, and one of the casualties of that dreadful summer was the commander-in-chief's confidence in 4th Army's commander.

ENTER THE TANKS

The first tanks – so called because they were shipped to France described as 'water tanks' – were developed in such secrecy that Haig did not know about them till Christmas Day 1915. He took an early interest in them, writing in April 1916 that they might prove useful in the northern part of the Somme front, to take the ridge around Serre, and discussing 'the surprise and demoralizing effect' likely to result from their first use. There would be too few available to use on 1 July, but during the summer stalemate GHQ remained anxious to accelerate their arrival with a view to using them in a decisive battle. Haig was not a free agent. Just as he had been pressed to initiate the Somme earlier than would have been ideal, so Joffre demanded a decisive resumption of Allied attacks on the Somme in order to keep the Germans at full stretch. The Russians were in growing difficulties, and if the Somme faltered the Germans might be able to shift some weight to the east. Haig realized that the attack would have to be properly prepared, and refused to launch it before 15 September, despite Joffre's pressure. But such was its importance that he felt it worth using as many tanks as were available. If the summer's fighting had turned into an attritional battle which had worn down the Germans, GHQ was clear that the next phase of the fighting was to be 'a decisive operation…'

Rawlinson was sceptical about the tanks. On 29 August, a fortnight before the battle, he told the King's assistant private secretary that:

> We are puzzling our heads as to how best to make use of them and have not yet come to a decision. They are not going to take the British Army straight to Berlin as some people imagine but if properly used and skilfully handled by the detachments who

work them they may be very useful in taking trenches and strong points. Some people are rather too optimistic as to what these weapons will accomplish.

Rawlinson was preparing his ground in case the coming battle did not produce the decisive result hoped for by Haig: there was still no meeting of minds between Querrieu and Montreuil. Nor was Gough any more optimistic, and neither of the army commanders engaged in the first tank battle was inclined to use them save in small groups dotted along the front. Kiggell told Rawlinson that Haig wanted tanks 'to be used boldly and success pressed in order to demoralize the enemy and, if possible, capture his guns'. It is hard to resist the conclusion that Haig and Kiggell figured among the 'some people' mentioned in Rawlinson's letter of 29 August.

The first tanks, part of the Heavy Section, Machine-Gun Corps, arrived in France in early September and were moved up by rail to Bray-sur-Somme. In the meantime 4th Army had at last taken Guillemont and Ginchy, helping the French to push on and reach the Bapaume–Péronne road at Bouchavesnes. Although the French, recovering after this advance, were unable to attack on 15 September, their heavy guns, reaching into the German flank and rear, made a valuable contribution.

Of forty-nine tanks available for the attack, thirty-two actually got into action. Tank D1 had the distinction of being first into battle on the morning of 15 September, when it went forward, shortly before the main attack began at 6.20, to clear a strongpoint on the edge of Delville Wood. Gough allocated his tanks to 2nd Canadian Division, which planned to use them to spearhead its attack on the sugar factory near Courcelette. The attack was successful, though the tanks broke down or moved too slowly to keep up with the infantry. On their right, 15th (Scottish) Division of III Corps, Rawlinson's left-hand formation, took Martinpuich with the help of half the Corps' eight tanks.

Further east, High Wood – 'ghastly by day, ghostly by night, the rottennest place on the Somme' – lived up to its evil reputation. Controversially, III Corps decreed that the four tanks allocated to 47th (London) Division would pass through the wood, despite the reasoned objection of the tank officers who argued that the ground was bad. Three ditched and the fourth reached the German support line, where it was destroyed by a shell. The first infantry attacks failed, and it was not until a trench-mortar battery had put 750 bombs into the wood that the morale of the Bavarian defenders cracked and the Londoners took the place at last. It did their commander, the well-respected Major-General Barter, no good. He was sacked, and his supporters attributed this to the fact that he had been right about the tanks while the corps commander was wrong.

Further east, XV Corps made for Flers. The New Zealand Division, on its left, was initially held up by fire from High Wood, but on the right the attack developed with far greater promise. Twelve of the seventeen tanks allocated to the attack here went into action together. There was panic among some defenders, and 41st Division took Flers with close support from some of the surviving tanks. A pilot, echoed by war correspondents, reported: 'A tank is walking up the High Street of Flers with the British Army cheering behind it.' On Rawlinson's right, XIV Corps made disappointing progress, largely because most of its tanks, for which gaps had been left in the barrage, failed to materialize.

By the end of the day the British had taken a great bite out of the German third position, seizing strongpoints which had held them up for months and capturing ground from which to renew their attack. They had not broken through, and the attack had cost 4th Army alone nearly 30,000 men. Success at Flers was, like success at High Wood two months before, to be over-celebrated: the truth of the matter was that the problem of exploiting success was still far from solution. The tanks could help break into the German position but, short-ranged, slow, prone to breakdown and ditching, bone-cracking and nauseating for their crews, they could not yet assist with the breakout.

THE END ON THE SOMME

If 15 September had brought no breakthrough it had at least continued with the remorseless process of attrition. On 25 September Charteris observed that German lads of the 1917 class, not due for conscription till the coming January, were appearing on the battlefield, 'and if the weather holds we shall have worked through them pretty quickly'. As usual he was optimistic. A bad summer blew into an awful autumn, and the conditions in which men lived and fought simply defy description. Even the Official History's prose rises to describe how, 'in a wilderness of mud, holding water-logged trenches or shell-hole posts, accessible only by night, the infantry abode in conditions which might be likened to those of earth-worms, rather than of the human kind'.

The British continued to make gains, taking Morval and Lesboeufs on 25 September and Thiepval – a 1 July objective – on the 26th, but their progress was painfully slow. The last blow in the battle was struck by Gough, whose men – renamed 5th Army on 1 October – took Beaumont-Hamel, another 1 July target, on 13 November. When Allied leaders met that month at Compiègne they agreed that it was time to halt for the winter. There would be another offensive in 1917, but it was evident to all that the burden of 1916 had, for British and French alike, been almost insupportable.

Even now it is impossible to say exactly what that burden was. Allied casualties on the Somme totalled about 600,000, two-thirds of them British. The Germans reported casualties on a different basis, and the British official historian, Sir James Edmonds, assessed them as 660,000–680,000. Even if, as some historians suggest, he was over-generous, it is hard to place them lower than 600,000. One German officer described the Somme as 'the muddy grave of the German field army, and of confidence in the infallibility of German leadership', while Ludendorff acknowledged that his army was 'completely exhausted' at its end.

One of the many virtues of Malcolm Brown's *Imperial War Museum Book of the Somme* is its identification of the ambivalence at the heart of the Somme experience. While one officer called it 'just slaughter', another, Charles Carrington, wrote:

> The Somme raised the morale of the British Army. Although we did not win a decisive victory, there was what matters most, a definite and growing sense of superiority over the enemy, man to man… We were quite sure that we had got the Germans beat: next spring we would deliver the knock-out blow.

Yet nobody reading Carrington's *A Subaltern's War* could doubt that he had indeed seen about the worst the battle had to offer.

This ambivalence extends to the generalship. Given the nature of Anglo-French relations and the emphasis that British politicians placed on maintaining the coalition, it is hard to see how Haig could have declined to attack on the Somme. Indeed, it took much of his moral strength not to be hustled into attacking sooner. Despite the advantages that the ground offered to the defender, and the lack of attainable objectives behind the front, the Somme was not inherently unsuitable for an offensive, and had the advantage of meeting French wishes to mount an Allied operation. Notwithstanding the losses of the first day, and the growing misery of the summer's fighting, the British could scarcely have stopped their attack: the need first, to relieve Verdun and second, to prevent the Germans slipping troops to the east, saw to that.

In terms of tactics if not morale, the British army which emerged from the Somme was better than that which had entered it. As Paddy Griffith has written: 'The five-month Somme battle taught the BEF many lessons and transformed it from a largely inexperienced mass army into a largely experienced one.' However, the management of the battle does not redound to the credit of the British high command. The first day's plan was the bastard child of the differing expectations of Haig and Rawlinson.

There was enough evidence to suggest that the scheme was unrealistically optimistic, and this was at best honestly discounted and at worst wilfully suppressed. Rawlinson's handling of the battle thereafter was deficient: he behaved like the corps commander he had been, not the army commander he was.

His own insecurity did not help. One example shows precisely how his relationship with Haig affected the battle. Lord Cavan of XIV Corps formally protested at an order to attack Le Transloy on 5 November:

> I assert my readiness to sacrifice the British right rather than jeopardize the French… but I feel that I am bound to ask if this is the intention, for a sacrifice it must be. It does not appear that a failure would much assist the French, and there is a danger of this attack shaking the confidence of the men and officers in their commanders. No one who has not visited the front trenches can really know the state of exhaustion to which the men are reduced.

Cavan pressed his point: Rawlinson went forward to see the ground, and agreed that the attack was impossible. After speaking to Foch, Haig reversed the decision, and XIV Corps attacked as ordered. Cavan lost 2000 men for no gains, and there is no evidence that his failure assisted the French.

The British won the battle on points and, as Sergeant R. H. Tawney – later a distinguished professor of economic history – wrote, were in danger of reducing 'the unspeakable agonies of the Somme to an item in a commercial proposition'. It seems certain that a knock-out blow was still well beyond them: their opponent was simply too tough. The British were right to be on the Somme: but so many of them would not lie there today had some of their leaders shown a moral courage equal to the physical valour of the men they commanded.

ENDURING THE
FRONT

A BLEAK YEAR

In the year 1917 the Russian Empire collapsed; America entered
the war; the French army mutinied; and Italy was badly beaten at
Caporetto. All these events were to bear upon the Western Front,
which was itself the scene of two major battles which cast long
and terrible shadows: the Nivelle offensive of April, and the Third
Battle of Ypres – usually known as Passchendaele, officially the
name of one of its component actions – which groaned on through
a wet summer and into a bitter autumn. A bleak year indeed: the
year of Passchendaele.

Men were dying of exposure on the bare uplands in front of
Bapaume, above the meandering Somme, when Allied military
leaders met at Joffre's headquarters at Chantilly on 15 November
1916. Their conclusions were scarcely revolutionary: Germany
remained the main enemy. Her rapid destruction of Romania in
the late summer had showed all too clearly that she remained a
formidable adversary, and the Allies were to mount 'general
offensive action' against her early in the New Year. Allied political
leaders met in Paris shortly afterwards and ratified this decision,
and in early December it seemed as if the recipe for the coming
year would be very much the mixture as before.

Then, in quick succession, key personalities changed. On
7 December Asquith was succeeded as prime minister by David
Lloyd George. Appointed minister of munitions as a result of the

'shells scandal' of 1915, Lloyd George had become secretary of state for war in July 1916. When he visited Haig that September it became evident that he and the commander-in-chief did not see eye to eye. Haig told his wife that 'I have no great opinion of L.G. as a man or a leader', while Lloyd George was later to say that he found Haig 'brilliant – to the top of his army boots'. The antipathy was scarcely surprising. Haig was reserved, patrician and reticent: Lloyd George flamboyant, populist and voluble.

Lloyd George's reservations about Haig's conduct of operations had been deepened by the losses of the Somme, and in particular by the mauling of 38th Welsh Division at Mametz Wood. When he visited the front in September he asked Foch his opinion of British generals, and Foch reported the conversation to Haig, who was horrified by what he regarded as 'ungentlemanly' conduct. In conversation with the journalist Charles Repington, Lloyd George described Haig as a 'military Moloch', and he went on to tell Maurice Hankey that in his view the Somme had been 'a bloody and disastrous failure'. When he became prime minister, therefore, there was every reason to expect that he would question the primacy of the Western Front and the character of operations conducted there: he was 'not prepared to accept the position of a butcher's boy driving cattle to slaughter'.

The slaughter of the past two and a half years had weighed heavily upon the French army, which felt its burden keenly: it had one man killed or captured for nearly every minute of the war. Much of the blame was levelled at old Joffre, whose oft-repeated assertion that he was nibbling away at the Germans rang increasingly hollow: the Germans seemed to be nibbling harder. Foch might have been considered as a replacement, but his star was not in the ascendant: he had commanded the French army group engaged in the Somme fighting, and it had (undeservedly) done little for his reputation. Nor did Pétain, the saviour of Verdun, with his methodical approach and chilly manner, seem the right choice.

NIVELLE TAKES COMMAND

The hour had a new hero. In mid-December General Robert Nivelle, who had recaptured Fort Douaumont, at Verdun, became *de facto* commander-in-chief, with Joffre still hanging on to his office at Chantilly. The fraud was transparent, and on Boxing Day 1916 Joffre went off to a meaningless advisory post in Paris and was appointed Marshal of France, the first since 1870. Nivelle – charming, persuasive and fluent in English – soon set about moving his headquarters to the splendour of the Château de Compiègne, rebuilt in the eighteenth century and later the favourite residence of Napoleon III. It was bigger, grander, and closer to the front: new man, new style.

Nivelle had a plan. It was based on the combination of overwhelming artillery support and well-prepared infantry attacks which had served him so well at Verdun. And it would succeed in just forty-eight hours – or it could be called off. No more Sommes: no more Verduns. It now seems glaringly obvious that what had worked so well as a battle plan – on a narrow front against a strictly limited objective – would be less likely to succeed as a campaign plan, on a far larger scale, designed to bring the war to a sudden end. But we must not be too harsh on Nivelle's backers. He was peddling victory, and the French army and nation alike wanted to believe him, just as a sick patient desperately needs to believe in a miracle cure. 'I have the secret,' announced Nivelle, and men trusted him.

So, at first, did Haig. When the two men met on 20 December Haig found him 'most straightforward and soldierly'. His plan seemed sound, at least in outline: a surprise attack against an enemy worn down by the Somme. Its detail, which arrived a few days later, was more worrying. Nivelle intended to strike his sudden, violent blow with a mass manoeuvre of twenty-seven divisions which, of necessity, must belong to one nation – France. The British would launch subsidiary attacks to pin down the Germans and, in order to free French divisions for the offensive, would have to extend their line southwards from the Somme to the Oise. Haig was welcome to plan for an offensive in Flanders, to be launched later should the need arise. For the moment Nivelle was anxious to gain agreement on the relief of French divisions between the Somme and the Oise: he wanted it completed by mid-January 1917.

BRITISH VIEWS

Haig was not impressed. Sickness and shortage of drafts from home meant that he had only about fifty divisions available instead of fifty-six: he felt unable to take over the new line and put in the holding attacks demanded by Nivelle. He was also concerned that the scheme meant the abandonment of his own plans for an offensive in Flanders. We have already seen how this sector had been Haig's preferred choice for an attack a year before, and he had been diverted to the Somme by the inexorable logic of Anglo-French relations in the year of Verdun.

The attractions of Flanders were twofold. First, the rail junction at Roulers lay temptingly close to British lines, a little over 12 miles (20 kilometres) from Ypres as the crow flies. Its capture, or even domination by artillery, would imperil the German hold on the whole northern sector of the Western Front. Second, the Channel ports of Ostend and Zeebrugge had been recognized as important objectives since the autumn of 1914, and in November 1916 Asquith had informed Sir William Robertson, Chief of the Imperial General Staff, that: 'There is no operation of war to which the War Committee would attach greater importance than the successful occupation, or at least the deprivation to the enemy, of Ostend and especially Zeebrugge.' German submarines based there not only sank warships and transports in the Channel, but forayed wider to add to the growing toll of merchant shipping sunk by U-boats based elsewhere. On 1 February 1917, at the considerable risk of alienating neutral opinion, Germany launched unrestricted submarine warfare, sinking suspect merchantmen on sight without applying the prize rules which had previously restricted their terms of engagement. On that day twenty-three of the 105 operational U-boats were based in Flanders.

Merchant shipping losses shot up, from around 300,000–350,000 tons a month in the winter of 1916–17 to 520,000 tons in March 1917 and an awful 860,000 in April. Losses on this scale raised the spectre of Britain being starved to death. The First Sea Lord, Sir John Jellicoe, was gloomy. In April, shortly after America's entry into the war – an event that unrestricted submarine warfare had done much to provoke – he told an American admiral that 'it is impossible for us to go on with the war if losses like this continue'. In June he went further, telling the War Policy Committee that: 'There is no good discussing plans for next spring – we cannot go on.' Jellicoe's views were neither precise nor consistent, and they were, in any event, not universally held. However, the purely military attractions of Flanders were substantial, and Haig's reliance on cross-Channel supplies helped make the maritime argument a powerful one. All the more reason why Nivelle's plan worried Douglas Haig, and why, in a well-argued letter of 6 January, he emphasized that he could not agree to Nivelle's proposals unless the clearing of the Belgian coast was provided for.

AN ALLIED ADJUSTMENT

And there were other worries. In December Robertson warned Haig that Lloyd George was 'off Salonika' but 'on Egypt, and wants to get to Jerusalem'. At the Rome conference in early January Lloyd George spoke warmly in favour of sending troops to the Italian front to attack Austria, on the grounds that 'if Austria were beaten Germany would be beaten too'. He was vexed to discover that neither the French nor the Italians backed the scheme. Later that month, at a meeting in London, Lloyd George spoke warmly in favour of French achievements, and was clearly impressed by the Nivelle plan.

Then, in yet another conference, this time at Calais in late February, Lloyd George went even further. He not merely agreed to the Nivelle plan, but decreed that the British army would be placed under Nivelle's command for the duration of the offensive. Robertson, who, after all, was the prime minister's professional adviser on such matters, was stunned: an observer described how 'his face went the colour of mahogany, his eyes became perfectly round, his eyebrows slanted outwards like a forest of bayonets held at the charge…' Haig took the news with no outward display, but immediately wrote to the King offering to resign his appointment. The King's private secretary wrote back to dissuade him, relaying royal confidence that the two generals would soon be working on 'the most amicable and open terms'.

GERMAN RE-ADJUSTMENTS

It was a vain hope. Although subsequent meetings repaired some of the damage done by Calais, it was hard to repair the mistrust which now existed between soldiers and politicians, British and French. And in the meantime the Germans were not idle. Ludendorff was later to admit that: 'our position was uncommonly difficult, and a way out hard to find. We could not contemplate an offensive ourselves, having to keep all our reserves available for defence'. The solution was twofold. Firstly, to shift troops from the Eastern Front, a process which was to become easier as 1917 wore on and Russia's commitment to the war weakened dramatically. Second, to give up the nose of the salient formed by the Western Front, falling back on to a well-prepared position and, by shortening the line, reducing the number of troops required to hold it.

ABOVE The telephone exchange at GHQ, in casemates at Montreuil, operated here by the signals branch of the Royal Engineers.

ABOVE Men of 15th Battalion the West Yorkshire Regiment, known as the Leeds Pals. The battalion suffered heavily attacking Serre on 1 July 1916, its experience typifying blighted hopes of quick victory.

ABOVE Australians, wearing steel helmets rather than the familiar slouch hats, manning a Lewis gun in the anti-aircraft role.

BELOW The ravaged site of Guillemont, September 1916.

ABOVE Somme mud. Sledges used to drag wounded down the main road at Le Sars, October 1916.

RIGHT General Robert Nivelle, the persuasive, half-English artillery officer who succeeded Joffre as French Commander-in-Chief.

RIGHT British soldiers posted to France passed through Etaples for training. Instructors, called 'canaries' because of their yellow arm bands, were notoriously unsympathetic and troops mutinied here in 1917.

BELOW An Australian tunneller demonstrates breathing apparatus used to filter gas or foul air. A caged canary gave warning of gas.

ABOVE A German pill-box near Zonnebeke, captured
by the Australians in September 1917.

ABOVE Tanks and New Zealand and British infantry, 25 August 1918.

ABOVE German stormtroops training for the spring offensive of 1918.
They move quickly, rifles slung, seeking weak spots in the defence.

ABOVE General Foch (left) appointed Allied Commander-in-Chief in 1918, with the American C-in-C General Pershing.

ABOVE Lieutenant-General Sir John Monash, ANZAC Corps commander, decorates an Australian soldier in 1918.

ABOVE Moment of victory. Brigadier-General J. C. Campbell addresses his brigade of 46th Division from the captured bridge at Riqueval. Some men are still wearing life jackets, and others have obtained German helmets.

German withdrawal to the Hindenburg Line was christened Operation Alberich, after the spiteful dwarf in the Nibelungen saga. It was well named. The retreating Germans left a desert behind them. Roads and railways were destroyed; bridges blown, orchards cut down, stately avenues felled across the roads they once shaded, wells poisoned and booby-traps left everywhere. One German, horrified by what his own side had done, left a signboard in Péronne saying: 'Don't be angry: Only wonder.' Crown Prince Rupprecht of Bavaria, commanding the northernmost German Army Group, personally interceded for the splendid castle at Coucy, its keep the largest in Christendom. It was wasted effort: Ludendorff sent engineers who packed 28 tons of explosive into the keep and blew it to bits.

THE NIVELLE OFFENSIVE

Although Allied propaganda made much of the German retreat, the well-handled withdrawal cast serious doubts over Nivelle's offensive. The Germans had pulled back from part of the attack sector. The newly liberated area was chaos, with roads to be rebuilt and the population fed. And Nivelle's political support slackened. The Briand government fell, and was replaced by an administration under Alexandre Ribot. Ribot's minister of war was the distinguished mathematician Paul Painlevé, and he discovered that even military support for the attack was less than firm. He then consulted the army group commanders, who were unenthusiastic. Painlevé made a last attempt to test Nivelle's resolve, and received a rhetorical *tour de force* in reply. Nivelle insisted that he knew what he was doing, and that his plan would work and win the war. Simply seizing the territory to be attacked would be only:

> a poor little tactical victory. It is not for so meagre a result that I have accumulated on the Aisne one million two hundred thousand soldiers, five thousand guns and five hundred thousand horses. The game would not be worth the candle.

The plan relied on surprise, a commodity in short supply. On 4 April the Germans captured a copy of Nivelle's plan which had unwisely been taken into a forward position. Soon they knew almost everything: date, times and objectives. Information was circulated to their gunners to enable them to shell French trenches at their most vulnerable moment, just before the attack started. As we shall see later, the Germans had used the experience of the Somme fighting to formulate tactics based in defence in depth, with a lightly held front line absorbing the impact of the attack while counter-attack formations moved up to deal with it. Their front along the Chemin des Dames and into the Soissonais region was already held in depth, well-suited to roll with the sort of punch Nivelle planned to deliver. The attack's prospects would have been poor even if security had remained intact: with security compromised, its chances of success dwindled.

By now the course to tragedy was irrevocably set. At a last difficult meeting at Compiègne on 6 April Nivelle undermined his opponents by offering to resign. The plan had now been so heavily over-sold that cancellation was unthinkable. And so, as Churchill was to put it:

> Nivelle and Painlevé found themselves in the most unhappy positions which mortals can occupy; the Commander having to dare the utmost risks with an entirely sceptical Chief behind him; the Minister having to become responsible for a frightful slaughter at the bidding of a General in whose capacity he did not believe, and upon a military policy the folly of which he was justly convinced.

As Edward Spears, a British liaison officer, observed, Nivelle had lost all touch with reality and was being swept along by his own rhetoric. And always at his elbow stood the chief of his personal staff, Colonel d'Alenson, mortally sick with tuberculosis and desperate to see the war won before he died.

The attack went in on the morning of 16 April, in icy rain which turned to sleet, with French infantry going forward, as they had so often in the past, with a courage worthy of a better cause. The plan's sternest critics soon saw their fears confirmed. The bombardment had often left the German wire uncut, and the creeping barrage buzzed and roared its way hopelessly ahead of the attackers. Even where they penetrated the defences they were taken on by flanking machine-guns which had escaped the shelling or briskly counter-attacked by Germans who had sat out the bombardment in the huge caverns which are a feature of the limestone landscape above the Aisne. By nightfall, far from being deep in the German rear, the attack had stalled. The medical services, counting on the light casualties envisaged by the plan, were overwhelmed. Spears saw French wounded depressed as never before. 'It's all up', they said. 'We can't do it, we shall never do it. *C'est impossible.*'

Nivelle refused to recognize failure. He ordered more attacks in the face of evident catastrophe and then tried to blame subordinates. By the time the battle formally ended on 9 May the French army had lost about 100,000 casualties. When he told Micheler, commanding one of his army groups, that he should be trying harder, Micheler rounded on him. 'You wish to make me responsible for this mistake: me, who never ceased to warn you of it. Do you know what such an action is called? Well, it is called cowardice.' Nivelle reeled like a drunken man as he walked to his car. And now his army, like a beast of burden flogged beyond endurance, began to mutiny.

THE FRENCH MUTINIES

On 29 April a battalion of the 18th Infantry Regiment refused to go back up the line. The ringleaders were arrested: four were shot and the remainder imprisoned. For a few days the episode was isolated. But soon similar outbreaks were reported elsewhere. The pattern was similar. Men, who had often drunk too much, refused to leave for the front or turned up at the transport without their rifles. Soldiers roamed the streets demanding more leave, better food, and above all no more attacks. This was quite unlike the sort of mutiny that the Russian army was undergoing. French officers might be jeered at or jostled – and even then usually not by men from their own units – but they were not murdered. True, somebody shot at a corps commander in Soissons, but that might have been simply to make the point.

The high command saw it as part of a deep-seated plot with links to extremist politicians, but this was never the case. The mutinies were spontaneous, and lacked organized leadership. They were more like strikes, carried out by citizen-soldiers who did not wish to see Germany win but would simply not throw away their lives in more hopeless attacks.

And it was not just the men who were disaffected. Private Louis Barthas, whose regiment had been kept at readiness to attack in appalling weather, saw a general order his colonel to attack. The tough, down-to-earth colonel took his pipe from his mouth, spat, and asked the general to look at his men. 'They would have marched on the first day, but now they won't: and I won't either.'

There was no doubt as to who should replace the broken Nivelle. On 17 May Pétain, soon heard to mutter 'they only call me in catastrophes', took over as commander-in-chief of an army which was beyond hope. His achievements over the months that followed are often, tragically, overshadowed by the role he played as head of the Vichy state in 1940–4. Yet there can be no doubt that Pétain deserved well of France that terrible spring. He immediately issued a directive forbidding major attacks: henceforth they were to be conducted 'economically with infantry and with a maximum of artillery'. Leave was increased: units out of the line might send 25 or even 50 per cent of their men home. Steps were taken to ensure that men did not waste their leave waiting for trains that never came, at stations whose buffets charged prices they could never afford. Leave trains became more regular, and soldiers' canteens widespread.

Pétain visited his regiments, talking to officers and men, assuring them of his commitment to small attacks and determination to await the arrival of the Americans before launching a major, properly co-ordinated, offensive. He announced a pay rise for veterans and the award of a decoration for distinguished units. He found out what men thought: monotonous food, and decorations which seemed to get hijacked by the staff were common causes of complaint. He looked hard at the rear areas, ensuring that troops at rest were not worn out with fatigue duties and had proper facilities for getting themselves and their uniforms clean.

And he gripped discipline. For while Pétain was fair, he was unquestionably firm. On 1 June he delegated authority to convene summary courts-martial, and Painlevé managed to persuade the President of the Republic to waive his right to reviewing their sentences 'in cases where discipline and national defence require an immediate penalty'. Pétain went on to assure officers that those who acted with 'vigour and energy' in suppressing mutiny were assured of his full support. Painlevé later claimed that only twenty-three men were shot. This is unquestionably an underestimate, but suggestions that whole batches of mutineers were led off to quiet sectors and wiped out by their own artillery err in the other direction.

There were two clear indications that the Pétain method was working. On Bastille Day, 14 July, the government risked routing the traditional parade through the working-class district of Paris. There were no jeers and catcalls at the President, and growing applause from the spectators as the men in horizon blue swung past. Two weeks later the French launched an attack north of Ypres, taking three lines of German trenches for the loss of fewer than 200 men killed. Other, meticulously prepared, attacks took the Fort de la Malmaison on the Chemin des Dames and the Mort Homme at Verdun. The French army was recovering its spirits.

It was to do so with weighty political support. On 22 July the 75-year-old Georges Clemenceau rose in the Senate to denounce what he called the 'anti-patriotism', and to attack ministers, who had failed to suppress the anti-military newspaper *Le Bonnet Rouge*. The government fell in September, and Painlevé headed a new administration which speedily ran into difficulties and folded in mid-November. President Poincaré summoned all the old names, but none would do: then, on the afternoon of 14 November, he invited Clemenceau to form a government. The old man did so, going on to tell a packed chamber that his policy was simple enough: 'to conduct the war with redoubled energy…' He was harsh, autocratic and remorseless. He stumped about the front in a battered hat and shabby coat, making it quite clear to all that his simple motto went to the heart of the matter: 'I wage war'.

ARRAS AND VIMY

The British army, meanwhile, was waging war on its own account. On 9 April it launched the Battle of Arras, intended to pin German troops to Artois and prevent reserves moving south to face Robert Nivelle. The first day of battle was remarkably successful. The Canadian Corps, attacking with its four divisions side-by-side, took Vimy Ridge, a remarkable feat of arms which not merely secured this dominant ground against which the Allied wave had lapped for nearly three years, but struck a mighty blow for Canadian national consciousness. 3rd Army made good progress east of Arras, its gunners laying on heavy, well-orchestrated barrages in which the new 106 fuse, which burst when it grazed barbed wire, played a prominent part. Further south, 5th Army's attack on Bullecourt was mishandled, leading to acrimony between the attacking Australians and the tanks whose support had misfired.

Yet even at Arras, where the British had bitten deep into German defences – Ludendorff acknowledged 'a bad beginning for the decisive struggle of this year' – success could not be reinforced. It was not until the afternoon of the 10th that Allenby, the army commander, realized quite what damage had been done to the Germans. That night he told his troops that they were 'pursuing a defeated enemy', and on the 11th sought to press the pursuit by sending in the cavalry.

By now the defensive crust had hardened, and the diary of the German 125th Regiment records: 'We stood up as on a rifle range and, laughing, greeted this rare target with a hail of bullets.' When a more formal attack went in on the 14th it was very roughly handled. The long ridges and shallow valleys enabled the Germans to employ elastic defence at its best, giving ground before the attack so that 'the deeper [it] penetrates into the defender's position, the more it will find itself faced by surprise and unforeseen conditions'. The collapse of the Nivelle offensive compelled Haig to continue the battle, and daily loss rates between 9 April and 17 May averaged 4070 men, a figure matched only by British losses in the German March offensive the following year.

SINEWS OF WAR

By now the British were administratively prepared for battle to a remarkable degree. Logisticians are the Cinderellas of warfare, whose efforts are usually only recognized, by soldiers and historians alike, when they fail. By this stage in the war British logisticians had mastered their prodigious task. In part this was due to Haig's recognition that civilian experts, invested with temporary military rank, could solve problems on a scale that might baffle professional soldiers. In 1916 Sir Eric Geddes, a railway magnate, was appointed Director-General of Transportation in France. His was an appropriate speciality, for by 1918 the BEF was using 900 locomotives, which travelled 9 million track miles (14 million kilometres) each month, carrying 800,000 tons of equipment and 260,000 of ammunition.

Increasingly efficient sea transport, docking and warehousing helped the BEF import stores of all sorts. During the whole war 5,253,538 tons of ammunition were shipped to France, but even this was exceeded by the 5,438,603 tons of fodder for the army's horses and mules. The BEF's animal strength peaked at 449,800 in 1917. In the army's enormous reliance on horses and mules, we see another facet of the war's ancient and modern character, for by 1917 the BEF was also using 6 million gallons of petrol every month. By mid 1917 Haig's logistics, and the procurement system upon which they in turn relied, were so robust as to give British planners the luxury of working with little constraint. For much of that summer British field gunners regularly fired 500,000 shells a day. Million-shell days were not uncommon and, during the Passchendaele battle, even this prodigious total was almost doubled on two occasions.

FLANDERS FIELDS

Haig, as we have seen, had long favoured an offensive in Flanders, and he now found himself in a position to attack on ground of his choosing. We cannot be certain of the degree to which the French mutinies provided him with an added incentive for the Flanders battle, but it seems likely that the scale of the indiscipline was not fully known at GHQ. On 15 May Haig's intelligence officer, John Charteris, wrote that Lord Esher, with whom he had dined, told him that 'the morale of the whole nation has been badly affected by the failure of their attack', and on the 19th he reported 'very serious trouble' in the French army. Haig was visited by Pétain's chief of staff in early June, and confided to his diary that the French army was 'in a bad state of discipline'. At the very least this meant that there would be little French help for the Flanders offensive: Haig could certainly not rely on the sort of reciprocity extended to Nivelle that spring.

In Haig's mind the offensive had two linked aims. The first, well outlined in a sketch-map handed to Pétain on 18 May, was for a two-phase advance from Ypres, the first extending as far as Passchendaele, and the second reaching out as far as Roulers and Thorout. A landing between Middelkerke and Ostend would be timed to coincide with the latter. The same month he told the War Cabinet that even if he failed in this aim, 'we shall be attacking the enemy on a front where he cannot refuse to fight, and where, therefore, our purpose of wearing him down can be given effect to'.

It was, in short, a repetition of the previous year's concept. There were objectives towards which the army would manoeuvre, and by doing so it would contribute to the steady attrition of German manpower. The notion of attrition continues to provoke shudders, but at the time its merits were, if not widely welcomed, then at least clearly articulated. When Lieutenant General Sir Ivor Maxse, whose biography is rightly called *Far from a Donkey*, addressed a platoon commander's course that May he told it: '*You have to defeat the German Army. You cannot measure your task by miles any more than you can measure a man's courage by his height.*' Early in May a conference in Paris concluded that the war-winning Allied offensive would have to wait until the Americans were present in strength in 1918. In the meantime, if they could not win the war, the Allies had to prevent the Germans from doing so, and could best accomplish this by mounting limited offensives. Haig briefed his army commanders on the 7th, confirming that the Arras operation would be scaled down as the army's weight was shifted to Flanders. There would be two distinct attacks: a curtain-raiser designed to take Messines Ridge, south of Ypres, and then, some weeks later, the 'Northern Operation' aimed at Passchendaele Ridge and beyond.

The whole of the Ypres salient was by now thoroughly battered after two and a half years of fighting, and Ypres itself, once crowned by its magnificent Cloth Hall, had been reduced to rubble. Yet the salient's topographical features endured. Although, like the planners of the period, we tend to speak of separate ridges, there is in fact one long, irregular ridge running down from Westroosebeke and Passchendaele north-east of Ypres, through Wytschaete to the town's south. Spurs, in effect smaller ridges in themselves, run off it. One goes almost north–south from Wytschaete to Messines, and another bulges eastwards in the very centre of the main ridge, to form the Gheluvelt plateau, with the Menin Road Ridge rising to its east. The ridge is low and undistinguished: the Gheluvelt plateau rises to only 213 feet (64 metres) and even Messines Ridge attains only 264 feet (80 metres).

There were woods in the salient, especially around the Gheluvelt plateau, where Polygon Wood, Glencorse Wood, Nonne Bosschen and Shrewsbury Forest still remained recognizable, though shelling was soon to change that. The many streams which drained the ridge's western slopes, like the Steenbeek and the Stroombeek, ran to join the little River Yser north of Ypres, their course often taking them across the British line of attack. As John Hussey has pointed out, the terrain is not dissimilar to, say, the area around York or Newark: low-lying, certainly, but not 'some monsoon-like tropical swamp'. However, the ground was not good for a war dominated by artillery: the drainage system was easily disrupted, and the soil – London clay, with layers of sand and silt – readily turned into mud.

None of this was a surprise to GHQ, which warned in May that a few hours of rain might swell the brooks and make operations impossible for twenty-four hours, while: 'A few weeks' rain may make the whole country impracticable for prolonged operations for at least one week.' This, coupled with John Charteris's assertion that in August the weather broke in Flanders 'with the regularity of the Indian monsoon' has led Haig's critics to suggest that the battlefield would inevitably become flooded. John Hussey's careful analysis in the very valuable *Passchendaele in Perspective* disproves this. From a meteorologist's standpoint, 'August might be expected to be reasonably dry, not abnormally wet'. This expectation proved false. As Haig's chief meteorologist, Lieutenant-Colonel Ernest Gold, later observed, the rainfall during the five months of the offensive was over five times heavier than for the same period in 1915 and 1916. The ground of the salient would certainly be rendered very difficult indeed by the combination of shelling and bad weather. The latter was not a foregone conclusion, however, and by attacking in the salient Haig took, as commanders sometimes must, a calculated risk. It did not pay off.

The German army's defence of the sector reflected the lessons of the Somme as embodied in its December 1916 pamphlet *The Principles of Command in the Defensive Battle in Position Warfare*. Anglo-American historians are sometimes given to over-celebrating German military excellence, but in terms of doctrinal development the Germans were clearly ahead of their opponents: they were good at analysing the results of a battle, turning this analysis into doctrine, and then training troops in the latest methods.

The new principles, embodying the elastic defence we have already seen used against Nivelle, stressed that the defender should seek to disrupt the attacker, not to hold his ground at all costs. Ground should be covered by fire, not held by men. The defender should never surrender the initiative, and must consider depth – in the sense of depth from front to rear – whenever positions were sited. There would be a number of defensive positions, each consisting of three lines. First came a lightly held outpost zone, giving security and observation, probably on a forward slope. Next was the battle zone, ideally situated on a reverse slope, with trenches and pill-boxes. Finally, the rearward zone or 'artillery protection line' came about a mile (2 kilometres) behind the battle zone, with the bulk of the field batteries in and just behind it. The next belt of defences, similarly organized, would be far enough behind for the attacker to have to shift his field guns after a successful attack on the first position. Although arrangements differed on Messines Ridge, where the narrowness of the ridge suggested slight changes, by the time the main battle opened the northern sector was held by a strong front position (the Albrecht and Wilhelm lines) with a third line and three successive belts of defences – codenamed Flandern I, II and III – behind it. Flandern I was complete, Flandern II marked out by wire entanglements and pill-boxes, and Flandern III simply sketched out.

In 1915 the Germans had dispensed with the brigade, and in 1917 their division consisted of three regiments of three battalions each, a three-battalion field artillery regiment, a heavy artillery battalion and assorted supporting units. It would usually post its regiments side by side, with a battalion each in the three defence zones. Battalions in the battle and rearward zones were expected to counter-attack when the opportunity offered. It was stressed that while immediate counter-attacks often worked, if they were delayed by more than perhaps half an hour the attacker would have brought up his own machine-guns and adjusted his artillery fire: then they were likely to fail.

Formal counterstrokes were to be carried out by counter-attack divisions, usually posted at the ratio of one for every two front-line divisions. They would try to choose the moment when the attacker was embedded in the battle-zone, nearing the limit of his own artillery support and getting through key trench-fighting resources such as hand-grenades. Then their barrage would wall him off from his supports and supplies while their infantry lunged forward. Counter-attack divisions were specially trained in their tasks, and when actually used came under the command of the line-holding division whose commander, it was argued, would have his finger on the battle's pulse.

MESSINES RIDGE

The Messines attack was to be carried out by Plumer's 2nd Army. Generals' nicknames are indicative of their troops' regard for them, and not for nothing was Sir Herbert Plumer known as 'Daddy'. Although his red face, white moustache and tubby build provided the model for the cartoonist Low's character Colonel Blimp, Plumer was an infantry officer with a deep understanding of trench warfare and a determination not to waste lives. His chief of staff, Sir Charles 'Tim' Harington, was a careful planner and, as is often the case with successful 'military marriages' between commanders and chiefs of staff, it was hard to see where one began and the other ended.

Plumer intended to take Messines Ridge by attacking on a 10-mile (16-kilometre) front with three corps in line and one in reserve. Each attacking corps would advance with three of its divisions up and one in reserve. Some preparations had been made for earlier planned attacks. Miners in particular had been at work since 1915, and there were now more than 30,000 men in Australian, British and Canadian tunnelling companies. The technical difficulties of digging around Messines were enormous, as miners had to penetrate a surface layer, then a layer of quicksand and finally enter blue clay, which expanded in contact with the air, to dig deep offensive tunnels beneath the German lines. A shallower defensive gallery, designed to detect and disrupt German mining, ran parallel with the front line. Mining was one area where the British enjoyed clear ascendancy, but German miners could not be disregarded, and hit back when they could, blowing in tunnels with small mines – camouflets – of their own, or breaking into them to fight at close quarters. The best modern research

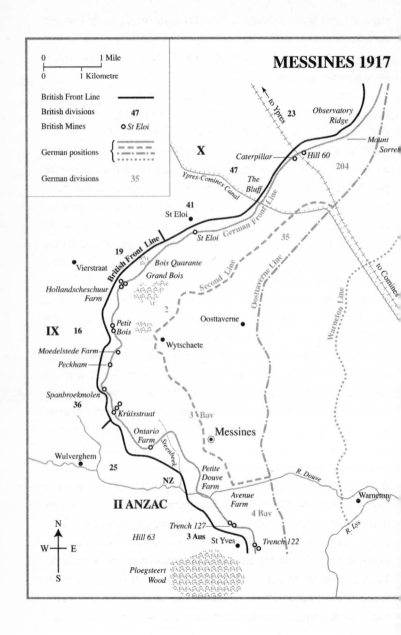

MESSINES 1917

| 0 | 1 Mile |
| 0 | 1 Kilometre |

British Front Line ——————
British divisions **47**
British Mines ○ *St Eloi*

German positions {
German divisions *35*

to Ypres **23** *Observatory Ridge*

X *Caterpillar* ○ *Hill 60* *Mount Sorrel*
47 *204*

Ypres-Comines Canal *The Bluff* *German Front Line*

41
St Eloi
○ *St Eloi* *35*

19 British Front Line *Second Line*
● *Vierstraat* *Bois Quarante* *Grand Bois* *Oosttaverne Line* to Comines

Hollandscheschuur Farm *2* *Warneton Line*

IX **16** *Petit Bois* ● *Oosttaverne*

Moedelstede Farm ● *Wytschaete*
Peckham

Spanbroekmolen
36 *Krùisstraat* *3 Bav*
Ontario Farm **Messines** ◉

● *Wulverghem* *Steenbeek*
25 *Petite Douve Farm* *R. Douve*
NZ ● *Warneton*

II ANZAC *Avenue Farm* *4 Bav* *R. Lys*

N
W—E
S *Trench 127* ○○
Hill 63 **3 Aus** *St Yves* ● ○ *Trench 122*

Ploegsteert Wood

suggests that there were in fact twenty-four mines loaded with a million pounds (nearly half a million kilograms) of ammonal explosive, much of it sealed into metal containers to protect it from the wet.

Sapper Jack Lyon of 171 Tunnelling Company Royal Engineers described how he worked as part of a twelve-man shift under a corporal. Three men worked at the tunnel face, one 'clay-kicking', lying on his back on a plank inclined between floor and roof, using both feet to jab a short spade into the clay. One of his mates put the clay into a sandbag, and the third dragged the bag back to the start of the trolley rails. Three men worked the trolleys, another operated the air-pump and the remainder helped get the sandbags up to the surface. All were volunteers, either Royal Engineers or 'permanently attached' infantry, usually miners who had joined the infantry at the start of the war. All worked three shifts in two days and then had a day's rest. After fifteen days, recalled Sapper Lyon, 'We went down for a bath and delousing operation, the latter being only partially successful.'

Other preparations were more recent. Water pipelines were laid to supply each corps with 150,000 gallons (680,000 litres) a day, and new light railways were built to carry ammunition and supplies forward. Plumer's own artillery was boosted by batteries from other armies to give him 2266 guns, 756 of them heavy or medium, with an average of 1000 rounds for each 18-pounder stacked on the gun-line and a total of 144,000 tons of ammunition dumped. Pill-boxes on the forward slopes of the ridge were engaged methodically by British heavy guns, and both trench lines and battery positions were repeatedly hammered: between 26 May and 1 June the Royal Artillery fired 3½ million shells into the German lines. When the attack began there would be a creeping barrage moving ahead of the infantry while standing barrages blocked off counter-attack divisions and counter-battery groups took on German batteries that had escaped the preliminary bombardment. The fire was unusually effective. British artillery spotters enjoyed good observation from Kemmel Hill, and supplemented this with captive balloons and observation aircraft. Plumer had 300 of the RFC's machines at his disposal, outnumbering the Germans by two to one. Seventy-two of the new Mark IV tanks were available, although in practice the terrain was too bad for them to prove very useful.

General von Laffert, of XIX Corps of the German Fourth Army, knew that an attack was on its way but was optimistic that he could deal with it. Because much British mining had been completed earlier, his own miners had been lulled into a false sense of security. At a meeting on 30 April the chief of staff of Rupprecht's army group suggested that Laffert might withdraw to the third (Oostaverne Line) or even the fourth (Warneton Line) of the defensive lines on and behind the ridge, but Laffert demurred: he would stay where he was.

At the end of May XIX Corps had four of its divisions (from the north 204th, 24th, 2nd and 40th) in line and two counter-attack divisions (35th and 3rd Bavarian) behind it. Such was the toll inflicted on his line-holding divisions that Laffert used the counter-attack divisions to replace the two hardest-hit, 24th and 40th. These were pulled out to refit, and two fresh divisions, 7th and 1st Guard Reserve, were given the counter-attack role. This decision was to cost Laffert his job. The new troops did not know the ground, while their predecessors had rehearsed the counter-attack task. The shelling also damaged Laffert's batteries: he had 630 guns, and had lost a quarter of his field pieces and nearly half his heavies before the battle started. Pill-boxes, which resisted everything but direct hits by heavy guns, stood the bombardment well, but the trenches between them vanished, and their garrisons were worn out by the strain.

A German soldier described the anguish of enduring the bombardment. 'All the trenches are completely smashed in,' he wrote, 'no more shelter is to hand, battery emplacements up to 6 feet [2 metres] thick are completely destroyed, and even 20-foot-deep [6-metre-deep] galleries are not safe from guns of heavy calibre – thus we are forced out into the open without any protection.'

At 3.10 on the morning of 7 June nineteen mines exploded below Messines Ridge with a blast so savage that it was heard in London and an observatory on the Isle of Wight detected it on its seismograph. The professor of geology at Lille University, over 12 miles (20 kilometres) away, sprang from bed thinking that there had been an earthquake, and looked out of his window to see German soldiers running panic-stricken about the streets. Some defenders were simply vaporized by the blast: others were buried by tons of earth. The war correspondent Philip Gibbs described the sight as:

> The most diabolical splendour I have ever seen. Out of the dark ridges of Messines and Wytschaete and that ill-famed Hill 60 there gushed out and up enormous volumes of scarlet flame from the exploding mines and of earth and smoke all lighted up by the flame spilling over into mountains of fierce colour, so that the countryside was illuminated by red light.

Survivors were pale and half-crazy: one British soldier recalled them 'running towards us shaking like jellies'.

The outpost line fell quickly, and the attackers regrouped for the assault on the second line, covered by a protective barrage. The second phase of the attack began at 7.00 a.m., and although some German units fought back with determination, they managed to hold their ground only on the far left of the attack. Frank Dunham, a stretcher bearer with a London battalion, saw just how successful the artillery had been in paving the way for the infantry.

> All the small dug-outs were bashed in and even some of the larger concrete ones were badly damaged... These prisoners were scared and fatigued, and we learned later that due to our

heavy shelling they had received very few rations and had
served longer in the front line as relieving troops could not
reach them.

As his company was making for its objective, a ruined château, he
saw his former company commander, Captain 'Gussy' Collins.
'He was strolling about the battlefield,' recalled Dunham, 'carrying his cane and wearing his renowned monocle as though doing
some training exercise. As he came level with our company he
shouted, "Haven't you captured the bally place yet?"'

The attackers paused again for the assault on the third line,
but, halting on the crest of the ridge, came under heavy fire as they
did so. Plumer, fearing that it would take longer than planned to
bring up the reserve division in each corps to launch the next
phase of the attack, postponed it by two hours, and it was not until
3.10 in the afternoon that it was delivered. It was generally
successful, and by nightfall most of the third line had been taken.

The two counter-attack divisions had been alerted at 3.30 that
morning, but concern about the direction of the British attack
persuaded 4th Army to retain control of them till after 7.00 and,
being new to the area, it took them some time to make their way
forward. Both were shelled as they moved up. 7th Division reached
the third line only to find the attackers already there, while 1st
Guard Reserve reached the outskirts of Messines just as the attack
on the third line went in: it was shoved back with heavy losses.

The day was a considerable success for Plumer. Although he
had lost nearly 25,000 men, most of them from II Anzac Corps, he
had taken more than 7000 prisoners, 48 guns and 218 machine-
guns, and killed or wounded at least 13,000 Germans. The battle
is a graphic illustration of the strengths and weaknesses of the
British army at this stage in the war, and sends echoes on into the
Second World War. It was a classic 'teed-up' battle, and the future
Field-Marshal Montgomery, then a junior staff officer, learnt
useful lessons serving with IX Corps. Preparation and planning

were first-rate, and briefing and rehearsal had been comprehensive. The artillery fireplan was well conceived and flawlessly executed, and in it we see one of the ingredients of Passchendaele: the growing dominance of British gunners. The infantry attacked with a resolution which again foreshadowed Passchendaele.

The training of British infantry had improved considerably since the Somme. Yet at Messines there were times – notably during the long and costly pause on the ridge – when British infantry seemed, at least to their opponents, to be lumpy and lacking in initiative. One German regiment, fresh from the Eastern Front, thought the tactical handling of British infantry to be worse than that of the Russian. Many German guns were in danger of capture on the reverse slope of the ridge, and the delay enabled most of them to be got away.

For all this the battle was an impressive victory. Even the redoubtable Rupprecht was shaken, and suspected that the next blow would fall without delay on what he regarded as the vital ground in his defences, the Gheluvelt plateau, where so many of his batteries were tucked into the woods or hidden behind the ridge. Why else, he argued, would the British have attacked Messines Ridge if not to exploit its capture promptly?

THE THIRD BATTLE OF YPRES

Haig was in no position to follow the capture of Messines Ridge with a swift second blow. The government had made it clear that the main Flanders offensive was conditional upon French support, and Haig knew that this would not be forthcoming on the scale for which he hoped. Lloyd George had flirted with other theatres of war, and feared that an attack at Ypres could well turn into a ghastly re-run of the Somme. However, Haig remained anxious to attack in Flanders for the reasons we have already explored, and on 12 June he told Robertson:

> if our resources are concentrated in France to the fullest pos-
> sible extent the British armies are capable and can be relied on
> to effect great results this summer – results which will make
> final victory more assured and may even bring it within reach
> this year.

Haig was authorized to 'continue his preparations for the present'
and it was not till 25 July, six days before the attack began, that he
was formally authorized to launch it.

Haig's instrument was Sir Hubert Gough of 5th Army, at
forty-seven the youngest of the army commanders, a cavalryman
with a reputation for dash which, it was felt, would prove useful if
a German collapse was followed by mobile operations. Gough felt
that it was a mistake to send him to 'a bit of ground with which I
had practically no acquaintance'. However, he duly handed over
the Croisilles–Havrincourt sector to 3rd Army at the end of May
and moved his headquarters to Louvie Château, 8 miles (12 kilometres) west-north-west of Ypres. GHQ gave him four corps, each
of four divisions – II, XIX, XVIII and XIV – with the single-divi-
sion VIII Corps in reserve and V Corps, also with a single division, in GHQ reserve. His artillery comprised 752 heavy and 1422
field guns. He had three tanks brigades of 72 machines each, and
406 aircraft. Staff officers used to 2nd Army's methodical ways
noted the change at once. Major Walter Guinness, a brigade-major
in 25th Division, noted that 5th Army seemed 'very haphazard in
its methods', and there is little doubt that the slapdash qualities of
Gough's staff played their part in what followed.

In outline the British plan made good sense. First, there were
the flanking thrusts. On Gough's right, the much-reduced 2nd
Army would attack the outposts of Flandern I to fix German
reserves. On his left, the French 1st Army would thrust towards
Bixschoote. Rawlinson, commanding the rump of 4th Army,
would attack in the coastal sector, and an amphibious landing,
with specially built landing craft, had been prepared. 1st Army

would send diversionary attacks towards Lens and Lille in an effort to attract Rupprecht's attention.

Gough's main attack, to be launched on 31 July, would take Pilckem Ridge north of Ypres and the Gheluvelt plateau to the town's east before swinging north-eastwards to reach the Roulers–Thourout railway on 7–8 August. At this period the tide would favour Rawlinson's coastal attack and the amphibious landing, and Gough and Rawlinson would then link up and push on through Bruges to the Dutch frontier. Gough was quite clear that Haig really intended him to break through:

> he quite clearly told me that the plan was to capture Passchendaele Ridge, and to advance as rapidly as possibly on Roulers. I was then to advance on Ostend. This was very definitely viewing the battle as an attempt to break through, and Haig never altered his opinion till the attack was launched, as far as I know.

Just as Haig and Rawlinson had disagreed over the plan for the Somme, so he and Gough differed over the detailed planning for Third Ypres. This time it was GHQ which was conservative and army headquarters radical. Gough decided to make the third line of the front position his first objective. After pausing there for a few hours, the attack would push on to the line Broodseinde–Gravestafel–Langemarck, and go even deeper if German resistance slackened. Haig's staff found this over-ambitious, and although Haig allowed it to stand he warned Gough that the Gheluvelt plateau was the vital ground and suggested to him that the Germans would pivot on it if they lost ground further north.

In the meantime, Colonel Fritz von Lossberg, the German army's leading expert on defensive tactics, arrived at Courtrai to take over as chief of staff of Fourth Army. Arnim, who knew him well, gave him a free hand, and he immediately rejected any idea of withdrawal to conform with the ground lost at Messines, and ordered work to be redoubled on the three Flandern lines. On 30 June Rupprecht's chief of staff suggested pulling back to Flandern I to disrupt British preparations, but Lossberg disagreed, arguing that the first line, where he would fight the battle as long as possible, would take much of the sting out of the attack long before it reached Flandern I.

His men would shelter from the inevitable bombardment in the large concrete bunkers which remain a feature of the Flanders landscape, and when the barrage lifted they would emerge to fight from the surrounding shell holes. Junior commanders were allowed as much initiative as possible, and could move about to avoid heavy shelling. The brunt of the attack would be borne by III Bavarian Corps, holding the 6 miles (9.5 kilometres) of front from Pilckem to the Menin Road, with three front-line divisions and two counter-attack divisions.

THE FIRST ATTACKS:
PILCKEM RIDGE, GHELUVELT PLATEAU AND LANGEMARCK

The bombardment began on 16 July, and in its course the gunners of 2nd and 5th Armies fired 4½ million rounds. The target was wider and deeper than at Messines, and air observation was hampered by the fact that the Germans fought hard for the sky: it was not until the end of July that the RFC had the edge. Although the shelling wrought severe damage to German positions, killed and wounded many of their defenders and pushed many more to the edge of collapse, it also broke up the drainage system and smashed the woods, making much of field and woodland alike impassable to tanks.

The long-awaited attack began at 3.50 on the morning of 31 July. On the right II Corps fought its way into Westhoek and Shrewsbury Forest, gaining a firm foothold on the Gheluvelt plateau, and XIX Corps, on its left, took Frezenberg and reached the line Zonnebeke–Langemarck. The two left-hand corps, XVIII

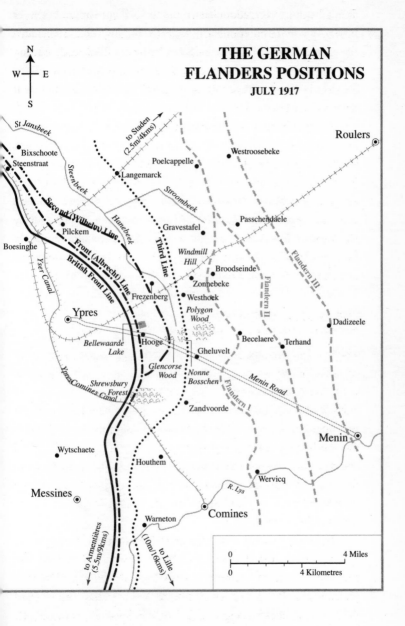

THE GERMAN
FLANDERS POSITIONS
JULY 1917

and XIV, did well at first, overrunning Pilckem Ridge, but were heavily shelled and counter-attacked in the afternoon. And then the weather broke, turning the Steenbeek, straddled by the northern corps, into a quagmire: a gunner officer reported that the infantry were up to their waists in water. The day's advance averaged some 3000 yards (2700 metres) at a cost of 30,000 casualties – roughly similar to those suffered by the Germans in bombardment and battle. But already half the tanks were out of action, knocked out or bogged, and the battlefield was breaking up.

In the days that followed Gough, heeding Haig's insistence that the Gheluvelt plateau was indeed the vital ground, renewed his efforts. However, the rain continued ceaselessly, converting the shelled area into a huge marsh, and German guns on the plateau were unusually effective. Second-Lieutenant Gerry Brooks, his memoirs preserved in the wonderful Liddle Archive at the University of Leeds, was commanding the tank *Fay* on 2 August, and describes just how difficult the ground was:

> The fun began when the tape we were following led through some very swampy ground. It was so wet we found it hard to swing. The four of us [tanks] got rather bunched and the *Foam* received a couple of direct hits and Harris her commander and two more of the crew were wounded. Harris was in great pain having his left arm nearly blown off from the elbow and also armour plate and rivets in his leg… We passed a good many dead who had fallen on July 31st. Soon we came up to our infantry who were hiding in shell holes with very heavy machine-gun fire. This pattered against our armour and some came through in a fine spray so that we were all soon bleeding from small cuts.

Fay bogged down shortly afterwards and her crew abandoned her: one was shot dead as he did so. Although Brooks found himself surrounded by counter-attacking German infantry, he managed to escape.

When II Corps attacked on 10 August its centre division, 18th, reached Westhoek and Glencorse Wood. That afternoon it was viciously counter-attacked from Nonne Bosschen and Polygon Wood and driven back with heavy loss. Although the corps commanders proposed to try again, the weather was so filthy that the attack was cancelled.

The weather prevented Gough from trying again till 16 August. He had already committed eight divisions held in reserve, and another two, sent across from 2nd Army, were soon caught up in the battle. II Corps tried to improve the results of the 10th by sending its battalions forward towards Polygon Wood on a front of only 250 yards (225 metres), pushing reserves through them as they paused on an intermediate line, but progress was poor. Further north, XIX attacked with 16th Irish Division on its left and 36th Ulster Division on its right. These formations had already fought hard at Messines, and had been living in the misery of the Ypres battlefield for a fortnight. It is to the enduring credit of soldiers from both sides of Ireland's cultural divide that they pushed well up the ridge beyond the Hanebeek and into the German pillboxes. Then the inevitable counter-attack swept them away, and the corps commander pulled the survivors back to the start line. In the north, XVIII and XIV Corps, attacking Langemarck on better ground and with artillery support well-observed from Pilckem Ridge, took the village. To their left the French 1st Army pressed forward on to the St Jansbeek.

There were further major attacks on 22 and 24 August, and a number of minor operations. 5th Army had now lost 60,000 men, and fourteen of its twenty-two divisions had been withdrawn to refit. Its gains had not been derisory, but the Gheluvelt plateau was still firmly in German hands. The weather was simply atrocious. Corporal Robert Chambers of the Bedfords wrote that it was 'raining like fury. Everywhere a quagmire. Fancy fighting

Germans for a land like this. If it were mine I'd give them the whole damn rotten country'.

These appalling conditions were no secret to commanders and their staff. On 16 August Gough visited Haig, and 'informed the Commander-in-Chief that tactical success was not possible and would be too costly under these conditions, and advised that the attack should now be abandoned'. The next day Charteris assured Haig that German morale was deteriorating steadily, and that German manpower could not stand the strain 'for more than a limited number of months (a maximum of twelve months) provided that the fighting is maintained at its present intensity in France and Belgium'. Haig was determined to continue the battle, but decided to place its conduct in the hands of Plumer.

2ND ARMY TAKES OVER:
MENIN ROAD RIDGE, POLYGON WOOD AND BROODSEINDE

Plumer was directed to take the Gheluvelt Plateau, and proposed a four-phase operation, spearheaded by X and I Anzac Corps with II Anzac in reserve. The southern part of his front was entrusted to IX and VIII Corps with only three divisions between them. He had 1295 guns to support the assault, and bid for 3½ million shells. Although he had been required to take over 5th Army's front as far as the Ypres–Roulers railway line, he was still attacking with twice the force over half the frontage assailed on 31 July, with about double the artillery support.

Plumer's staff had thought hard about the problem of dealing with deep defence backed by counter-attack divisions. Artillery would not merely destroy defences, neutralize defenders and suppress German guns: it would protect the attackers from counter-attack with standing barrages and also reach out to disrupt counter-attack divisions on their way forward. Loosely grouped skirmishers would lead the advance, followed by main assault parties, with mopping-up groups moving at the rear. Each attack would have three bounds, with pauses between them to permit consolidation and allow fresh units to move up through those which had led on the previous bound. Reserves were on hand at the rate of a platoon per company and so on up: behind each attack division stood a reserve division. This was attack in depth, and with units extended back for almost 8 miles (13 kilometres) it looked not dissimilar to the defensive system it proposed to break. Characteristically, Plumer's staff paid special attention to sorting out roads and light railways in the rear areas. They were also lucky: the rain stopped, and troops found themselves basking in the sun.

The bombardment began on 31 August and the infantry attacked at 5.40 on the morning of 20 September. They moved quickly behind the creeping barrage, and by midday 2nd Army had reached most of its objectives on the ridge, overrunning much of the Wilhelm Line. 5th Army, attacking on its left, also made good progress. Then, when the counter-attack was launched, British guns drew a curtain of fire in front of the newly captured positions and raked the three fresh divisions as they came up, rendering them ineffective. General von Kuhl, Rupprecht's chief of staff, admitted: 'our counter-attack divisions arrived too late. Their blow came up against a defensive position already organized in depth and protected by an artillery barrage'. Most remaining objectives were seized in the next few days, and Plumer's first step had taken much of the vital ground.

The battle looked different to participants. Lieutenant Firstbrooke Clarke of the North Staffordshires wrote:

> I suppose to people at home it is a fine victory. Well, so it is but they don't see the dead and wounded lying out and they don't have 9.2s bursting 10 yards away, machine-gun bullets scraping a parapet. I lost 17 of my platoon (4 killed) besides the casualties in the rest of the Coy [Company]. I was so sick of it and upset that I cried when I got back.

The second step, taken on 26 September, saw Plumer's Australians take Polygon Wood while 5th Army took Zonnebeke. These gains made it easier for British observers to see counter-attack divisions moving up, and the Germans now changed their policy, pushing more troops forward and emphasizing the need for full artillery preparation before formal counter-attacks went in. The new system was put to the test when Plumer took his third step on 4 October. The sheer vigour of the two Anzac Corps took them deep into Flandern I east of Zonnebeke. The prominent Windmill Hill, north-west of Zonnebeke on the Langemarck road, was stormed by 3rd Australian Division on one of the few occasions when large-scale bayonet fighting took place. 5th Army kept pace, gaining a foothold in Flandern I and taking Poelcappelle.

It was a bad day for the Germans. Ludendorff acknowledged that 'the idea of holding the front line more densely... was not the answer'. The Germans were now losing more men than the British, and they redrafted their defensive tactics yet again, this time relying on a thin line of sentries with a few machine-guns, backed by a main line of resistance spread deeply about the shell-holes and pill-boxes behind it. There would now be one counter-attack for one line-holding division, the latter on a frontage of only just over a mile (2 kilometres).

By now the experience of Ypres, fighting in stinking mud littered with the ruins of farms and villages, the shattered stumps of trees, and the corpses of men and horses, had etched itself deeply into the minds of the soldiers on both sides. The mud was so deep that a gun-platform for an 18-pounder needed a foundation of fascines (bundles of brushwood) and road-metal, with two layers of thick planks laid on top: even then it might last for only twenty-four hours. Men who lost their footing moving up in the dark risked drowning in the mire. One unnamed soldier told how he and his comrades tried to rescue a man sinking slowly in the mud. They could not, and eventually: 'I shot this man at his most urgent request, thus releasing him from a far more agonizing end.'

Lieutenant Edwin Campion Vaughan of the Royal Warwicks sheltered in a captured pill-box while:

> From the darkness on all sides came the groans and wails of wounded men; faint, long, sobbing moans of agony, and despairing shrieks. It was too horribly obvious to me that dozens of men with serious wounds must have crawled for safety into shell-holes, and now the water was rising above them and, powerless to move, they were slowly drowning.

An Australian officer, Lieutenant Russell Harris, recalled: 'The feeling of frustration at having been unable at times to go to the help of men trapped in those mudholes... It was impossible to shut one's ears to their cries, and when silence came it was almost like a physical blow, engendering a feeling bordering on guilt.'

Both sides used gas from time to time, and its insidious presence added a further ghastly complication. Alan Hanbury-Sparrow sat in a dugout as it rocked with the bombardment, feeling only half a man in his gas-mask. 'You can't think; the air you breathe has been filtered of all save a few chemical substances,' he wrote. 'A man doesn't live on what passes through the filter, he merely exists.'

The Germans were driven to 'grey desperation' by the conditions which most reckoned to be worse even than those at Verdun. 'The hard times experienced here exceed everything which we have gone through before,' wrote one soldier.

> It is horrible. You often wish you were dead, there is no shelter, we are lying in water, everything is misery, the fire does not cease for a moment night and day, our clothes do not dry. The worst, however, is the setting in of vomiting and diarrhoea.

Although the bunkers withstood direct hits, they sometimes slid into nearby shell-craters, trapping those inside. 'There was no way of rescuing them,' recalled an officer, 'and we suffered rather heavy casualties this way, not to speak of the painfully slow death of those trapped inside.'

LAST GASP:
POELCAPPELLE AND PASSCHENDAELE

The weather broke again after 4 October, and on the 5th both Gough and Plumer told Haig that it was time the campaign ended. It was evident that its tactical objectives could no longer be achieved. Rawlinson's coastal operation had been thwarted by well-timed German shelling in mid-July (a deserter had given vital information), and the amphibious assault had been shelved. It now seems clear that Haig ought to have stopped, and Charteris admitted that most of those at the 5 October conference 'though willing to go on, would welcome a stop'. But the Australian Official History is more generous, saying: 'let the student, looking at the prospect as it appeared at noon on 4 October, ask himself: "In view of three step by step blows, what will be the result of three more in the next fortnight?"'

The Battle of Poelcappelle began on 9 October and went wrong from the start. Charteris watched it – so much for the gilded staff which never left the château. He thought it: 'the saddest day of the year. It was not the enemy but the mud that prevented us doing better... Yesterday afternoon was utterly damnable. I got back very late and could not work, and could not rest'. Gains were negligible and losses high. The New Zealand Division had suffered heavily, losing 2700 men in four hours on 'New Zealand's blackest day'. Its commander complained that 'the artillery preparation was insufficient, the barrage poor... Our casualties are heavy, [Lt Col] Geo. King among others – I am very sad'. Private Leonard Hart of the Otago battalion recalled that on reaching the crest of the ridge they found:

a long line of practically undamaged German concrete machine-gun emplacements with barbed wire entanglements in front of them fully fifty yards deep... Dozens got hung up on the wire and shot down before their surviving comrades' eyes.

Three days later II Anzac Corps, attacking in driving rain behind a thin barrage, strengthened its grip on Passchendaele Ridge. An Australian infantry officer gave a graphic description of the battle:

On the night of the 11th we marched off at 6.30pm and walked till 5am on the morning of the 12th... Before 5am we had lost men like rotten sheep, those who survived had most marvellous escapes. I nearly got blown to pieces scores of times. We went through a sheet of iron all night and in the morning it got worse. We attacked at 5.25 and fought all day at times we were bogged up to our arm pits and it took anything from an hour upwards to get out. Lots were drowned in the mud and water.

Conditions in the whole salient were now so unreservedly terrible that the battle had clearly reached its dying fall. Haig pressed for one last try – his 3rd Army was preparing an offensive at Cambrai, and the Germans had to be pinned down – but agreed to wait until the weather improved slightly and even more artillery was available. The newly arrived Canadian Corps began its drive on Passchendaele on 26 October, and actually took the village on 6 November. The battle shuddered to a halt on 20 November. Conditions were too dreadful to permit its continuation and, as we shall see in the next chapter, Haig now had other concerns.

The casualty figures for 3rd Ypres are just as controversial as those for the Somme. Sir James Edmonds declared that the British had lost 244,897 killed, wounded and missing, and estimated German losses at 364,320. He reached the latter figure by taking the admitted German loss of 217,000, and adding 'wounded whose recovery was to be expected within a reasonable time' who were not included in German statistics. Churchill, however, thought that the British had lost 400,000 men, while Lloyd George put the figure at 399,000. It is probably safest to say that losses were about equal, at about 260,000 each.

THE MAINSPRINGS OF MORALE

Anyone visiting the salient can hardly fail to be struck by the short distances involved – it is 6½ miles (10.5 kilometres) from the Menin Gate at Ypres to Passchendaele Church – and the crushing weight of cemeteries and memorials. Tyne Cot, just below the crest of Passchendaele Ridge, is the largest Commonwealth war cemetery in the world, with nearly 12,000 graves, and the panels behind it list the names of over 34,000 British missing. Almost 55,000 more Australian, British, Canadian, Indian and South African missing are commemorated on the Menin Gate memorial. In the winter, with the beeks running deep and the wind whipping the rain past the dour, brick-built farms, the fundamental question insistently demands an answer. How did flesh and blood stand living and fighting in such a landscape?

Keith Simpson suggests that: 'Ultimately the British soldier obeyed his officers and military authority out of a combination of habit, social deference, the fear of the consequences of disobedience, and personal loyalty and respect.' Discipline undoubtedly played its part, and recent work on the capital sentences inflicted on British soldiers during the war points to the fact that death-sentences had a greater chance of being confirmed when a major battle was in progress and morale, in the high command's opinion, needed stiffening.

During the whole war more than 3000 officers and men were sentenced to death. Most had their sentences commuted by the commander-in-chief, but 306 were executed for military offences such as desertion or casting away arms. In 1998 the British government decided against pardoning these men, arguing that, as far as the extant documents show, most seemed to have been justly convicted *by the law as it then stood*. It declared, however, that 'those executed were as much victims of war as the soldiers and airmen who were killed in action, died of wounds or disease; as the civilians killed by aerial or naval bombardment; or those lost at sea'.

This humane declaration did not go far enough for those who continued to demand a blanket pardon, which was eventually granted in 2006. However, tragic though these individual cases remain, it is clear that an army which saw about 5,700,000 men pass through its ranks was not dragooned into battle by fear of the firing-squad. While formal discipline, backed by the brutal sanction of the death penalty, did indeed play its part in keeping men at their duty, it was part, as Keith Simpson suggests, of a much more complex package.

Soldiers brought part of this with them into the army. In his very important chapter in *Passchendaele in Perspective*, John Bourne maintains that by 1917 the Regular army had failed to impose its values on a huge citizen force. 'The urban working class volunteers and conscripts of the First World War,' he writes, 'did not enter the alien authority system of the Regular army naked and without tried and tested survival strategies.' Most of these had originated in the workplace. The British working man was used to tedium, regimentation, subordination and physical hardship. He found solace in the military community, comrades and distractions like sport, entertainment and gambling, and often took pride in his trade. Working class values, Bourne concludes, helped produce 'an army with a remarkable degree of social cohesion, imbued with a resilient optimism, built to resist and to endure'.

Good leadership also helped. Norman Gladden, a private in 7th Royal Northumberland Fusiliers, remembered his company commander, Captain West, as 'a good, brave and truly gentle man'. And he wrote approvingly of Lieutenant Hewitt, a Guardsman promoted from the ranks – as so many officers were by then. He was strict on parade, 'yet off parade he was friendly without being condescending, an attitude which many of his amateur colleagues would have done well to emulate...' Nor should we forget the impact of NCOs, and those 'big men' among the private soldiers whose own quiet bravery meant so much to less courageous hearts. Siegfried Sassoon gives us a snapshot of Corporal Griffiths:

> doing his simple duty without demanding explanations from the stars above him... Vigilant and serious he stared straight ahead of him, and a fine picture of fortitude he made. He was only a stolid young farmer from Montgomeryshire; only; but such men, I think, were England in those dreadful years of war.

This leadership was not confined to the regimental officers with whom men came into contact. Many senior commanders and their staff were well aware what the battlefield did to those who survived it, and recognized that units had to be rotated so that men spent some time in the line before coming back into reserve or, best still, to rest. In his chapter in *Passchendaele in Perspective*, Peter Scott stresses the importance of maintaining some kind of equilibrium between men's physical demands like food, tobacco, sanitation, shelter, medical attention, a reliable postal service and regular leave, and the awful realities of life at the front. He notes that when the men of 113rd Infantry Brigade of 38th Welsh Division came out of the line they were met by the division's senior logistic staff officer with a complete change of uniform, clean underwear, whale oil to rub into their feet, matches, cigarettes and biscuits.

These creature comforts were extraordinarily important. The daily rum ration, in particular, looms large in British personal accounts. One soldier wrote of a smell of 'rum and blood', and Robert Graves suggested that his men's rum tot, issued in his battalion as they stood to their arms at dawn, was 'the brightest moment of their twenty-four hours'. Sometimes it was used to prepare men for battle, but wiser units used it afterwards. 'For the boys who wanted rum there was plenty,' remembered one Australian. 'In the AIF [Australian Imperial Force] the rule was, no rum before a fight; the rum was given afterwards when the boys were dead beat.'

Buoyed up by the knowledge that if they survived the next two days they might live for another forty years, some men simply switched themselves off, and faced battle with sheer resignation. Advancing behind the barrage, Gladden experienced 'a peculiar, almost dreamlike, illusion. Though my feet were moving with all the energy needed to carry me with my burden across the ground, I felt that they were, in fact, rooted to the earth, and that it was all my surroundings that were moving of their own accord'. Charles Carrington felt much the same. He had a split personality just before the battle, and then withdrew himself altogether, 'leaving a zombie in command of B Company, the 1/5th Royal Warwickshire Regiment'. When the battle opened, 'the Zombie took charge and I felt nothing at all. I think I should not have known if a bullet had struck me'.

Regimental loyalty played a part in the equation. The future Field-Marshal Slim remembered his men being rallied to a shout of 'Heads up, the Warwicks, and show the blighters your cap-badges.' They had no cap badges – they were wearing steel helmets – but this appeal to ancient pride worked. For conscripts, or wounded returning to the front through a replacement system which filled gaps in the roster without much thought for a man's regimental identity, the regiment often meant little. But even they formed part of a complex world of loyalties and responsibilities that started with the infantry section. C. E. Montague was right to say how small a man's world really was: 'all that mattered to him was the one little boatload of castaways with whom he was marooned on a desert island making shift to keep off the weather and any sudden attack of wild beasts'. At its best, this spirit could produce a spirit of corporate identity which went well beyond polished boots or bright badges. 'We were bonded together by a unity of experience that had shaken off every kind of illusion, and which was utterly unpretentious,' wrote Charles Carrington, who earned his Military Cross at Passchendaele. 'The battalion was my home and my job, the only career I knew.'

Few men were overtly patriotic: there was a generalized feeling that the Allies were right and Germany was wrong, and a belief that refusing to do one's bit was like failing a mate who was down on his luck. Real hatred of the enemy was comparatively rare. Both sides killed prisoners from time to time, usually in the heat of the moment, if they had maintained a stout defence too long. 'No soldier can claim a right to quarter if he fights to the extremity,' argued Charles Carrington. Ernst Junger, on the other side of the hill, agreed: 'the defending force, after firing their bullets into the attacking one at five paces' distance, must take the consequences.'

The loss of a close friend – or the sheer difficulty of getting prisoners back through the barrage – might cause lapses. Private Frank Richards of the Royal Welch Fusiliers saw a comrade set off out down the Menin Road with six prisoners. He came back soon afterwards and admitted: 'I done them in… about two hundred yards back. Two bombs did the trick.' The man was killed seconds later. Richards, who served at the front throughout the war, thought this behaviour unusual, and believed that 'the loss of his pal had upset him very much'.

These coping mechanisms helped bring the British army through the nightmare of Passchendaele with its morale strained but unbroken. Yet those who knew it well saw how tired it really was. 'For the first time,' wrote Philip Gibbs, 'the British army lost its spirit of optimism, and there was a sense of deadly depression among many officers and men. They saw no ending of the war, nothing except continuous slaughter…'

BREAKING THE
FRONT

TANK ATTACK

1917 – the year of the Nivelle offensive, the French mutinies and
the long, wearing slog towards Passchendaele – ended with a spec-
tacular blaze which was to make the coming winter seem darker
still. After 3rd Army's patchy performance at Arras in the spring of
1917 its commander, General Sir Edmund Allenby, was sent off to
command the Egyptian Expeditionary Force. He was not pleased
for, as his biographer Lawrence James explains, he saw himself
'exiled to a peripheral and moribund front…' In the event he was
to distinguish himself there, and his energy and cavalryman's flair
for manoeuvre were to be rewarded with a series of victories over
the Turks. His successor, Sir Julian Byng, had commanded the
Canadian Corps, whose capture of Vimy Ridge had been an
unqualified success. While Passchendaele ground on, his staff
developed plans for an offensive towards Cambrai.

That spring the British had followed up the German withdrawal to the Hindenburg Line to occupy a line running from St
Quentin, past Cambrai and then turning to run north-north-west-
wards in front of Arras. The front cut across the Cambrésis,
whose sand and loam on chalk produces a landscape very like
that of the Somme. The St Quentin Canal, built by Napoleon, was
incorporated into the Hindenburg Line, and west of Cambrai the
Canal du Nord, so recently constructed that it was not yet filled
with water, also formed part of German defences. The whaleback

mass of Bourlon Wood, between the two canals, still dominates the whole area.

Defences were strong, with an outpost line running west of the Canal du Nord, crossing it at Havrincourt and then swinging east in front of Ribécourt to pick up the line of the St Quentin Canal. The front system, Siegfried I, lay 1–2000 yards (1–2 kilometres) behind it, its trenches dug so wide as to make them uncrossable by tanks, with four rows of wire, 95 yards (90 metres) deep in all, slanted out in great wedges in front of them. The support system, also well dug and wired, was 2–2½ miles (3–4 kilometres) behind, with the Siegfried II system still further back.

Impressive though these defences were, in the autumn of 1917 there seemed good reason for risking an attack on them. Breaking the Hindenburg Line at Cambrai would severely disrupt its northern run towards Monchy, and taking Cambrai itself would badly damage German communications. There were also more local agendas. 3rd Army, and its new commander, had been overshadowed by the fighting further north. General Sir Aylmer Haldane suggested: 'The tail wags the dog, and army commanders who have their own advancement in mind submit schemes instead of GHQ.' The Tank Corps, under the energetic Brigadier-General Hugh Elles, with Lieutenant-Colonel J. F. C. Fuller – later to emerge as one of Britain's outstanding military thinkers – as his chief of staff, sought an opportunity to show its mettle on firm ground, not the mud of the Ypres salient, and Cambrai seemed an ideal spot. Finally, Brigadier-General Tudor, commanding the artillery of the 9th Division, had developed a method of marking artillery targets, and the gun positions from which they would be engaged, by accurate survey, so that they could be quickly and effectively engaged without the need for preliminary registration by fire. Tudor suggested that tanks, not guns, should cut the wire, and that an attack could be preceded by a short bombardment.

On 16 September Haig discussed the plans for an attack at Cambrai with Byng, but did not feel able to formally authorize the attack until the Passchendaele battle had ended. Losses in the fighting there, coupled with the need to send troops to Italy, where the Italian army had been routed at Caporetto, made him reluctant to hand Byng a blank cheque. One of the attractions of the Cambrai project was its limited liability. Fuller had envisaged a large-scale tank raid on to the German gun-line. 3rd Army's plan was more ambitious. Two of its five corps, II and IV, would attack between Bonavis Ridge and the Canal du Nord, using 216 tanks to reach the St Quentin Canal at Masnières and Marçoing. The Cavalry Corps would then push through this gap to take Cambrai and the crossings of the River Sensée. Further north, IV Corps, with 108 tanks, would take Flesquières Ridge and Bourlon Wood.

In all there were to be 378 fighting tanks, 54 supply tanks pulling sledges, 32 fitted with grapnels for dragging wire to make gaps for the cavalry, two carrying bridging equipment and five wireless tanks. Most would carry fascines (large bundles of brushwood), which would be dropped into trenches to provide crossing-points. Infantry and tanks practised drills for working together so that mopping-up parties would be on hand to capitalize on the shock inflicted by the tanks. Over 1000 guns, using Tudor's new methods, would support the attack. Byng emphasized that if early results were not impressive, the operation could be halted after forty-eight hours before it had become too costly.

Security was good. The tanks were moved up to their rail-heads by night, and crawled to assembly areas whence, after dark on 19 November, they edged cautiously, in bottom gear with engines barely ticking over, to the forming-up line. At 6.20 on the morning of the 20th, with a glimmer of light revealing the German outpost line, the barrage crashed down and the tanks went forward. The surprise and shock were too much for many defenders: some bolted and others gave up without a fight. By midday the outpost line and main battle line were overrun on much of the attack frontage.

There was a reverse at Flesquières, where 51st Highland Division became separated from its tanks. Most authorities have blamed the divisional commander, Major-General 'Uncle' Harper, for this, but it has recently been argued that bad luck and unhelpful ground were far more to blame. The defending division, 54th, was commanded by Lieutenant-General von Watter, whose brother had encountered tanks on the Somme and warned him what to expect. He had trained his field gunners to pull their 77mms out of their gunpits and take on tanks with direct fire: they had even practised on moving targets. When the tanks crossed Flesquières Ridge, with the infantry now some distance behind them, they were taken on by determined gunners. Haig's official dispatch paid tribute to a German officer who had manned his gun single-handed until killed. The 'gunner of Flesquières' story is largely myth. As the tanks lurched over the crest-line they were at a temporary disadvantage: 51st Division lost twenty-eight of its tanks. If there was a particular German hero that day, it may have been Lieutenant Müller or Sergeant-Major Kruger of the 108th Field Artillery Regiment.

Although the break-in had gone well, the break-out (familiar story) was disappointing. II Corps got up on to the canal, and crossed it at Marcoing, but the tank 'Flying Fox' had crashed through the bridge at Masnières. The handling of the cavalry was less than slick, and it was not until sunset that, hampered on its move forward by cluttered roads and uncertainty as to which villages were already occupied, it received orders 'to push on with full strength through Marcoing and carry out the original plan of a breakthrough at that point'. B Squadron of the Canadian Fort Garry Horse, given a special independent mission, had already crossed the canal near Masnières, ridden down a battery of 77mm guns and galloped through parties of German infantry. The squadron's survivors returned after dark, bringing eighteen prisoners with them. Its senior surviving officer, Lieutenant Harcus Strachan, wrote that 'there would have been a remarkable opportunity for a great cavalry success had the operation in its original form been carried out'. Nevertheless, the British had captured 7500 prisoners and 120 guns, and had pushed some 7000 yards into one of the strongest parts of the Western Front. It was such a palpable success that church bells were rung in England for the first time during the war.

The battle went flat over the days that followed. Tank losses had been heavy – 179 of the 378 fighting tanks were out of action, 65 of them destroyed and the others ditched or broken down. On the 21st, III Corps began what was to become a long and debilitating battle for Bourlon Wood, for that evening Haig told Byng to persist with the offensive. His reasons were threefold. First, he was encouraged by Charteris to believe that the Germans showed 'a disposition to retire' because they were 'soft' as a result of the wearing-out battle of the past two years. Secondly, he was optimistic about the cavalry's chances, although the chance for bold action – such as it was – had now passed. And lastly, he hoped that the success would embarrass Lloyd George who had been increasingly critical of the British command.

In the end it was Haig who was embarrassed. The battle for Bourlon Wood imposed a heavy drain on 3rd Army's manpower – the youngest British general of the war, Brigadier-General R. B. Bradford VC MC, was killed there at the age of twenty-five – and the British soon found themselves holding a salient with tired troops. By sheer bad luck orders were given for commanders to rest and hand over to their seconds-in-command, so when the German counter-attack came on 30 November it caught the British flat-footed. The Germans tried the classic ploy of attacking both shoulders of the salient in an effort to pinch it out. They made poor progress on the Bourlon–Moeuvres front in the north,

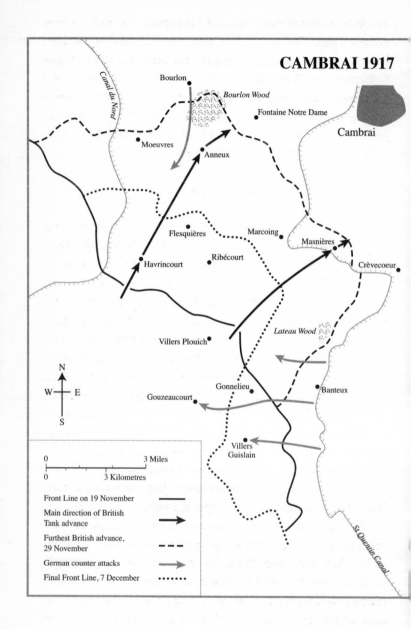

CAMBRAI 1917

Canal du Nord

Bourlon

Bourlon Wood

Fontaine Notre Dame

Cambrai

Moeuvres

Anneux

Flesquières

Marcoing

Masnières

Crèvecoeur

Ribécourt

Havrincourt

Lateau Wood

Villers Plouich

Gonnelieu

Banteux

Gouzeaucourt

Villers
Guislain

N
W — E
S

0		3 Miles
0		3 Kilometres

Front Line on 19 November

Main direction of British
Tank advance

Furthest British advance,
29 November

German counter attacks

Final Front Line, 7 December

St. Quentin Canal

but on the southern flank they broke in between III and VII Corps around Villers Guislain. Things were very bad, and would have been worse had 1st Guards Brigade not been on hand to regain Gouzeaucourt. When the battle ended on the night of 4/5 December the British retained part of the old Hindenburg system around Flesquières, but had relinquished their other gains and lost fresh ground in the south. Both sides had lost about 40,000 men, with 158 British guns lost to 145 German.

PRINCES OF THE TRENCHES

Cambrai was not merely a disappointing battle for the British: it was an instructive one for the Germans. Just as the defensive fighting on the Somme in 1916 had helped them refine the defensive doctrine that was to cause the Allies such difficulties in 1917, so their experience of launching attacks of their own, most notably on the Eastern Front – where the city of Riga had been taken in a textbook assault by General Oscar von Hutier's Eighth Army in September 1917 – had helped them develop offensive doctrine. It is now clear that the differences between German, British and French doctrine were less clear than most historians once suggested, and we must steer clear of imagining that all British officers were hidebound martinets while their German opponents were clear-thinking innovators. Two of the most useful books on the subject, Paddy Griffith's *Battle Tactics of the Western Front* and Martin Samuels's *Doctrine and Dogma: German and British Infantry Tactics in the First World War*, come at the argument from opposite ends.

But in offensive as in defensive tactics, the Germans were better than their opponents at codification and doctrinal development. They were also clearer in the identification of tactical concepts, like the need to designate a *schwerpunkt* (focus of energy), the advantage of *aufrollen* (flank attack), and the importance of *schlagfertigkeit*, which was to tactics what quickness of repartee was to conversation. To promote the latter the Germans reduced the number of levels of command until by 1917–18 there were in essence only two tactical levels, battalion and division: others were primarily administrative.

The practice of giving the commander on the spot authority over reinforcing units also helped. By 1918 the average age for promotion to captain in the German army was 29½, and an officer this age might find himself the *kampftruppenkommandeur* in a sector, controlling the three battalions of his regiment and any reserves sent there, effectively exercising the authority of a British brigadier-general who might be ten years older and would have a more complex chain of command to tug. We have already seen the problems imposed on the British army by rapid pre-war expansion which inevitably diluted the trained manpower available and resulted in the promotion of the unfit as well as the fit. The Germans had not only a deeper pool of regular and reserve officers, but a formidable NCO corps. One British general reckoned that a pre-war German NCO, on completing the two-year course at NCO school, was 'as efficient as the average British subaltern of, say, five years' service'. During the war NCOs commanded most platoons and, by 1917–18, were routinely commanding companies. They might be commissioned after further training, but in order to preserve the social exclusivity of commissioned rank the Germans developed the rank of *offizierstellvertreter* (deputy officer): these worthies had the responsibilities, though not the status, of subalterns.

When the Germans counter-attacked at Cambrai they did so behind a creeping barrage which could be accelerated by signal lights fired by the infantry it supported. And in most divisions the attack was led by élite assault units. These had been developed from small beginnings after the Guard Rifle Battalion pioneered fluid assault in retaking a captured trench on New Year's Eve 1914. In March 1915 an assault detachment, of about half-battal-

ion size, was created, and soon came under the command of
Captain Willy Rohr, who had served with the Guard Rifles. Rohr
developed tactics based on section-sized 'stormtroops', supported
by machine-guns, mortars, flamethrowers and artillery, all co-
ordinated at the lowest possible level to ensure the effective
suppression of enemy defences. Once stormtroops had made a gap
in these defences, they rolled up enemy trenches by attacking
along them with hand grenades.

The experience of Verdun encouraged the Germans to build
assault detachments into larger assault battalions and to create
more of them. Several *Jäger* (rifle) battalions were converted
wholesale, and there were also regimental stormtroop detachments. Establishments varied as the war went on, but a storm
battalion might comprise up to five infantry companies, one or
two twelve-gun machine-gun companies, a flamethrower section,
an infantry gun battery with four to six guns, and a mortar
company with eight mortars. The Germans had a functional
approach to the various arms: troops and their weapons were
considered for what they did, rather than what they were. Storm
battalions needed to generate *Stosskraft* (assault power) as well as
Feuerkraft (fire power), and it was logical to mix infantry and
artillery within them, without letting traditional inter-army rival-
ries get in the way.

These units were more than just practitioners of the most up-
to-date tactics: they were filled with the fittest, keenest officers
and men, imbued with a spirit that made them 'princes of the
trenches'. The soldier-poet Franz Schauwecker describes the ideal
stormtrooper:

> he moves from shellhole to shellhole in raging fire, by leap
> and bound, by creep and crawl like a seal, close to the earth
> like an animal, never discouraged, never irresolute, never for-
> feiting intent, always full of recourse, schemes and self-
> reliance, answering every blow with a counterblow… a new

kind of man, a man in the highest exaltation of all manly qualities so harmonized and from a single caste that one sees a
man in the word 'fighter'.

The Crown Prince of Prussia gave stormtroopers his personal
support, and when Ludendorff visited his headquarters at Stenay
in September 1916 it was natural that a company of Rohr's assault
battalion should form the guard of honour. Ludendorff was
intrigued by their dress: the coal-scuttle helmet, fast replacing the
spiked helmet in the infantry, puttees, mountain boots and leather-
patched tunics. This, thought Ludendorff, should become the
model for the rest of the German infantry.

Stormtroop tactics paid dividends at Cambrai. The short
bombardment did not forfeit surprise, and behind it came the
stormtroops, supported by pioneer units dealing with obstacles
and ordinary infantry to mop up by-passed positions. There was
no sudden British collapse, and isolated groups of defenders
fought back hard, forcing the Germans to take them on in detail.
Well-prepared stormtroopers were closely supported by 'infantry
accompanying batteries', one four-gun battery per attacking regiment, moving up with the infantry to provide direct fire, as well
as by their own machine guns and mortars. They were followed
by 'assault blocks', up to battalion-sized teams of infantry,
mortarmen and machine-gunners, briefed to exploit success and
maintain the momentum of the attack. The triumph of these
methods at Cambrai suggested to Ludendorff that they were
indeed the way ahead.

'BREAKTHROUGH MÜLLER'

There was another useful lesson of Cambrai. The artillery fire
support of stormtroop attacks had been developed by Georg
Bruchmüller. He had been a regular gunner officer with a modest
background, and was on the retired list as a lieutenant-colonel

when the war began. Re-employed in 1914, he soon found himself commanding the artillery of an infantry division, and in 1916 masterminded a centralized artillery fireplan when a German corps counter-attacked the numerically superior Russians at Lake Narotch. On 1 May 1917 he was awarded the Pour le Mérite, an unusual decoration for a staff officer, before being sent off to be artillery adviser to Hutier for his attack on Riga. In the German army appointment mattered less than formal rank, and the fact that Brüchmüller was still only a re-employed retired lieutenant-colonel mattered not a jot. He soon had the nickname *Durchbruchmüller* – 'Breakthrough Müller' – and, as General Max Hoffmann, chief of staff on the Eastern Front, was to write, troops 'went forward with a fuller sense of confidence when Bruchmüller and his staff were in charge'.

Artillery assets were divided into four groups. Close support for the infantry was provided by the *Infanteriebekampfungsartillerie* (IKA), with 75 per cent of guns assigned to it. Some 20 per cent of batteries formed counter-artillery groups (*artilleriebekamfungsartillerie* – AKA) whose task was counter-battery fire. The long-range guns of the *Fernkampfartillerie* (FEKA) reached out to hit command posts, ammunition dumps and reserve concentrations. Finally, the *Schwereste Flachfeuerartillerie* (SCHWELFA) consisted of the heaviest guns, grouped to include their own air observation and survey units, which took on critical hard targets like railway bridges and reinforced command posts.

In addition, there were infantry assets: trench-mortars; infantry-accompanying batteries of 77mm guns; and infantry guns (captured Russian 76.2mm guns with cut-down barrels), which were parcelled out at the rate of one per attacking battalion and manhandled forward with the assault. Neither the infantry accompanying batteries nor the infantry guns fired in the preparatory bombardment: their job was to take on targets like machine-guns and snipers which had escaped other fires.

The essence of Bruchmüller's tactics was the centralization of control at the highest level consistent with the communications available, so that the artillery assigned to an operation played to the baton of a single conductor. His bombardments were short and violent, designed to neutralize rather than destroy the defender, and mixed gas, shrapnel and high explosive shells. Bombardments were divided into phases, each with a specific tactical objective, and could be mixed and matched as required. Bruchmüller understood the psychological effects of artillery fire, and often organized fireplans so that the same positions were hit time after time, making it hard for the defender to work out when it was safe to man his trenches to meet the real assault.

A creeping barrage – *feuerwalze* – would move ahead of the attackers, and although they were able to speed it up (by firing green flares) no method was devised for slowing it down. In the first half of 1918 Bruchmüller slowed the pace of the barrage, and by June it moved only 220 yards (200 metres) in ten minutes. He also authorized commanders to pull batteries out of the *feuerwalze* to deal with pockets of resistance, and made sure that they had enough assets to do this. By May 1918 Bruchmüller had developed the double creeping barrage, the nearer line of fire, consisting of high explosive, moving uniformly just ahead of the infantry, while the further line, consisting largely of gas, dwelled longer on likely lines of resistance.

Bruchmüller was increasingly suspicious of the need to register targets before an attack, as that inevitably compromised surprise. Captain Erich Pulkowski developed a method of adding daily meteorological influences to the special characteristics of individual guns and ammunition batches to make un-registered fire more accurate, and the British themselves had shown, with their barrage at Cambrai, just how effective un-registered fire could be. Bruchmüller backed the Pulkowski method against much high-level opposition, and managed to secure its partial adoption in February 1918.

LUDENDORFF'S DECISION

On 11 November 1917 Ludendorff met a select group of his advisers at Mons, the little Belgian town where British and Germans had first clashed in 1914 and now the seat of Rupprecht's army group headquarters. Among them were Major – soon to be Lieutenant-Colonel – Georg Wetzell, OHL's chief of operations on the Western Front, and Captain Hermann Geyr, a leading offensive ideologue and author of the pamphlet *The Attack in Position Warfare*. American entry into the war changed the entire strategic balance. Although Ludendorff and his officers were not to know it then, the tiny US Army was to grow so swiftly that it would have a million men in France by July 1918 and over two million by the year's end. If the details of America's contribution were still unknown to the Germans, its general effect was not. Even if Germany succeeded in closing down the Eastern Front altogether, which she was already close to doing, she would inevitably be swamped by men and material pouring in from the United States. Her only chance, believed Ludendorff, was to attack before the Americans were present in strength.

One decision was simply made. Beating the French would still leave Britain in the war, and there was always the danger that an uncowed Britain, supported by the USA, might continue the naval blockade which was doing Germany so much harm. Defeating the British, however, would turn the northern flank of the Western Front and provoke a French collapse. Ludendorff concluded that 'we must beat the British'.

Ludendorff's staff made several plans. Among them were schemes for attacks on both sides of Ypres – 'George I' and 'George II' – which would join at Hazebrouck and then swing north-westwards to encircle a large part of the British army. Although there was much to be said for this scheme – for even a short advance would put important targets within German reach –

the British had demonstrated with agonizing clarity that it was not easy to attack in Flanders. All might be well if Ludendorff could wait until the battlefield had dried out, but the need to strike before the Americans arrived in strength helped rule out 'George' as a first option. Attacking in the Arras–Vimy sector – 'Mars' and 'Valkyrie' – would prove difficult because of the British hold on Vimy Ridge and the cluttered character of the ground.

Ludendorff's glance slid further south, to the land between the Rivers Sensée and Oise. Here the attackers could concentrate behind the Hindenburg Line, and for much of the attack front the defenders would have the wilderness of the old Somme battle-field to their backs. In the south, General von Hutier, back from the Eastern Front, would mount 'Michael I' with Eighteenth Army securing the Crozat Canal as the attack's left shoulder and advancing astride St Quentin. In the centre, General von der Marwitz's Second Army would make for Albert ('Michael II') while General von Below's Seventeenth Army unleashed 'Michael III' towards Bapaume. Once the front was broken, the attackers could swing northward cutting deep into the British rear. Below's right wing could then launch 'Mars South' against Arras and, if the weather improved, 'George' could be sprung last of all, exposing the British to a concentric attack which they would have little hope of resisting.

Ludendorff paid careful attention to morale. Many senior offi-cers feared that the German army had degenerated into a mere militia, and part of the morale-building process included the re-introduction of the formal 'goose-step' parade drill. Decorations were lavishly distributed, and military bands gave concerts featur-ing patriotic tunes. Ludendorff encouraged his men to believe that this mammoth offensive, the *Kaiserschlacht*, the Kaiser's battle, would win the war and end their miseries.

The balance of forces certainly looked encouraging. Some seventy-four German divisions, backed by 6608 guns and 3534 mortars, were to attack on a front of about 50 miles (80 kilometres). They would be supported by over 700 aircraft, some, in the recently renamed battle squadrons, dedicated to ground attack, and others flying against British and French aircraft. Facing this panoply were the British 4th and 5th Armies, with thirty divisions between them. But Ludendorff was too experienced a commander not to recognize the flaw in his project. He was attacking where short-term tactical success was most likely, but in a sector where he could drive very deep into the British lines without necessarily doing fatal damage. Much would depend on how the British fought; how well his own men endured the pressure of the battle; and, above all, whether the alliance would hold together under its impact.

AWAITING THE BLOW

The blow was to fall on a British army which was feeling the strain of a long war. If Passchendaele had worn down the Germans, it had also hit the British army hard. On 1 March 1918 Haig's infantry was just over half a million strong, only 36 per cent of his total strength as opposed to 45 per cent only six months before. Shortage of manpower compelled the reduction of battalions per brigade from four to three in British divisions (Dominion troops retained four), and 141 wartime-raised battalions, which could no longer be kept up to strength, were disbanded. Morale seemed to have recovered from its lowest ebb in the wake of Passchendaele, but the nation was scraping the bottom of its manpower barrel. In 1915 the German cavalry officer Rudolf Binding suggested that the quality of British troops compensated for their small numbers, but a year later he was complaining that prisoners were 'rickety, alcoholic, degenerate, ill-bred and poor to the last degree'. By 1918 many observers, British and German, testified to the growing numbers of schoolboys in the ranks, and a new military service act, which came into operation in April 1918, conscripted men aged forty-one to fifty.

Haig had reluctantly agreed to take over more ground from the French, and by January 1918 had extended the British front another 42 miles (68 kilometres), as far as the River Oise. This placed fresh demands on manpower, because French defences were not organized on the scale required by the British. Moreover, British defensive tactics were themselves in the process of changing, and the new doctrine, heavily influenced by German experience, required existing trench-lines to be remodelled. A GHQ memorandum of 14 December 1917 ordained that there would be three layers of defences. A Forward Zone would be based upon well-wired redoubts, whose machine-guns covered the ground between them. A sprinkling of 17-pounders, sited individually, protected against tank attack. A mile or two further back came the Battle Zone, with more redoubts, the bulk of the artillery, and counter-attack units to support the Forward Zone. Still further back was the Rear Zone, in theory organized much like the Battle Zone, protecting heavy batteries and supply dumps. Tanks, it was decided, would be grouped behind the front for counter-attacks, not posted as individual strongpoints, or 'savage rabbits'.

There were two major weaknesses in this new structure. In the first place, it had not been properly taught, and there was a good deal of consumer resistance. 'It don't suit us,' grumbled one experienced NCO. 'The British Army fights in line, and won't do any good in these bird cages.' Many commanders, used to holding ground as far forward as possible, pushed too many men – and far too many machine-guns – into the Forward Zone. They also failed to appreciate that the German system hinged on an unwritten contract between troops in the line and the high command. The former would hold on even if surrounded, and the latter would launch counter-attacks as soon as possible. There are limits to men's tenacity, and a defence without hope of relief is something few citizen armies will sustain.

The second weakness turned on manpower shortages. Gough's 5th Army, holding the southern end of the British line had only 14 divisions to hold 42 miles (67 kilometres) of front, and only 8830 labourers in addition to fighting troops. When the German attack began there were no dugouts in his Battle Zone, and it was incomplete south of St Quentin. The Rear Zone consisted only of its forward trench, the Green Line, simply marked out on the ground. Things were better further north, where 3rd Army had 16 divisions for 28 miles (45 kilometres), but even here the Battle Zone was unfinished and the Rear Zone incomplete.

Gough pointed out the weakness of his line and, once he had discovered that Hutier was his opponent, predicted that his army would be in the path of the main assault. In February he was given permission to 'fall back to the rearward defences of Péronne and the Somme' if heavily attacked, but it was made clear that Péronne should be held at all costs. Haig visited the 5th Army front in early March, and recognized that things were far from ideal. 'The French handed over to him a wide front with no defences,' he wrote, 'and Gough has no labour for the work.'

Haig was in growing difficulties. Cambrai had done very serious damage to GHQ's standing in the eyes of politicians: Haig himself, Kiggell, his chief of staff, and Charteris, his intelligence officer, were all under scrutiny. Kitchener had died in 1916, drowned on his way to Russia. On 7 December Lord Derby, now secretary of state for war, told Haig that: 'the War Cabinet are constantly saying that the statements and views you have put forward at different times regarding the moral and numerical weakening of the enemy are not borne out by the opposition your troops encounter, and so it seems to me and the General Staff here'. Haig did his best for Charteris, but in December replaced him with Major-General Herbert Lawrence, who had left the army after the Boer War when Haig had been promoted over his head to command the 17th Lancers. The two worked well together, but the fact that Lawrence was his own man, with a career to resume when the war finished, made him more robust in his dealings with the commander-in-chief than had often been the case at GHQ. Shortly afterwards Kiggell went too, and Lawrence stepped up to become chief of staff.

Haig's own position was far from secure. Lloyd George later admitted that the problem in replacing him was to find somebody who would do better. 'It is a sad reflection,' he wrote after the war, 'that not one among the visible military leaders would have been any better. There were amongst them plenty of good soldiers who knew their profession and possessed intelligence up to a point. But Haig was all that and probably better within limits than any others within sight...' In January 1918 he sent the South African premier J. C. Smuts and the War Cabinet's secretary Maurice Hankey to the front in an effort to see who might replace Haig. Lloyd George described their report as 'very disappointing', for it endorsed Haig. Robertson, who had for so long sought to cover Haig's back in London, was more vulnerable: in February he was replaced by General Sir Henry Wilson. Wilson, a clever, voluble francophile, was widely mistrusted by his own army and had been shunted off to be liaison officer to the French in 1915. In 1917 Lloyd George had appointed him British representative on the Allied Supreme War Council, and his promotion to Chief of the Imperial General Staff was bad news for Haig.

GHQ had little doubt that the Germans would attack. In December 1917 its intelligence branch, then still under Charteris, had given them an assessment which tallied accurately with Ludendorff's own: in the early spring the Germans would 'seek to deliver such a blow on the Western Front as would force a decisive battle which she could fight to a finish before the American forces could take an active part...' News of German concentrations around Mézières persuaded Haig that this might presage an attack towards Amiens and 'an advance in force south-west of St Quentin'. In January he warned the War Cabinet that the next four months would be 'the critical period of the war'. This frank statement failed to ensure that his army was brought up to strength, and as Charteris gloomily opined on 26 January it entered the year with a longer front to hold, a reduced establishment with which to hold it, no hope of reinforcements and the prospect of a heavy German attack.

THE MARCH OFFENSIVE

At 4.40 on the morning of 21 March the German artillery shook the front between the Sensée and the Oise with the wild, impersonal malice of some natural disaster. German guns fired over 3 million rounds that day. Lieutenant Herbert Sulzbach, a German artillery officer, wrote that it was:

> as if the world was coming to an end… During the firing I often have to interrupt my fire direction duties because I can't take all the gas and the smoke. The gunners stand with their sleeves rolled up and the sweat pouring down. Round after round is rammed into the breech, salvo after salvo is fired. I don't have to give orders any more because the men are so enthusiastic; they fire at such a rapid rate that no commands are necessary.

A British machine-gunner on the receiving end thought that it 'seemed as though the bowels of the earth had erupted, while beyond the ridge there was one long and continuous yellow flash'. Lance-Corporal William Sharpe had four youngsters who had only just turned eighteen in his section: this was their first experience of battle. 'They cried and one kept calling 'mother!' and who could blame him, such HELL makes weaklings of the strongest

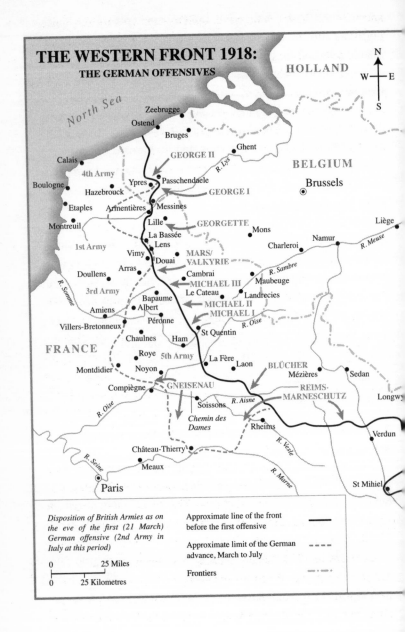

THE WESTERN FRONT 1918:
THE GERMAN OFFENSIVES

HOLLAND

North Sea

Zeebrugge
Ostend
Bruges
Ghent

GEORGE II

R. Lys

BELGIUM

Calais

4th Army

Brussels

Boulogne

Ypres Passchendaele
Hazebrouck

GEORGE I

Etaples
Armentières
Messines
Montreuil
Lille
GEORGETTE
Mons

La Bassée
Lens
Liège

1st Army
Vimy
Douai
MARS/
VALKYRIE
Charleroi
Namur

R. Meuse

Arras
Doullens
Cambrai
R. Sambre
Maubeuge

3rd Army
Bapaume
Le Cateau
Landrecies
MICHAEL III

Amiens
Albert
MICHAEL II
Péronne
MICHAEL I

Villers-Bretonneux
Chaulnes
Ham
St Quentin
R. Oise

FRANCE
Roye
5th Army
La Fère
Laon

Montdidier
Noyon
BLÜCHER
Mézières
Sedan

Compiègne
GNEISENAU
REIMS-
MARNESCHUTZ
Longwy

R. Oise
Soissons
R. Aisne

Chemin des
Dames
Rheims
Verdun

R. Vesle

Château-Thierry

R. Seine
Meaux
R. Marne

St Mihiel

Paris

Disposition of British Armies as on
the eve of the first (21 March)
German offensive (2nd Army in
Italy at this period)

Approximate line of the front
before the first offensive

Approximate limit of the German
advance, March to July

0   25 Miles
0   25 Kilometres

Frontiers

and no human's nerves were ever built to stand such torture, noise, horror and mental pain.' Their trench was blown in, and although Sharpe searched for the lads he never saw them again.

An artillery officer, almost blown off his bunk 'by concussion like an earthquake', tried to telephone his batteries, only to discover that all the telephone cables, buried 6 feet (2 metres) deep, had been cut. The German artillery specialists Bruchmüller and Pulkowski had done their work well.

The German infantry loped forward behind the barrage. It was a foggy morning, which gave them protection from the surviving machine-guns in the Forward Zone, but presented command and control problems which bugle-calls, specially taught for just such an eventuality, only partially solved. Across much of the British front the picture was the same. Groups of stormtroopers slipped in between the redoubts like wraiths, and the first many British soldiers saw of their enemies was when attacks curled in from flanks and rear. Under these circumstances some men fought to the last extremity, but the majority, fighting what was all too evidently a losing battle, surrendered. Most Germans behaved surprisingly well. Private J. Parkinson was changing the belt on his machine-gun when he felt a bump in his back. It was a German officer's pistol, and its owner said: 'Come along, Tommy. You've done enough.' 'He must have been a real gentleman,' admitted Parkinson.

The personality and determination of individual leaders made a real difference. Manchester Hill, just west of St Quentin, was held by elements of 16th Battalion The Manchester Regiment under its commanding officer, Lieutenant-Colonel Wilfrith Elstob. A burly former schoolmaster who had joined the battalion as a private in 1914, Elstob knew, like so many others, that the attack was coming. When his men marched up to the line a few days before, their band played them out of camp, and as it turned about to return Elstob remarked: 'Those are the only fellows who will come out of this alive.' He had pointed out the position of battalion headquarters on a map, emphasizing: 'Here we fight, and here we die.'

The battle began early for the Manchesters when a scream from the fog told them a sentry had been bayoneted. There was then some firing, but no serious attacks, and when the fog lifted late in the morning the Manchesters could see German troops moving westwards on both sides of them. Attacks proper started at about 3.00, as follow-up troops arrived. Elstob, wounded three times, was the heart of the defence, darting about with revolver and grenades. His field telephone allowed him to maintain contact with brigade headquarters, and he eventually reported that he had few men left, but declared: 'The Manchester Regiment will hold Manchester Hill to the last.' He was killed as he went back with more grenades.

Elstob's gallant stand earned him a well-deserved Victoria Cross, but his battalion had far more men captured than killed: there were limits to what even stoutly led men could achieve. In other cases leadership was less vigorous, often because officers believed that there was simply no point in ordering their men to fight on. Lieutenant-Colonel Lord Farnham surrendered Boadicea Redoubt: the Germans reported the capture of one lieutenant-colonel, a small white dog, three captains, seven subalterns, 241 men, and 41 machine-guns and mortars. This sort of thing was scarcely last-ditch defence, and one nameless sergeant was scathing. 'I must confess that the German breakthrough on 21 March 1918 should never have occurred,' he maintained. 'There was no cohesion of command, no determination, no will to fight, and no unity of companies or of battalions.'

By nightfall the Germans had inflicted over 38,000 casualties on the British, including some 21,000 prisoners. They had lost slightly more men, with hardly any prisoners, and had taken part of 3rd Army's Battle Zone south of the Scarpe, though the Flesquières salient was still secure, while 5th Army had lost a huge tract of ground north of Ham. The advance was less impressive on the 22nd, though Hutier made such good progress along the Crozat Canal that he suspected he might have caught Gough in the process of withdrawing. He had not, but the pace of his advance showed that 5th Army was now in real difficulties. That morning Gough declared that 'corps will fight rear-guard actions back to forward line of the Rear Zone, and if necessary to rear line of Rear Zone'. Given the fact that the Rear Zone consisted at best of 'an immaculately patterned mock trench', this was pure moonshine.

All that week 5th Army slid back in defeat. One junior staff officer reported that:

> The troops were walking down a main road. They were in no formation and units were mixed up in strange confusion. Officers and men were together and it was just a rabble, but there was no panic, no hurry, not much talking, no shouting – just a dogged steady slogging towards the rear.

The divisional artillery commander ordered him to stop the rabble and make a line, but it was no use: 'You might as well have tried to stop the sea.' Guy Chapman saw similar sights. 'The privates were all children,' he wrote, 'tired, hardly able to drag their aching shoulders after their aching legs. Here and there an exhausted boy trudged along with tears coursing down his face.' Experienced officers knew that things were desperate. Captain Douglas McMurtrie of the Somerset Light Infantry strove to keep his men in hand when his colonel ordered him to retreat on 24 March. 'I was determined not to let the men start running,' he wrote, 'for once they did so in such a situation it was impossible to hold them. I had my revolver out and anyone who tried to run I immediately threatened to shoot. This stopped all running but it was the worst hour I have ever had with the only exception perhaps of the Cambrai counter-attack on Nov 30th [1917].' And there were even more worrying signs. Some soldiers now doubted whether there was any point in the war: 'The Boche can have this country as far as I'm concerned.'

These worrying remarks were paralleled in the Allied command. Pétain, the French commander-in-chief, had honoured an earlier agreement and sent six divisions to shore up Gough's right flank. On the 23rd, the day that Péronne fell, Haig asked Pétain to concentrate another twenty divisions around Amiens, only to discover that Pétain, concerned that the Germans might attack him, could not spare them. He made it clear that, *in extremis*, the French army would fall back to cover Paris. His reserve army group would fall back from Montdidier to the south-west if seriously attacked, and was not to be cut off with the British if the Germans succeeded in reaching Amiens and cutting the major rail link between the Allied armies. Haig had already faced the possibility that 'the British will be rounded up and driven back into the sea', and now he wrote that he was 'confronting the weight of the German army single-handed'.

THE DOULLENS CONFERENCE

On 26 March Haig met some of his army commanders at Doullens, not far behind the shifting front. Gough was too busy to be there, and though Byng attended old Plumer muttered that he ought to have been with his army, and then, helpful as ever, offered to send fresh troops south. Haig was then summoned to the town hall, where Lord Milner, a member of the War Cabinet, and Henry Wilson, the new Chief of the Imperial General Staff, were meeting a senior French delegation. Haig said that he proposed to hold Amiens and hold north of the Somme: he had placed elements of 5th Army south of the Somme under French command. Pétain, deeply pessimistic, observed that there was now very little left of 5th Army. Foch, rising to the occasion, burst out: 'We must fight in front of Amiens, we must fight where we are now. As we have not been able to stop the Germans on the Somme, we must not now retire a single inch.' Haig then said that if Foch was prepared to give him advice he would happily follow it, and after some discussion a document was drafted giving Foch authority to co-ordinate all Allied armies on the Western Front. It was the genesis of a unified command, in circumstances of far greater danger than had prevailed at the Calais conference which had subordinated Haig to Nivelle a year before. Yet this time the arrangement suited Haig, for it was Pétain who was overruled. Amiens would be held at all costs. United, the Allies might just stand: divided, they would certainly fall.

THE KAISERSCHLACHT ENDS

Although the Allied leaders were not to know it, the attack was already running out of steam. In part this was due to what the Prussian military thinker Clausewitz had long ago called 'the diminishing power of the offensive': as the attackers moved further from their bases they became ever more tired, and it became more and more difficult to supply them. German soldiers gorged themselves on captured food and drink, and discipline wavered. On 28 March Rudolf Binding entered Albert, which had just fallen, and saw:

> men driving cows before them on a line; others who carried a hen under one arm and a box of notepaper under the other. Men carrying a bottle of wine under their arm and another one open in their hand… Men dressed up in comic disguise. Men with top hats on their heads. Men staggering. Men who could hardly walk.

He ordered an officer to press on with the advance, but was told: 'I cannot get my men out of this cellar without bloodshed.' As the momentum of the offensive faltered, Ludendorff kept tinkering with the lines of advance given to army commanders, sacrificing the grand plan of rolling up the British to capitalize on short-term local advantage, and on 28 March he unleashed Mars: it made little progress. Nevertheless, during those critical days many British soldiers felt themselves staring defeat in the face. On 11 April Haig issued an order of the day which concluded:

> There is no other course open to us but to fight it out! Every position must be held to the last man: there must be no retirement. With our backs to the wall, and believing in the justice of our cause, each one of us must fight on to the end. The safety of our homes and the freedom of mankind alike depend on the conduct of each one of us at this critical moment.

'Michael' at last sputtered to a halt, but not before Villers-Bretonneux – from whose long ridge the spires of Amiens can be seen on the horizon – had fallen. The Germans took it on 24 April, using thirteen of their own tanks, the monster A7V *Sturmpanzer-wagen* , to help them do so. South-west of the town that morning a section of three British tanks moved out to engage them, and Second Lieutenant Frank Mitchell's Mk IV 'male' (armed with 6-pounder guns, whereas Mk IV 'females' had only machine-guns) took on an A7V in the world's first ever tank-versus-tank battle: Mitchell won it. Later the same morning seven British 'whippet' light tanks, alerted by a reconnaissance aircraft, caught two German battalions in the open and drove right through them, machine-gunning as they went. That night three brigades, two Australian and one British, counter-attacked, and by dawn on the 25th Villers-Bretonneux was back in Allied hands. 'Michael' was over. It had taken over 90,000 prisoners and 1000 guns, and had overrun more territory than all the Allied advances of the past three years. But it had not won the war.

LUDENDORFF KEEPS TRYING

Yet the strategic logic which had persuaded Ludendorff to attack in March had not changed. He tried again, mounting 'Georgette' – an attenuated version of 'George' – on 9 April. The brunt of the attack fell on an over-extended Portuguese division holding the line around Neuve Chapelle, and the Germans advanced 6 miles (10 kilometres) that day. They went on to make a deep dent in British lines, running from Givenchy on the La Bassée Canal to Merville on the Lys, and then on up to Ypres, where all those painfully earned gains of 1917 were snuffed out. The Germans even wrested Kemmel Hill from the French. But if the British blamed the French for this, many Frenchmen were no less critical of the English. 'Everyone says the same,' wrote Captain Henri Desagneux. 'The English are useless, it's the Scots, the Australians and Canadians who do all the work.'

Foch sent three divisions north to replace five British divisions which had been badly mauled in the fighting, and these were sent down to rest on the Chemin des Dames, now such a quiet sector that it was nicknamed 'the sanatorium of the Western Front'.

These divisions, constituting Lieutenant-General Gordon's IX Corps, held part of the ridge under the command of the French 6th Army. But far from having time to rest and refit in a quiet sector, they found themselves directly in the patch of the next of Ludendorff's offensives, 'Blücher', which began early on the 27th. As we have seen from German experience at Vimy, holding a ridge was rarely easy, for it was always tempting to pack the vital but vulnerable ground with troops. This is just what General Duchêne of 6th Army did, and Bruchmüller's bombardment was so effective that in some cases the principal opposition to the Germans came from the ripped-up ground. By nightfall the Germans were across the Aisne, and by 1 June they had taken both Soissons and Château-Thierry. Tim Travers suggests that there was a 'noticeable drop' in British morale, but highlights the fact that there were still examples of inspired and inspiring leadership. Lieutenant-Colonel Dean of 6th South Wales Borderers was carried into an artillery headquarters, hard hit. Although 'grievously wounded, obviously dying, and unable to speak, he made signs for writing materials – he managed to scrawl "To my battalion – Stick it, Boys", and died within a few minutes'.

ENTER THE AMERICANS

Yet the story was the same as before – substantial tactical gains but no strategic success – with an added twist. General John J. Pershing, the commander of American forces in France, was insistent that his troops should fight as a unified American army and not be parcelled out amongst the Allies. Nevertheless he was prepared to listen to reason and support Allied endeavours where the situation genuinely demanded it. American ground troops had their baptism of fire on 3 June, when machine-gunners of the US 3rd Division shot up Germans trying to cross the Marne at Château-Thierry. Three days later 4th Marine Brigade assaulted Belleau Wood, west-north-west of the town. The Marines attacked in long, straight lines, with the sort of tactical innocence that European armies had long since lost. It took them until 25 June to secure the wood, and they lost 5000 men, including half their officers.

Yet their victory was a portent for the future. The Americans were inexperienced. Their logistics were clumsy. Their commander was not blown along by Foch's enthusiasm. Still, they had won one battle, and would win more. Henri de Pierrefeu coined a simile which many felt to be absolutely appropriate: the Americans were like a transfusion of blood arriving to reanimate the pallid body of France. The French Captain Desagneux's heart lifted when he saw his first Americans, 'twenty strapping great fellows, sappers, admirably turned out with brand new equipment'.

And as Allied spirits rose, so German resolve wavered. Ludendorff, like a driver pumping desperately at the accelerator as he feels the engine falter, launched two more attacks. On 9–14 June Operation 'Gneisenau' pushed past Montdidier. Then on 15 July came the last attack, officially the 'Reims– Marneschutz' but tellingly known as 'Friedensturm' – the Peace Offensive. The now-familiar tactical ploys, stormtroops coming in behind a lightning bombardment, gained ground on either side of Rheims. But that was all: the Germans had shot their bolt.

THE ALLIED RIPOSTE:
MANGIN, ST MIHIEL AND MEUSE-ARGONNE

Successive German attacks, which led to Foch and Haig demanding reserves to solve their own particular problems, made it hard for Foch to co-ordinate a cohesive Allied counter-attack. Haig wanted reserves to reinforce the Lys sector in Flanders. And Pétain had prepared an attack by Mangin's 10th Army, but then cancelled it to send reserves across to help contain the 'Friedensturm' west of Rheims. Foch recognized that Mangin's proposed attack would focus Ludendorff's attention on the huge salient now in his possession, preventing him from attacking elsewhere. So he ordered Pétain to let Mangin's attack proceed. It thrust up from the forests of Compiègne and Retz on 18 July. Although it had little chance of cutting off German forces in the salient, it took 25,000 prisoners and forced Ludendorff to give up captured ground between Soissons and Rheims.

In late July and August Allied strategy coalesced. There would be a convergent offensive, with the Americans operating in Lorraine on the Allied right flank while the British took the lead in an attack eastwards through Cambrai. *'Tout le monde à la bataille'* – 'Everybody to battle' – declared Foch. The Americans began by pinching out the St Mihiel salient south of Verdun on 12–15 September. They then shifted their grip, attacking into the

Argonne, parallel with the Meuse, on 12 September in a battle the Americans call Meuse–Argonne. Pershing had been offered the choice of attacking either there or into the more open country between Rheims and the Argonne. He chose the Argonne because, he thought, no troops but his own would have the fighting spirit for such a task.

It was certainly a battle which demanded fighting spirit aplenty. Although some Americans divisions had gained combat experience fighting under Allied command, Pershing's was still a largely untried army, and it was engaging an experienced opponent on ground ideal for defence. The Americans took Montfaucon Ridge on 27 September, but two days later were sharply rebuffed at Exemont. They were now up against the main positions of the Kriemhilde line, and the Americans paused before launching an attack which saw them reach the Grandpré gap, where the valley of the River Aire divides the Argonne. On 12/13 October Pershing reorganized his command – getting bigger all the time – to form an Army Group, with two armies, 1st under Hunter Liggett and 2nd under Robert Bullard. It took more heavy fighting, with the Germans falling back yard by yard, before Liggett's men reached the Meuse just opposite the little town of Sedan, scene of a stunning German victory in 1870.

HAMEL AND AMIENS

Well before Pétain's scheme for a convergent Allied offensive was even sketched out, the British took important steps towards making it possible. The poor showing of 5th Army, which the condition of its defences only partly justified, finished Gough. On 28 March Rawlinson replaced him, and the 5th Army disappeared from the British order of battle, to be replaced by a reconstituted 4th Army under Rawlinson. Haig's own position remained insecure, with Henry Wilson, the Chief of the Imperial General Staff,

THE WESTERN FRONT 1918:
THE ALLIED ADVANCE

HOLLAND

North Sea

Zeebrugge
Ostend
Nieuport
Bruges
Ghent

Calais

Boulogne Hazebrouck

Etaples

Montreuil

2nd

Passchendaele

Ypres

Messines

Armentières

Laventie Lille

La Bassée

Lens

Vimy Douai

Arras

Cambrai

Bapaume

Albert Péronne

Amiens

Villers-
Bretonneux

St Quentin

FRANCE

Montdidier

Compiègne

Soissons

Château-Thierry

Meaux

⊙ Paris

5th

Mons

Charleroi

Forest of Mormal

1st

Maubeuge

Landrecies

3rd Le Cateau

4th

R. Oise

3rd till 14 Sept La 1st
Noyon Fère Laon

10th till 27 Nov then 3rd
Chemin des Dames

R. Vesle

5th

Rheims

R. Marne

Army Group
Rupprecht

Brussels

BELGIUM

Liège

Namur

R. Meuse

R. Sambre

Army Group
Boehn

Army Group
Crown Prince

Army Group
Gallwitz

Mézières Sedan

R. Aisne

4th

US 1st

Argonne Verdun

US 2nd

St Mihiel

**10th from 27 Nov
then 8th**

Army Group
Albrecht

R. Seine

R. Oise

R. Somme

R. Lys

| 0 | 25 Miles |
| 0 | 25 Kilometres |

German forces in Army Groups
under name of commander   Albrecht

Approximate line of the Western
Front, August   - - - -

Approximate line of the Western
Front, 11 November

British and American armies   1st

French and Belgian armies   1st

telling Lloyd George that he would fight a good defensive battle, 'and that the time to get rid of him was when the German attack was over'.

Rawlinson was pessimistic when he arrived, believing that a determined German attack would take Amiens. However, as we have seen, Ludendorff turned his attention elsewhere, and as he did so Rawlinson worked hard to improve his defences, instituting a properly thought-through system of deep defence based on a serious study of German methods of attack. It soon became evident that these defences would not be put to the test. A variety of evidence – notably a large raid carried out by the Australians near Morlancourt on 10 June – suggested that German troops in the sector were of poor quality and their defences ill-prepared.

As he considered the feasibility of launching an attack of his own, Rawlinson noted that the British army's diminishing manpower (for which, it must be said, his own efforts on the Somme were in part responsible) suggested that 'all possible mechanical devices' should be used to increase the offensive power of divisions. The only two areas where such developments might be expected were in the increase of machine-guns, and in extended 'numbers and functions of tanks'. He did not mention artillery, perhaps because he considered that the most significant developments – which we have previously traced – had already occurred.

An early demonstration of the Rawlinson method came on 4 July when the Australian Corps attacked the village of Hamel, north-east of Villers Bretonneux. Because the Australians were badly below strength, Lieutenant-General Sir John Monash, their newly appointed corps commander, proposed to attack with his infantry thinly spread: artillery, machine-guns and tanks would give the blow its real punch. The tanks were the new Mk V, slightly faster and more easily driven than the Mk IV, carrying its fuel under armour and, perhaps most important, more reliable than earlier models.

The original plan, which did without a creeping barrage, did not commend itself to some of those involved, whose experience of tanks had been marked by the Bullecourt fiasco in 1917. Monash and Rawlinson were flexible enough to permit 'bottom up' influence on their plans. The final scheme embodied a lightning bombardment, which paid careful attention to German batteries, and then a creeping barrage moving ahead of the infantry and tanks. There was one hold-up where tanks failed to reach an objective which the infantry had to storm in the old style, but elsewhere the day was a triumphant success.

In the weeks that followed further raids suggested that German troops and the defences they held remained poor, encouraging Rawlinson to plan for a much larger attack. The scheme, sent to GHQ on 17 July, embodied an attack by eleven divisions on a 19,000-yard (17,000-kilometre) front from just north of the Somme to Demuin, south of the Amiens–Villers-Bretonneux road. There was to be a three-phase advance, its first objective the German front line and its third the outer Amiens defence line, built by the French in 1916. Troops taking the first objective would secure it while those attacking the second passed through, and after another brief pause these same troops would go on to the third. To ensure smooth command (and minimize national frictions) the three corps involved – the British III Corps north of the Somme, the ANZAC to their right and the Canadians to the extreme south – would have their own sectors, with Canadians leapfrogging Canadians, and so on.

Both Foch and Haig tinkered with the plan. Foch decreed that the French 1st Army, on Rawlinson's right, would attack as well. Haig, in a dull echo of the Somme, visited Rawlinson just before the attack and told him to aim at going far deeper. The line Chaulnes–Roye, 7 miles (11 kilometres) beyond Rawlinson's final objective, was to be taken, and Ham, another 15 miles (24 kilometres) further on, was the general direction of the advance.

The odds were stacked in Rawlinson's favour. His Canadian and Australian divisions were first rate, and he had 342 Mk V tanks and an assortment of other supply and infantry-carrying tanks. In addition to the 800 aircraft of his own, some dedicated to attacking German anti-tank guns and others to dropping ammunition to advancing troops, there were enough French aircraft on his right to give the Allies almost 2000 aircraft against fewer than 400 German. Lastly, there were 2000 guns, which were to eschew preliminary bombardment but maintain a heavy creeping barrage in front of the advance. Robin Prior and Trevor Wilson observe that the ratio of artillery required per yard of attack front – for field guns, one gun per 25 yards (22 metres) firing four rounds per minute for the creeping barrage – was actually exceeded: 'As a formula for victory, this could hardly have been bettered.'

Rawlinson was meticulous about maintaining security: in particular, it was important that the presence of the Canadians should not be revealed as the Germans, with good reason, regarded them as 'shock troops' whose presence indicated a major offensive. It is likely that the Germans had some inkling of what was afoot, but news did not filter down the chain of command until it was too late.

The attack began at 4.20 on the morning of 8 August. Sir John Monash recalled how:

> A great illumination lights up the Eastern horizon: and instantly the whole complex organization, extending far back to areas almost beyond earshot of the guns, begins to move forward: every man, every unit, every vehicle and every tank on the appointed tasks and to their designated goals, sweeping on relentlessly and irresistibly.

There were a few temporary setbacks, but determined men took them in their stride. A Canadian artillery sergeant was riding forward when he saw that a gun-team in front had been hit:

The first thing I saw was one of the drivers lying face down in the dust, dead. Some horses were lying in a heap, where the shell had landed. On the left I saw someone pulling one of the other drivers, also dead, out of the way into a shell hole. A man's feelings get blunted at these sights, and his mind being fully occupied by the work in hand he has no time to consider such things in the sad and awful light of what they really are. All I remember is that I turned round and shouted to the lead driver of my gun to swing out, so as to avoid the man in the road and the dead horses.

Captain Henry Smeddle's tank company went forward through batches of wounded and German prisoners, and it was clear that 'very little infantry opposition was being met with'. The scale of the surprise struck him when he reached Harbonnières station to see an ammunition train pull in as if nothing was happening. 'It was immediately shelled by all the 6-pder guns of the approaching tanks,' he wrote. 'One shell must have struck a powder van for suddenly the whole train burst into one great sheet of flame.'

Well might Rawlinson report that 'we have given the Boche a pretty good bump this time', for his men advanced 8 miles (12 kilometres) and inflicted 27,000 casualties. Only in the north, where III Corps was attacking over difficult ground with tired troops, were there serious disappointments. The German Official History called this 'the greatest defeat which the German army had suffered since the beginning of the war... The position divisions between the Avre and the Somme which had been struck by the enemy attack were nearly completely annihilated'. Ludendorff himself was horrified. 'August 8th was the black day of the German army in the war,' he wrote. 'This was the worst experience I had to go through.' One black day, however, was followed by a hundred more, many scarcely less gloomy.

THE HUNDRED DAYS

The Amiens battle slowed down in the days that followed, though not before the US 131st Infantry Regiment, fighting under III Corps, had helped take the important Chipilly spur overlooking the Somme. Foch pressed Haig to hustle on both 3rd and 4th Armies, but Haig was concerned about stiffening resistance. Rawlinson, far more mature as an army commander than he had been two years before, was disinclined to be pushed into premature action. The official historian maintains that he asked Haig: 'Who commands the British Army, you or Foch?' Haig himself was inclined to be less rigid, and not without reason, for while so many of the men under his command were 18-year-olds, his senior commanders knew their business as never before. On 22 August Haig told the army commanders:

> It is no longer necessary to advance in regular lines step by step. On the contrary, each division should be given a distant objective which must be reached independently of one's neighbour, and even if one's flank is thereby exposed for the time being.
>
> Reinforcements must be directed on the points where our troops are gaining ground, not where they are checked.

It was not until 21 August that Byng was ready to attack north of Albert, and found that the Germans had already begun to give ground. Rawlinson kept pace, taking Albert, and soon both armies were hustling the Germans back across the wilderness of the old Somme battlefield. On the 26th 1st Army joined in, attacking east of Arras. The New Zealanders took Bapaume on the 29th, and the next day the Australians began their attack on Péronne, a strong position lying behind the Somme with its blown bridges. They took the dominating Mont St Quentin on 1 September, and Péronne itself fell the next day. Ludendorff's gloom deepened: he had hoped to winter in an intermediate line west of the main Hindenburg Line, but now there was no alternative but to fall back on to the line itself. However, it remained formidable. The British army had lost 80,000 men in August, and even the Mk V tanks found it hard to keep up with the pace of battle. There seemed every chance that the front would freeze hard again, as it had so often in the past.

Things were different that summer. Haig's armies managed to maintain the tempo of their advance, and although the Germans never broke – day after day machine-gun rearguards sacrificed themselves to buy time – the old spirit had gone. We must not detract from the achievement of the last Hundred Days – during which the British armies suffered over 300,000 casualties, a growing number of them a consequence of the influenza epidemic sweeping Europe – but German performance from August to November was undermined by the loss of the million men in the Ludendorff offensives, as well as by the long strain of the wearing-out fight.

In late September 4th Army broke the Hindenburg Line north of St Quentin in a battle where 46th North Midland Division, a Territorial formation, many of whose soldiers came from mining and pottery towns, distinguished itself by taking the bridge at Riqueval intact. As the sun broke through the mist, Major H. J. C. Marshall, one of the division's officers, described how:

> Over the brow of the rise opposite to us came a great grey column. Half an hour later a similar column appeared, and then another and another. We had broken the Hindenburg Line, and 4200 prisoners, seventy cannon and more than 1000 machine-guns were the trophies of the fight gathered by our single division!

Further north the US 27th and 30th Divisions, fighting under Australian command, suffered heavy casualties: the 107th Infantry

Regiment lost 377 killed and 658 wounded, the heaviest US regimental loss in the entire war. Captain O. H. Woodward, an Australian tunnelling officer, thought that 'as individuals the Americans were not to be blamed, but their behaviour under fire showed clearly that in modern warfare it was of little avail to launch an attack with men untrained in war, even though the bravery of the individual may not be questioned... No wonder the German machine-gunners had a field day'. By nightfall on the 29th the German defensive system was in ruins, and Ludendorff warned that only an immediate armistice could avert a catastrophe.

In October the Germans were elbowed back, still struggling hard, across the downland of the Cambrésis, up to Le Cateau and past the Forest of Mormal. There was vicious fighting on the Sambre Canal, where the poet Wilfred Owen was killed, and November saw the British armies back at Mons, where they had fired the first shots of the war in August 1914.

Despite all the efforts of the combatants on both sides over the previous four years, the Western Front was never truly broken. Even at this late stage in the war the Germans were pushed back in increasing disarray, but with their front intact. There was a very real probability that the Allied armies would shortly outrun their supplies, bringing their advance to a halt on the very borders of Germany. But it was not to be, for the Germans, undermined by military defeat and naval blockade, had reached the end of their tether.

THE ARMISTICE

In Germany, to starvation at home – largely a consequence of the blockade – was added unremitting bad news from the front. The government fell, and on 1 October a new one, headed by the moderate Prince Max of Baden, came to power. On 23–4 October the Italians beat the Austrians at Vittorio Veneto. The Ypres salient had already been expunged, and on 28 September Plumer began to clear the Flanders coast: King Albert of the Belgians entered Bruges on the 25th. Ludendorff resigned on 27 October; on 1 November Turkey capitulated. Three days later the High Seas Fleet began to mutiny, and Austria signed an armistice.

On 7 November a German armistice delegation arrived at a railway junction in the Forest of Compiègne. Foch received its members for a wintry interview in his carriage, and on the 10th the German government authorized acceptance of Allied terms. The armistice was signed at 5.15 on the morning of the 11th: it came into effect at 11.00 that day. Lieutenant R. G. Dixon of the Royal Garrison Artillery put that moment into words of which many would have approved:

> No more slaughter, no more maiming, no more mud and blood, and no more killing and disembowelling of horses and mules – which was what I found most difficult to bear...
>
> There was silence along the miles and miles of thundering battle-fronts from the North Sea to the borders of Switzerland... The whole vast business of the war was finished. It was over.

A Canadian soldier, Private Price, had the melancholy distinction of being the last man in the British armies killed in the war. He died at 10.58 on the morning of 11 November 1918, just two minutes before the armistice came into effect. Price lies in the little cemetery at St Symphorien, just east of Mons. Nearby are the first and last British soldiers killed in the war: Private Parr of the Middlesex, killed on cycle patrol on 21 August 1914, and Private Ellison of the 5th Lancers, who died on 11 November 1918. I know of no more poignant comment on the Western Front.

RETROSPECT

I was completing this book, and the television series it accompanies, over the eightieth anniversary of the armistice. At 11.00 on the morning of 11 November 1998 we were filming on Manchester Hill, near the spot where Wilfrith Elstob died. It was a beautiful autumn day, with the light slanting past the trees that circle the quarry where he had his command post. I have never known two minutes' silence seem more natural.

Much of the discussion surrounding the anniversary focused on whether the war was necessary or not. My old colleague John Keegan was among those who saw it as: 'Unnecessary, because the train of events that led to its outbreak might have been broken at any point during the five weeks of crisis that preceded the first clash of arms…' Alan Massie argued that Britain should not have fought in the war, and that the Russian Revolution, Fascist Italy, Nazi Germany, and the war of 1939, were among its baneful consequences.

It seems unquestionably true that, in common with so many other wars, the First World War could have been averted by astute diplomacy or more common goodwill. But we must neither credit our ancestors with knowledge of the future, nor seek to judge them by our standards. The threat to Britain seemed real enough to them in 1914, and a sense of national honour tugged their conscience harder than it does ours today.

This debate cannot obscure the central truth of the Western Front. For the only time in her history, Britain took the field in a major war against a first rate adversary and confronted that enemy's main strength in the war's principal theatre. She not only bore the enormous strain of the war, but also played a leading part in winning it. Well might Foch say of the Hundred Days: 'Never in any time in history has the British army achieved greater results in attack than in this unbroken offensive.'

Nearly 750,000 Commonwealth soldiers, sailors and airmen died on the Western Front. They rest in more than 1000 military and 2000 civil cemeteries. More than 300,000 of them have no known graves, and are commemorated on memorials to the missing: there are seven in Belgium and twenty-two in France. Some of these, like the Menin Gate and Tyne Cot at Ypres, and the Thiepval Memorial on the Somme, are well known and visited regularly. Others, like the Indian memorial at Neuve Chappelle, its 'Indo-Saracenic' architecture incongruous among the lush fields and pollarded willows, are more lonely. Those they commemorate were Regulars, Territorials, volunteers and conscripts, aged from fourteen to sixty-eight and ranging in rank from private soldier to lieutenant-general.

Some had done their duty without flinching:

Not uncontent to die
That Lancaster on Lune might stand secure.

Others found military service itself a long agony, and would have sympathized with an unknown soldier whose letter, opened by the censor in June 1918, admitted: 'everybody is fed up with the war and don't care who wins so long as we can get it over'. Death came in his capricious ways. Men were sniped, machine-gunned, shelled, bombed, bayoneted and mortared. They were kicked by horses, electrocuted by generators, and suffocated by charcoal braziers in winter dug-outs. One NCO died of a heart attack behind the lines just as the Battle of Loos started. A military policeman was shot dead by a deserting officer, who was himself executed for the crime.

Some men were snatched away in an instant. Charles Carrington saw Corporal Matthews die on the Somme:

I was looking straight at him as the bullet struck him and was profoundly affected by the remembrance of his face, though at the time I hardly thought of it. He was alive, and then he

was dead, and there was nothing human left in him. He fell
with a neat round hole in his forehead and the back of his
head blown off.

Others died in pain and terror that we can only guess at. An
Australian at Pozières saw 'a shapeless black thing, flapping... I
ran over, ducking and weaving, till I got close. And it was a man,
blackened, not a bit of flesh not burnt, rolling around, waving an
arm stump with nothing on it'. An unhappy few died by the hands
of their comrades, and even here there was no consistency. Some
stood square-shouldered, filling their lungs to face the volley,
while others were tied to a chair, drunk and sobbing.

The sheer quantity of loss numbs our comprehension. Over
73,000 missing are commemorated at Thiepval, and almost
55,000 on the Menin Gate. Whatever the motive for their service
or the manner of their death, they are united by the common
humanity which we too share. As Lieutenant-Colonel John
MacRae, who himself died in the war, wrote, they:

> ... *lived, felt dawn, saw sunset glow*
> *loved and were loved...*

As we now are, so once were they; as they now are, so must we
be. Let us remember them all, not with bravado or bombast, but
with the respect that their sacrifice demands.

THE WAR IN OUTLINE

This brief summary aims to put the Western Front in the context of the war as a whole. While the battles there would have seemed all-consuming to those taking part, there were many other campaigns around the world, many other bloody battles, many other casualties on both land and sea.

On the Eastern Front, Germany and Austria-Hungary fought the Russians. Early in the war, in August–September 1914, the Russians suffered serious reverses at the hands of the Germans at Tannenberg and the Masurian Lakes, but did much better further south against the Austrians in Galicia. 1915 began badly for the Austrians, with the expensive failure of an attempt to relieve the beleaguered fortress of Przemysl. In the north, however, the Germans captured Warsaw and pushed on to Brest-Litovsk and Vilna. The Russian army was terribly mauled, and it is a tribute to its sheer dogged resilience that it remained in the field at all.

Following the early failure of the German army commander on the Eastern Front, Field-Marshal Paul von Hindenburg was sent to command German forces there, ably seconded by Lieutenant-General Erich Ludendorff and Major-General Max Hoffman. From November 1914 Hindenburg exercised overall authority over Austrian forces too, although the Austrian chief of the general staff, General Franz Conrad von Hötzendorf, took a close personal interest in the campaign. The association was not altogether happy, and soon the Germans were to complain that their alliance with the Austrians was like being 'fettered to a corpse'.

In 1916 the Russians responded to French appeals to distract the Germans from their offensive at Verdun by attacking them at Lake Narotch. Although this was a bloody failure, a bigger attack –

known, from the name of the commander of the Russian south-western army group, as the Brusilov offensive – was spectacularly successful. The Austro-Hungarian Fourth Army was almost destroyed, and German reinforcements had to be rushed in from the west to stabilize the situation. Brusilov's triumph encouraged Romania to join the war on the Allied side, but the ensuing counter-offensive saw Romanians and Russians alike badly beaten. Most of Romania was overrun, and even long-suffering Russia had reached the end of its tether. Hindenburg and Ludendorff departed for the Western Front, but German authority in the east was strengthened, leaving the Italian Front as the main concern of Conrad von Hötzendorf, who was himself relieved of his post as chief of staff in March 1917 and sent off to command in the South Tyrol.

In March 1917 the tsar abdicated, and a Provisional Government took power. It strove to remain faithful to the Allied cause, and launched another offensive in Galicia in July. German counter-strokes administered what was in effect the *coup de grâce* to Russia's military effort. In November a communist coup overturned the Provisional Government, and in December Russia concluded an armistice which was confirmed the following year. Civil war followed in Russia, and although the Germans left some troops to watch their eastern frontiers, they were able to shift most to the Western Front.

Turkey entered the war in late October 1914, and her armed forces received considerable support from Germany, who had sent a substantial training team there in 1913. A Turkish invasion of Russian territory in the Caucasus was sharply rebuffed at Sarikamish in December 1914–January 1915. The war ebbed and flowed in 1915–16, with the Russians having rather the better of it, capturing Erzerum and Trebizond. Even this otherwise unimportant front cast a long shadow, for the initial Turkish success in 1914 encouraged the Russians to ask for Allied help against the

Turks. This request played its part in initiating a campaign which had an appreciable impact on the Western Front: Gallipoli.

The Gallipoli peninsula, with its characteristic dog-leg outline, forms the northern coastline of the narrow Dardanelles, which connect the Aegean Sea with the Sea of Marmara. Allied attention was drawn to the area by Turkey's plea for help, and the 'easterners', who sought a more profitable theatre than the Western Front, advocated forcing the passage of the Dardanelles to enable an Allied fleet to reach the Turkish capital Constantinople (now Istanbul) and drive Turkey out of the war. There were initial naval attacks in February and March, and landings in April and August. Although there were moments when the allies might have taken Gallipoli, a combination of hesitance and misjudgement among their commanders coupled with dogged resistance and some inspired leadership on the part of the Turks produced stalemate. The Allies withdrew in December 1915 and January 1916.

Italy joined the Allies in May 1915 in the hope of making gains at Austria's expense. Her strategy was to hold the Trentino, Austrian territory jutting down into Italy north of Verona, while attacking into the Isonzo salient Italy's north-east frontier. In a long and bitter series of battles on the Isonzo, too often ignored by Anglo-American historians, the Italian army made painful progress at great cost, but by the summer of 1917 the Austrians, worn to a thread, asked for German help. General Krafft von Dellmensingen's German contingent played a leading part in winning the Battle of Caporetto in October 1917. The Italians lost more than half a million men, and were bundled back to a defensive line just north of Venice. Six French and five British divisions were sent from the Western Front to support the Italians.

The rapid deterioration of Austria's economy and growing exhaustion of her army in 1918 did not prevent further attacks, but the Italians were now able to parry them. In October the Italians launched their own final offensive, beating the Austrians at Vittorio

Veneto and pushing on, against diminishing resistance, in an advance ending in an armistice which took effect on 4 November.

The war originated in events in the Balkans, and fighting began early there. An Austrian invasion of Serbia initially made good progress, taking Belgrade, the Serbian capital, but soon stalled in the face of fierce Serbian resistance. In late September the Serbs counter-attacked, retaking Belgrade and driving the Austrians from Serbian territory with considerable loss. However, Allied failure at Gallipoli encouraged Bulgaria, with her own territorial ambitions in the Balkans, to join the Central Powers, and in the autumn of 1915 a combined German, Austrian and Bulgarian offensive crushed Serbian resistance, driving remnants of the Serbian army through Montenegro and down into Albania. The survivors were rescued by Allied ships in early 1916.

Bulgaria's entry into the war had alarmed the Greeks, who feared for their province of Macedonia, and called for Allied assistance. An Allied force was duly sent to Salonika, in north-east Greece, only to discover that Greece's pro-German king, Constantine, dismissed his pro-Allied premier, Venizelos, and declared Greece neutral. The Allies, however, retained a substantial force at Salonika, which at least provided a command for the French General Maurice Sarrail, an ardent republican for whom a substantial post had to be found. There was some inconclusive fighting against the Bulgarians in 1916–17. In June 1917 King Constantine abdicated, and his successor, Alexander, reappointed Venizelos who brought Greece back into the war.

Sarrail's successor, General Guillaumat, reorganized Allied forces and successfully integrated the Greeks into his command. With the Allies on the Western Front showing signs of buckling under the strain of the German offensive, he was recalled to serve as military governor of Paris. However, his replacement, the resourceful General Franchet d'Esperey, began the Battle of the Vardar in mid-September. The Bulgarians, now denuded of

German support, were swiftly beaten, and surrendered on 30 September.

There were two theatres of war in the Middle East. Egypt was a British protectorate, and in February 1916 the Turks launched a half-hearted attack on the Suez Canal. The British followed up its repulse by advancing into Sinai, and prepared positions there for a possible advance into Palestine, part of the Turkish Empire. Turkish attention was distracted by an Arab revolt against their rule, which gained momentum in the second half of 1916 and included guerrilla attacks (in which the British Colonel T. E. Lawrence – 'Lawrence of Arabia' – played a distinguished part) on the long and vulnerable Turkish lines of communication.

In March 1917 the British, under General Sir Archibald Murray, launched the first Battle of Gaza in an attempt to get into Palestine, failed, tried again the following month and failed once more. Murray's successor was General Sir Edmund Allenby, who had commanded an army on the Western Front. In October–November 1917 he outflanked the Gaza positions by swinging through Beersheba on the desert flank and going on to take Jerusalem. Allenby's preparations for a renewal of the offensive were impeded by the steady leeching away of his troops to the Western Front, but in September 1918 he sprang a brilliantly successful attack on the Turks at Megiddo, and took Damascus on 1 October: an armistice was concluded at the end of the month.

The second front in the Middle East was in Mesopotamia, now Iraq. General Sir John Nixon's expeditionary force from India landed at Basra, and began to advance, with inadequate supplies and no real campaign plan, along the Tigris towards Baghdad. Its leading elements took Kut-al-Amara in September 1916, only to be besieged there in December. Attempts at relief failed, and Kut surrendered in April 1916, a serious blow to British prestige, coming as it did so soon after failure at Gallipoli.

Nixon's successor, General Sir Frederick Maude, resumed the

advance, winning the second Battle of Kut in February 1917 and taking Baghdad in March. He pushed on up the Euphrates and beat the Turks at Ramadi in September, only to die of cholera. His successor, Sir William Marshall, consolidated the gains, and although expeditions were sent out to the oilfields at Baku and Mosul, there was little more serious fighting.

There was sporadic fighting in Africa, the Allies overrunning German colonies in Togoland and South-West Africa. The Cameroons held out till early 1916, but in South-West Africa the talented German commander, Colonel Paul von Lettow-Vorbeck, remained in the field for the whole war. In a brilliant guerrilla campaign, he held down 130,000 Allied troops.

Although the war at sea contained fewer of the main fleet actions than pre-war theorists had expected, it was none the less important. In 1914 German maritime colonies worldwide – like Tsingtao on the Chinese coast – were snapped up quickly. Admiral Maximillian von Spee's German China Squadron, on its way home by way of South America, destroyed a British squadron off Coronel on the Chilean coast on 1 November 1914, but was caught off the Falklands eight days later and almost entirely destroyed. German commerce-raiders caused some losses, and on 22 September a German submarine pointed the way ahead by sinking three old cruisers in the Channel.

In January 1915 a German squadron raided into the North Sea, but the British, alerted by radio intercepts, met it at the Dogger Bank. The action was inconclusive, but the Germans profited by the experience to improve precautions against internal explosions in their ships. The following month the Germans began an unrestricted submarine campaign against all merchant shipping, including neutral vessels, in the waters surrounding Britain. In May the Cunard liner *Lusitania* was sunk with the loss of over 1000 lives, arousing a storm of international protest, and the campaign was suspended.

Allied vessels were still attacked, and during 1916 there were raids on the British coast. The year's main clash at sea was the Battle of Jutland, fought between the British Grand Fleet and the German High Seas Fleet on 31 May. The Germans inflicted greater losses than they suffered, but were aware that they had courted great risk, and never again ventured out of port.

In February 1917 the Germans again adopted unrestricted submarine warfare, hoping that its effect on Britain would outweigh the risk of bringing the United States into the war. Although Germany had neither sufficient U-boats nor adequate tactics for their use, the campaign did terrible damage: in April 1917, its worst month, the Allies lost half a million tons of shipping. Adoption of the convoy system and increased Anglo-American naval co-operation – for the Americans did indeed enter the war in April 1917 – helped reduce losses. However, the U-boat threat had its effect on the Western Front. One of the objectives of the Third Battle of Ypres, the British offensive launched in the summer of 1917, was taking the German submarine bases at Ostend and Zeebrugge, and the latter was the scene of a gallant raid on 23 April 1918 when the light cruiser *Vindictive* and smaller craft assaulted the port and inflicted some damage.

The war at sea was inconclusive, and certainly did little to justify the expenditure lavished on surface fleets. However, if the German submarine campaign managed neither to starve Britain out of the war nor to prevent the passage of American troops to Europe, the Allied blockade of Germany was a different matter. The Central Powers ran short of food and military raw materials, and although the blockade no more broke German morale than did Allied bombing a generation later, it led to growing problems on the home front and contributed to demands for an end to the war.

The First World War was indeed a conflict that spanned the globe, and its growing appetite for resources spread ripples of war even where armies and navies themselves did not reach. Yet from the British point of view, then as now, the war had one primary focus, the Western Front.

THE BRITISH CHAIN OF COMMAND

This simplified outline deals primarily with the infantry. Supporting arms (artillery and engineers) and ancillary services were to be found at divisional level and above. Establishments changed as the war went on. Terminology varied between arms: a company-sized body of cavalry was called a squadron, and a similar body of artillery (usually with six guns) a battery. The word regiment had no tactical significance in the infantry, though different battalions of a given regiment might find themselves in the same brigade. Confusingly, artillery batteries were grouped into brigades, although these artillery brigades (really the equivalent of infantry battalions) were designated by roman numerals in an effort to minimise confusion.

The BEF was effectively one army in 1914, becoming five by 1918. Commander-in-Chief was Field-Marshal Sir John French till Dec 1915, then General (later Field-Marshal) Sir Douglas Haig.

ARMY	(Commanded by a **General**) comprised about four corps, but precise numbers depended on the army's role.
CORPS	(Commanded by a **Lieutenant-General**) usually comprised three or four divisions.
DIVISION	(Commanded by a **Major-General**) usually had three brigades.
BRIGADE	(Commanded by a **Brigadier-General**) had four battalions to winter 1917 and three thereafter.
BATTALION	(Commanded by a **Lieutenant-Colonel**) had four companies.
COMPANY	(Commanded by a **Major** or **Captain**) had four platoons.
PLATOON	(Commanded by a **Subaltern – a Lieutenant** or **Second-Lieutenant**) had four sections.
SECTION	(Commanded by a **Corporal**) with 8–10 men.

FURTHER READING

This is in no sense a comprehensive bibliography, simply a short guide for those wishing to read further. I have restricted myself to suggesting a handful of favourite books per chapter. Since the first edition of this book appeared the first volume of Hew Strachan's masterly *The First World War* (Oxford, 2001) has been published and must be regarded as required reading, as must Jack Sheldon's trio of books on the German experience of the Western Front.

INTRODUCTION

Of the books marking the 80th anniversary of the armistice, both John Keegan *The First World War* (London 1998) and Niall Ferguson *The Pity of War* (London 1998) are likely to stand the test of time – though I disagree with their judgement on the war's origins. The former, beautifully written and illuminated by wisdom and humanity, is the best general account of the war. Although we must question some of its interpretations, for tactical narrative it remains hard to beat the British official history, Sir James Edmonds *Military Operations: France and Belgium...* There are several distinctive red-jacketed volumes for each year of the war, together with volumes of excellent maps. John Ellis *Eye-Deep in Hell* (London 1976) remains the most accessible review of life at the front. Of the many anthologies of war experience, Guy Chapman *Vain Glory* (London 1937, 1968) still repays the reader. The serious visitor to the Western Front will profit from taking Peter Chasseaud *Topography of Armageddon* (London 1991), a selection of trench maps. Hugh Cecil and Peter H. Liddle (eds) *Facing Armageddon* (London 1996) is a mine of valuable essays by many of the foremost contemporary scholars, and Brian Bond (ed) *The First World War and British Military History* (Oxford 1991) is especially useful in charting the reputations of generals. Ian Malcolm Brown *British Logistics on the Western Front* (London 1998) is a long-overdue study of an important subject. Readers who wish to trace relatives can do no better than consult Simon Fowler, William Spencer and Stuart Tamblin, *Army Service Records of the First World War* (London 1996).

MAKING THE FRONT

Paul Kennedy (ed) *The War Plans of the Great Powers* (London 1979) is a useful introduction. My *Riding the Retreat: Mons to the Marne 1914 Revisited* (London 1995) tells the story of a ride from Mons in the footsteps of the BEF. For an evocative account of the opening campaign see the Moltke chapter in Correlli Barnett *The Swordbearers* (London 1963). Among the many memoirs, Edward Spears *Liaison 1914* (London 1930) and Walter Bloem *The Advance from Mons* (London 1938) deserve mention. Lyn Macdonald *1914* (London 1987) is a marvellous anthology, and the well-illustrated Keith Simpson *The Old Contemptibles* (London 1981) remains the best overview of the British army of 1914. Michael Howard illuminates expectations and doctrine in 'Men Against Fire: The Doctrine of the Offensive in 1914' in Peter Paret (ed) *Makers of Modern Strategy* (Oxford 1986).

FEEDING THE FRONT

Tim Travers *The Killing Ground* (London 1987) is good for the war as a whole, and its chapter on the cult of the offensive is especially useful. Shelford Bidwell and Dominick Graham *Fire-Power: British Army Weapons and Theories of War 1904–1945* (London 1982), Ian F. W. Beckett and Keith Simpson *A Nation in Arms: A Social Study of the British Army in the First World War* (Manchester 1985), and John Turner (ed) *Britain and the First World War* (London 1988) are useful for various aspects of the British background. For the New Armies see Peter Simkins *Kitchener's Army: Raising the New Armies 1914–1916* (Manchester 1988). Of David French's many contributions to our understanding of the war, see particularly *British Strategy and War Aims 1914–1916* (London 1986). Robin Prior and Trevor Wilson *Command on the Western Front: The Military Career of Sir Henry Rawlinson* (Oxford 1992) is invaluable for the spring offensives of 1915, Loos, the Somme and 1918.

HOLDING THE FRONT

Despite its age, and the doubts that modern scholarship has thrown onto its views on Falkenhayn, Alistair Horne *The Price of Glory: Verdun 1916* (London 1962) remains a superb study. For the French military background see Douglas Porch *The March to the Marne: The French Army*

1871–1914 (Cambridge 1981), and for France and the war see J-J Becker *The Great War and the French People* (Leamington Spa 1985). *Les Combattants des Tranchées* (Paris 1986), Stéphane Audoin-Rouzeau's wonderful work on French trench journalism, is now available in English. For an important study of a French infantry division see Leonard Smith *Between Discipline and Obedience...* (Princeton 1994). The way the army was seen – and, no less important, saw itself – before the war is beautifully depicted in Francois Robichon *L'armée Francaise vue par les peintres* (Paris 1998).

COMMANDING THE FRONT

Gerald Gliddon *The Legacy of the Somme* (London 1996) is a carefully annotated bibliography of fact and fiction on the Somme. Martin Middlebrook *The First Day on the Somme* (London 1971) is not simply a good book, but is one which changed the way many people felt about military history. Lyn Macdonald *Somme* (London 1983) is the best general anthology, while Malcolm Brown *The Imperial War Museum Book of the Somme* (London 1996) skilfully uses letters and diaries in the museum to reflect the two faces of the Somme, 'the mud and the stars'. Paddy Griffith *Battle Tactics of the Western Front: The British Army's Art of Attack 1916–18* (London 1994) sees the Somme as a key stage in the British army's learning process. The best general study of the battlefield is Martin and Mary Middlebrook *The Somme Battlefields* (London 1991), and several good slim volumes are published by Leo Cooper as an imprint of Pen and Sword Books in the Battleground Europe series.

ENDURING THE FRONT

Peter H. Liddle (ed) *Passchendaele in Perspective* (London 1997) is the essential starting-point for any serious study of 1917. For a penetrating view of the French army see Edward Spears *Prelude to Victory* (London 1939). John Terraine *The Road to Passchendaele:* The *Flanders Offensive of 1918: A Study in Inevitability* (London 1977) is one of the most important of its author's many studies of the war. Lyn Macdonald *They Called it Passchendaele* (London 1978) gives the view from the mud. Ian Passingham *Pillars of Fire* (Stroud 1998) is a good account of Messines Ridge. For the Australians see C. E. W. Bean *Anzac to Amiens* (Canberra 1983).

BREAKING THE FRONT

Tim Travers *How the War Was Won: Command and Technology in the British Army on the Western Front* (London 1992) is the most useful starting-point for the British army, and for the year in general see John Terraine *To Win a War: 1918, the Year of Victory* (London 1982). For the Germans see Bruce I. Gudmundsson *Stormtroop Tactics: Innovation in the German Army 1914–1918* and David T. Zabecki *Steel Wind: Colonel Georg Bruchmüller and the Birth of Modern Artillery* (London 1994). Shane B. Schreiber does justice to the Canadians in *Shock Army of the British Empire: The Canadian Corps in the Last 100 Days of the Great War* (Westport, Conn. 1997). In *The Kaiser's Battle* (London 1978) Martin Middlebrook does for 21 March 1918 what he did earlier for the First Day on the Somme. The most recent of Lyn Macdonald's anthologies, *To The Last Man* (London 1998) is arguably her best.

INDEX